Honoring Trans and Gender-Expansive Students in Music Education

Honoring Trans and Gender-Expansive Students in Music Education

Matthew L. Garrett (he/him) and
Joshua Palkki (he/him)

Oxford University Press is a department of the University of Oxford. It furthers the University's objective of excellence in research, scholarship, and education by publishing worldwide. Oxford is a registered trade mark of Oxford University Press in the UK and certain other countries.

Published in the United States of America by Oxford University Press
198 Madison Avenue, New York, NY 10016, United States of America.

Library of Congress Cataloging-in-Publication Data
Names: Garrett, Matthew L., author. | Palkki, Joshua, author.
Title: Honoring trans and gender-expansive students in music education /
Matthew L. Garrett, Joshua Palkki.
Description: New York : Oxford University Press, 2021. |
Includes bibliographical references and index.
Identifiers: LCCN 2021013449 | ISBN 9780197506608 (paperback) |
ISBN 9780197506592 (hardback) | ISBN 9780197506622 (epub)
Subjects: LCSH: Music—Instruction and study. | Transgender youth—Education—United States. |
Gender-nonconforming youth—Education—United States.
Classification: LCC MT1 .G24 H66 2021 | DDC 780.71—dc23
LC record available at https://lccn.loc.gov/2021013449

DOI: 10.1093/oso/9780197506592.001.0001

3 5 7 9 8 6 4 2

Paperback printed by Marquis, Canada
Hardback printed by Bridgeport National Bindery, Inc., United States of America

This book is dedicated to trans and gender-expansive students in school music programs.
Live your truth.

Contents

Acknowledgments

With deep gratitude, we thank many special people in our lives who have helped us bring this resource to life.

Thank you to Norm Hirschy for honoring trans and gender-expansive students with this project. Your excitement and encouragement inspired us to curate years of experiences into one place. More importantly, you afforded us with opportunities to cultivate fabulous relationships with our collaborators, in an effort to empower trans and gender-expansive students to learn.

This book would not have been possible without the invaluable feedback from beloved colleagues. Thank you for taking the time to read our draft chapters and provide suggestions to improve the quality of this important work: Genny Beemyn, Bruce Carter, Shae Miller, Jessica Nápoles, Jake Nousomme, Carl Oser, Stephanie Prichard, Jared Rawlings, William Sauerland, Ryan Shaw, Jason Silveira, Melanie Stapleton, Cynthia Taggart, and Mari Esabel Valverde.

Peer mentoring has also been essential to us, as we moved from a pattern of writing article-length publications to writing a book. Daniel Goldmark and Bridget Sweet: thank you for your insight, advice, and for your good humor. Michael Peters, Matthew's partner: thank you for all of your encouragement, love, and patience. Your combined constructive input pushed us to explore our ideas, uncover practical solutions to real world challenges, and to finish writing! We also offer a special thank you to Susan McClary, who saw great value in the underlying concept of this book from an early stage, and who essentially said, "Do it!"

Being a successful college music teacher requires strong connections with school music teacher colleagues. Matthew is grateful for the creativity of Karly Bowman-Morron, Kristopher Morron, Loraine Sims, Julienne Thornell, and John Egger. Joshua wishes to thank Maria Dowell, Roger Emerson, and Michael Hayden. Thank you for sharing ideas that you have found to be successful in celebrating and honoring gender diversity. We also wish to thank and honor Melanie Stapleton: a trailblazing music educator who is helping to lead our profession to be more inclusive of trans and gender-expansive students (blurringthebinary.com).

Thank you to our research assistants, Dennis Feinland and Kelsey Giotta. Your careful reading and thoughtful contributions aided substantially to the completion of this project. Thanks also to the California State University, Long Beach Academic Affairs and Office of Research and Sponsored Programs and the Case Western Reserve University Baker-Nord Center for the Humanities for grant support of these assistants.

Finally, thank you to all of our amazing collaborators, we are better people for learning from you. Their stories and lived experiences are the lifeblood of this book, and the heartbeat of why we teach people through the art of music.

About the Companion Website

www.oup.com/us/htgesme

In an effort to amplify the voices of the trans and gender-expansive (TGE) persons who collaborated with the authors, Oxford University Press has created a website to accompany *Honoring Trans and Gender-Expansive Students in Music Education*. Readers can listen to the recorded voices to gain a more complete understanding of TGE persons' lived experiences. The authors encourage readers to access the companion website in conjunction with reading the written narratives highlighted in Chapter 7.

Introduction

Teaching People to Learn through the Art of Music

Chapter Guide

MELANIE (pronouns, she/her; gender identity, Transgender woman; racial identity, white): "The most important thing is how comfortable [trans and gender expansive students] feel and that they feel loved and respected by you. Because at the end of the day, you might be the only person that shows them that love. You might be the only person that shows them that they matter—that who they are is valid. . . . And if your trans kid knows that you care about them and that you're supporting them in whatever way that you can, or at least trying to learn, they're going to have a lot more patience and a lot more understanding than if they think that you're not."

Who We Teach and What We Teach, *in That Order*

Why is it important for music teachers to consider gender diversity? Students represent a multitude of differences, and gender diversity is but one of those

Honoring Trans and Gender-Expansive Students in Music Education. Matthew L. Garrett and Joshua Palkki, Oxford University Press. © Oxford University Press 2021. DOI: 10.1093/oso/9780197506592.003.0001

possible differences. We, as music teachers, should not intentionally exclude certain students from learning activities or music-making experiences. Valuing gender diversity and demonstrating that value through inclusive teaching is one way to support all students potentially present in music classrooms. Music educator Judith Jellison (2015) advocates, "children who are more understandable as individuals are more teachable as learners" (p. 2). Individual students learn more deeply when they feel comfortable enough to experience a sense of vulnerability when engaging with music. Unfettered by fear of failure or unnecessary reprimand, students can more easily connect with classroom experiences—interactions that may transfer beyond classroom walls and strengthen lifelong engagement with music. A common argument against considering gender diversity stems from the claim, "I'm here to teach music, not sociology or health science." This view, unfortunately, advocates that teachers should concentrate on content, with a potentially narrow goal of developing students' musicianship skills above all else. From this perspective, gender diversity is deemed tertiary to student success. A major goal of this book is to reframe this argument, placing our students *before* the content. Music teacher educators often proclaim to future teachers, "We don't teach music, *we teach people through music*." Translated into a slightly different context, we might consider the idea: *there is no music without people, and there is no music-making without safety*. This mentality is summarized beautifully by middle-school band teacher Tavia (pronouns, she/her; gender identity, cis[gender]-het[erosexual] female; racial identity, white), a middle-school band teacher:

> First off, support the kid. Oh my goodness, support the kid. [. . .] One of the conversations that I'll always have with students [is] "okay, you want me to address you as this? Should I do that in communications home? Is that how you want to be [recognized] in the program?" That kind of thing. Cause some kids are like, "yeah, I'm supported." And others like, "no, please don't. I will get kicked out of my house." [. . .] So yeah, it's about the kids.

Imagine a music classroom in which students were motivated to learn because they felt heard and valued as people, before engaging in the art of music. As authors, we are not suggesting that music teachers should understand the nuances of each individual student *before* teaching begins. We regard teaching and engaging with students as an ongoing process that takes time, practice, and refinement. Part of the teaching process, however, should include efforts to honor students' gender identity and expression. In summary, we teach people, who value musical experiences, by engaging in school music.

Celebrating Our Differences through Communal and Collaborative Musical Experiences

The students in music classrooms of US schools are diverse in many ways, and music teachers can find ways to celebrate and honor the gender diversity of trans and gender-expansive (TGE) youth so that they can engage fully with collaborative musical experience. The tenets outlined in this book mirror, and in some ways draw upon, Culturally Responsive Pedagogy (CRP)—an approach to teaching in which students' backgrounds are taken into consideration when teachers plan instruction (Gay 2013; Ladson-Billings, 1995, 2011; Lind & McCoy, 2016). Incorporating contextual knowledge about students aids educators in personalizing student learning. Furthermore, learning about students' backgrounds helps us, as teachers, meet them where they are in their musical development. Music education professor Vanessa Bond (2017a) speaks of CRP "as a constructivist practice" in which learning "becomes an emancipatory process that frees students from the notion that a particular kind of cultural capital is worth having; difference does not equal deficit" (p. 155). We, as authors, believe that music education can be part of an emancipatory, radically inclusive educational experience for TGE students. To that end, this book is intended to serve as a resource for pre-service music teachers, professional music teachers, and music teacher-educators.

Teaching Trans and Gender-Expansive Persons in Music Education

This is a book about honoring transgender (trans) and gender-expansive (TGE) persons, subsets of the LGBTQA/queer community. Acronyms like LGBT, LGBTQ, and LGBTQIAA+ often are used without much clarity about what they mean and how subsets of the queer community relate. As authors, we have chosen to use the acronym LGBTQA: L (lesbian), G (gay), B (bisexual), T (trans), Q (queer, questioning), and A (agender, asexual, aromantic, etc.; ally) to represent populations within this larger community. We also use the term *trans* rather than *transgender*. When used in other forms (e.g., LGBT or transgender), we are quoting the term or acronym used by another author to accurately represent their writing. We also use the term "queer" for the entirety of the LGBTQA community, though not all LGBTQA persons identify with this term (e.g., Kean, 2020). We have chosen these six letters (representing at least 10 terms) because at this juncture, we consider it a fairly comprehensive representation of the many facets of the non-cisgender and non-heteronormative population, while being aware of the fact that these letters are not all-inclusive. All language about gender and sexuality is reductive and choices are necessary for clear communication, and these choices are fraught with challenges. We discuss labels and language in more detail in Chapter 1.

We have made choices in this book that reflect our values as authors and educators. First, we decided that TGE voices must be honored by featuring directly quoted stories and lived experiences. Second, since publications do not always list the pronouns of authors, we have chosen to use singular "they" when referring to authors' work to be as inclusive as possible (Airton, 2019). Finally, at the time of this writing, Americans are interrogating ideas of racial injustice and discriminatory acts that represent systemic and institutionalized racism. Following the lead of major newspapers and publishers (e.g., Coleman, 2020), we have chosen to capitalize "Black" and not "white" as a small gesture to remedy the injustices that people of color face daily in the United States. As you read this book, we encourage you to be open to learning about queer persons in music classrooms and realize that LGBTQA and non-LGBTQA persons have a great deal in common with one another.

Honoring TGE Persons through Music Education

Increased Visibility

In recent years, the visibility of TGE persons in the United States has increased dramatically. Authors have posited that the nation is at a gender "tipping point" (Steinmetz, 2014a) and is undergoing a "gender revolution" (Henig, 2017). Inherent in this larger cultural shift is a movement expanding beyond the concept of gender as a binary. In recent years, there has been rapid progress toward equal rights for many members of the LGBTQA community in the United States and abroad. During the writing of this book, a decision by the US Supreme Court made gay, lesbian, bisexual, and transgender persons a protected class in work environments—signifying that LGBTQA Americans no longer can be fired simply for their gender identity or sexuality. In popular culture, gay, lesbian, bisexual, and trans issues have become increasingly present, and the "T" is becoming more prominent. Considering an intersectional view of popular culture, the narratives of trans women of color have been highlighted in peripheral ways on shows like *Orange Is the New Black*, and foregrounded in the FX series *Pose*, the Netflix documentary *Disclosure*, and the HBO reality series *Legendary*. Similarly, the Netflix series *Queer Eye* chronicled the story of a trans man. Alex Blue Davis, an actor who identifies as a trans man, joined the cast of *Grey's Anatomy* in season 14; and trans man Chaz Bono shared his experience in *Becoming Chaz* on the OWN network.

Greater numbers of TGE youth are "coming out," or publicly claiming their gender identity—some at very young ages. TGE individuals appear more frequently in news stories, television programming, and in social media, which may account for an increase in self-identifying, or "coming out." Caitlyn Jenner's story and Katie Couric's *Gender Revolution* introduced many American households to the experiences of trans youth, as have podcasts like *How to Be a Girl*. The public transition of trans activist Jazz Jennings led to a children's book about her life: *I Am Jazz* (Herthel & Jennings, 2014) and a television show of the same name on TLC. Not all discussions around gender diversity in popular culture have been positive, however. Authors have noted that the journey toward equality for TGE persons is the next battleground for civil rights (e.g., Schoenberg, 2015).

Some TGE youth have never known a world in which TGE persons were not present in the zeitgeist of news and popular culture. Thus, it seems that "general public attitudes have become more accepting of the idea of a 'gender creative' person" (Ehrensaft, 2016, pp. 7–8). The results of one research study affirm that "transgender children do indeed exist and that their identity is a deeply held one" (Olson et al., 2015, p. 473). TGE youth are more openly present in school environments. Music teachers should seek ways to support and honor the gender diversity represented in their schools, realizing that TGE young persons inevitably will be present in music classrooms. If we, as music educators, teach people first, then realizing inclusive learning will be a matter of meeting students where they are and helping them to move forward.

Intersectionality

Who are you? This is a seemingly simple but exceedingly complex question, because each of us has a multifaceted history and multiple identities. For example, an Asian-American music teacher with a graduate degree may have grown up in a foster-family system. Those intersecting identities and experiences combine to represent a fascinating individual. As individuals, we are not defined solely by a single facet of our identity. In Chapter 1, we describe in more detail the *intersectional* approach utilized in this book (Crenshaw, 1991). This approach includes interrogating how our identities as authors might influence research and writing processes. As part of this approach, we include parenthetical information about each of our collaborators when we highlight their quotes. We identify their pronouns, self-identified gender identity, and self-identified racial identity. Refer back to the quote at the opening of this introduction to learn more about Melanie, (she/her; transgender woman; white).

Empowering People to Learn Music Together

Positionality as LGBTQA Community Members

It is important that we, as authors, disclose our positionality in this work in order to be transparent about the power dynamics at play. Scholars seeking to further social justice aims must "identify how their identity relates to class, ethnicity, gender, sexuality, and age, and the power/privilege inherent in those intersecting identities" (Parson, 2019, p. 18). We, as authors, are two white, openly gay, cisgender music educators who experience a reiterative "coming out" process in our personal and professional lives. That reiterative process means that we continue to "out" ourselves, even though the first time we did so occurred many years ago. Writing the last two sentences is another form of "coming out" to you, the reader. We both come from middle-class families, earned college degrees, work as college faculty, and acknowledge the many layers of privilege associated with those experiences. Matthew was raised in white-collar suburbs of the Southeastern United States and currently lives in a suburb of Cleveland, Ohio. He identifies as Christian, liberal, and gay. Joshua was raised in the rural upper Midwest, and concurrently identifies as queer, progressive, and having come from a blue-collar family. He lives in metro Los Angeles. We as authors both believe that our TGE collaborators' identities are authentic as reported, and we advocate for music learning environments as safe spaces, developed and maintained by safe people. As members of the LGBTQA community, we recognize our position of privilege and the need to appropriately employ that privilege to help raise the voices of TGE community members.

We as authors believe that it is possible for researchers like us—remaining ever aware of our cisgender privilege—to use that position and privilege in a positive way to bring attention and respect to trans experiences and trans issues. We recognize that some scholars (e.g., Namaste, 2000, 2009; Pennington, 2019) take issue with cisgender scholars "studying" trans persons, and we acknowledge these concerns. As Peter Cava (2014), instructor of women's, gender, and sexuality studies at Louisiana State University, writes:

> If *trans* means more than a minority, then trans politics do not end at minority rights; rather, as trans activist Leslie Feinberg has emphasized, trans politics call for universal liberation. When we achieve that goal, it will be a cause (that is, a reason) for celebration. Until then, it is a cause (that is, an activist initiative) *worthy of everyone's participation*. (p. 10, emphasis added)

The opportunity to create a resource with and for music educator colleagues realizes Cava's argument for broader participation in the drive for equity among underrepresented minorities.

As education professor Laura Parson (2019) writes, "The goal, in the positionality process, is to understand the multiple ways that privileged aspects of a researcher's identity act as 'power over' research participants" (p. 21). Such power and privilege differentials cannot be ignored; yet, in this book we strive to honor participants by highlighting their lived experiences to reveal reality from their perspectives—shining a light on things that may have remained uncovered. We as authors are imperfect and we acknowledge that we will make mistakes. Our fear, however, did not stop us from taking part in work that has the potential to make life better for TGE youth.

Negotiating positionality and power differential is complicated. The desire to be constructive and empowering must be measured as being contextually appropriate. The self-reflective component of the process requires time to think through potential actions. As one of our collaborators, Dane Figueroa Edidi (she/her; trans woman; Black [African, Cuban, Indigenous]), says:

> You have to always realize (as white people): it's not your story to tell, right? It's not your story to tell. [. . .] What people have to realize is that they can't be gatekeepers, right? And we already have a blueprint of what gatekeeping looks like, because it is the way our society has already created a gateway into people of color's lives. And so, I think that you just have to look at the checklist and be like "is that gatekeeper-ey"? "Is that gatekeeper-ey"? "Is that gatekeeper-ey"? And then check it off. Because also some things are academic and you're doing a study, and it is academic, but then it's like, "well, does that then mean that you're the only person who can speak about this," right? [. . .] And so, I think what you do have is that you have the opportunity to shift the way in which we think about—the way in which we honor the lived experiences of people.

Dane's comments remind us that multiple intersecting characteristics should be considered when choosing what to say and do to empower people. Similarly, Keizen (they/them; gender creative; Han Chinese) comments:

> Just in general, I advised people with privilege who want to be—*want* to use their privilege in a sensitive way. I've told them to just shut up and learn how to make space for people with less privilege. I mean, we all have privilege. And as a teacher, it's tricky because we do have to balance where we have authority and where we have to give up space.

When a teacher decides to focus on student-centered learning activities, like asking ensemble leaders to help select repertoire, they act on the idea of giving up some teacher-centered privilege to impact student learning. We as authors believe that narratives can be powerful in creating larger social change, as highlighted by Marshall Ganz (2011) from the Kennedy School of Government at Harvard University:

> Narrative is the discursive means we use to access values that equip us with the courage to make choices under conditions of uncertainty, to exercise agency. [. . .] Narratives thus become sources of learning, not only for the head, but also for the heart. Public narrative links the three elements of self, us, and now: why I am called, why we are called, and *why we are called to act now*. (p. 274, emphasis added)

The rich stories and experiences from our collaborators have caused us, as authors, to frequently consider our positionality as writers and to truly listen to what is being said; as Jessica (she/her or they/them; trans feminine non-binary; white) states, "I feel like all too often we aren't given a fair crack at that representation. It's typically not a place where it comes from us. It's sort of like a cis person's perspective of us most of the time."

Goals of This Book

Celebrate and Honor TGE Persons *in Their Own Voices*

Throughout this book you will find quotes and vignettes from TGE persons, as well as from teachers and parents working with TGE youth. Music education professor Karen Salvador (2019) writes that, in trying to be more equitable, "sharing factual information can help, but stories are often more convincing and effective in building empathy and solidarity" (p. 60). We interviewed collaborators so that we, as two gay men, were not using our voices to speak on behalf of a population to which we do not belong. We do this not to tokenize these collaborators or to exploit their stories—we share their narratives and experiences with you in order to humanize the lived experience of TGE persons. The words of our collaborators represent the heart of this book as we attempt to humanize and personalize issues surrounding TGE students in music education. We also need to make clear that *TGE individuals are not a monolith*. There is no one "correct" way to live as a TGE person—each individual has a different story to tell. Our interviews uncover but a sliver of the TGE experience in the United States today. We offer the following example from an interview with an eight-year-old trans girl, Gabriella (she/her; trans female; white), and her parents Victoria (she/her; cis female; white) and Quincy (he/him; cis male; white), both secondary music educators, as an example of the power of these narratives.

VICTORIA: So, we went to a Facebook page of a friend here in the area who is transgender. Do you remember that picture of Anne and she's an adult trans woman. And she had posted last year a picture of her before her transition. And Gabriella said, "well, why didn't she transition as a kid like me?" And I said, well, because not everybody has supportive parents, right?

GABRIELLA: Yeah.

VICTORIA: And there's even a couple of kids at elementary school, right? Whose parents sometimes say things. What did they say?

GABRIELLA: I didn't know if there's any kids at elementary school like me.

VICTORIA: Well, there's not any trans kids but there's a couple of kids who have said that their parents have said things, right? Who was it that you told me the other day that their mom said that she didn't approve?

GABRIELLA: I don't remember.

VICTORIA: Somebody you said because of, because God—remember? There's a couple of parents in the district that . . .

QUINCY: . . . have vetoed play dates . . .

VICTORIA: They say God made you this way and . . .

GABRIELLA: Oh yeah!

VICTORIA: Do you remember that?

GABRIELLA: My friend Arianna, she's very nice. And she supports me, but her mom doesn't support me. Her mom said that a man is the way that God made me. . . . And I was just created in the wrong body.

JOSHUA: How does it make you feel when adults say things like that?

GABRIELLA: It makes me feel bad.

There is no way for any researcher or author to better describe the feeling of an eight-year-old trans girl navigating her gender in an elementary-school environment than to let her do it herself. Perhaps equally important to TGE persons sharing their experiences is for people to *listen* to and *learn* from the stories. We as authors hope that narratives and dialogues help you to perceive TGE individuals as living, breathing, three-dimensional persons—persons not dissimilar from you, the reader.

Create a Resource with and for Music Teacher Colleagues

Gender-diverse individuals may or may not be visible in our classrooms. A person may identify a certain way but until they speak it into existence, that identity may remain entirely internal. As a result of this, too many school officials assume that TGE persons do not exist in their schools, and they do not proactively plan to support TGE persons. Based on professional literature and research (e.g., Mangin, 2018, 2020; McQuillan & Leininger, 2020; Singh & Jackson, 2012; Travers, 2018), we as authors recommend that all schools and teachers proceed *as if TGE students exist in your schools*—because they do. We draw on our own experiences talking with TGE persons, our research in LGBTQA studies and music education, and our many conversations with music teacher colleagues before, during, and after professional development workshops to create a resource for working with TGE students in music classrooms.

Our Collaborators

Process

Considering the power and positionality issues described earlier, we as authors sought to collect a wide variety of individual narratives from TGE persons. Over the course of nearly two years, we conducted interviews with 30 TGE persons and several parents and teachers of TGE musicians. We became connected with these collaborators via social media posts, personal/professional connections, and recommendations from other collaborators.

We conducted interviews either in person or via Zoom videoconferencing (partially a result of the Covid-19 pandemic). With the help of a research assistant, we reviewed transcripts using an online transcription program, then we selected the sections that we would highlight. We undertook a sorting process for these interview segments by the chapter in which they would be most appropriate. Then, we utilized a process of Holistic and In-Vivo Coding (Saldaña, 2013) to arrange interview data within the chapter. The narrative data presented in this book are foundational to this project and for future research.

After choosing which interview segments we could potentially incorporate, we sent transcript segments to our collaborators for verification and/or editing—a process known as *member checking*: "Member checking is a requisite part of research conducted with marginalized groups by privileged outsiders to ensure that researcher representation of the participant's words reflects the participant's lived experiences from their standpoint" (Parson, 2019, p. 29). We made all edits requested by the collaborators before including their words in this manuscript and had all participants self-identify their pronouns, gender identity, and race. When we introduce quotes from these collaborators, we list these as they typed them, so you may notice some disparity in terms (e.g., nonbinary vs. non-binary, female vs. woman). While this may seem like a small semantic issue, it also is a small way to honor those whose lived experiences form the basis of this book.

It is important to understand that we do not purport to speak for all TGE persons or present them as a monolith. We echo the sentiments of music education professor Bridget Sweet (2016) in that the "sharing of these perspectives and stories is not to claim their thinking as right or wrong, but rather to provide a variety of perspectives from which the reader may glean ideas, validation, and encouragement" (p. xii). The real names of people and places are used to delineate these collaborators and their settings, unless they requested a pseudonym (as noted in the following).

Teachers/Parents of TGE Collaborators

Elizabeth Singer is a public school choral music educator in Northeast Ohio.

Jaqueline (Jaqui) Giltner is a private vocal instructor and member of the National Association of the Teachers of Singing who works with students identifying as trans or nonbinary.

Peter Mullins (pseudonym) is a high-school choral educator in the Northeastern United States.

Quincy and Victoria Granger (pseudonyms) are high-school choral music educators in Michigan and parents of Gabriella.

Roger Emerson is a professional composer and arranger with over 900 choral titles in print and over 30 million copies in circulation.

Susan Nace is a private school and community choral music educator in San Jose, California.

Tavia Zerman recently completed her twentieth year of teaching middle-school band at Hayes Middle School in Grand Ledge, Michigan.

Travis Gratteau-Zinnel, a former middle-school band and choir educator, is currently the Waterloo Community School District's instructional coach for fine arts in Waterloo, Iowa. He is also a doctoral student at Iowa State University in the Social and Cultural Studies of Education program.

TGE Collaborators

Aaliyah is a vocalist who sings with the South Coast Chorale in Long Beach, California.

Abdullah (Abby) Rahsheen Hall is artistic director of the Trans Chorus of Los Angeles.

Andrew Sage Mendez-McLeish is a lecturer in education and child development, a special education teacher, and a consultant and advocate for TGE youth and young adults. He holds a teaching credential and Master of Arts degree in Special Education from California State University, Dominguez Hills.

Andy is an instrumentalist who recently graduated from high school and is planning to attend college in Ohio.

Avery Brown is a singer, trumpet player, and pianist who has studied at Orange Coast College and the University of Massachusetts.

Brendan M. is a music educator with experience teaching in Denver Public Schools and in Pennsylvania school districts.

Camden Padilla is a Women, Gender, and Sexuality Studies major at the University of Redlands in Redlands, California.

Dana Hargrave is a choral singer in Southern California who performs with Los Cancioneros Master Chorale.

Dane Figueroa Edidi is a singer, dancer, actor, writer, advocate, and educator. She has self-published several books, is a six-time Helen Hayes Award nominee, and is the co-editor of the *Black Trans Prayer Book*.

Elliott Zerman is completing high school in Michigan and hopes to pursue an undergraduate degree in psychology.

Emily Goldman (pseudonym) is a choral conductor-singer on the East Coast and holds a master's degree in choral conducting.

Gabriella Granger (pseudonym) attends Fairlane Elementary School in her hometown in Michigan; she transitioned the summer before second grade.

Hayley Abramowitz is a Washington, DC-based soprano who holds a Bachelor of Music from the University of Maryland and a Master of Music from the Jacobs School of Music at Indiana University.

JB Levine is an alum of the University of Houston, a former high-school choir teacher in the Houston metro area, and current graduate student in choral conducting at San Jose State University.

Jessica Joyce is a musician and actress who performs mostly in the Los Angeles area. She is currently completing her Master of Music in Tuba Performance at her alma mater, California State University of Long Beach, and is a section leader for the Trans Chorus of Los Angeles.

Keizen Li Qian recently completed a Master of Science degree in Biology at California State University, Fullerton, where they were a part of the CSUF Singing Titans.

Kim Mendez-McLeish is currently completing a Master of Music degree in voice performance at Herb Alpert School of Music at University of California, Los Angeles, where they recently received a Bachelor of Music in the same area of study.

Lu Tesarowski is a graduate of San Jose State University and the Associate Conductor of iSing Girl's Chorus in the San Francisco Bay Area.

Mari Esabel Valverde is an award-winning composer predominantly of vocal music. She holds degrees from St. Olaf College and San Francisco Conservatory of Music.

Marshall Agagas Mojica is a choral student at Renaissance High School for the Arts in Long Beach, California.

Mason (pseudonym) is a music education major (instrumental) at a large university on the West Coast.

Max Berland is an instrumental music educator at Ysmael Villegas Middle School in Riverside, California.

Melanie Stapleton is a choral director in the Houston Independent School District and recently completed her Master of Music Education degree at the University of North Texas.

Michael Bussewitz-Quarm is an actively commissioned composer living in New York with her wife and two children. She can be reached through her website at www.MBQStudio.com.

Michelle Guzowski is a composer and sings with the Cleveland Transgender Choir.

MJ Rawls is an actress/singer/dancer/choreographer based in Chicago, Illinois. She is also a teaching artist and has taught a series entitled Trans 101 to local CPS students and teachers.

Mystic Rose (pseudonym) is an undergraduate music major at the University of North Texas in Denton, Texas.
Percy Mendiola is a student at Renaissance High School for the Arts in Long Beach, California.
Phoebe Singletary is a nonbinary public educator and activist for trans youth; she studied at the University of Central Florida, Orlando, Florida.
Rex W. is a nonbinary LGBTQ+ speaker and educator who studied music in college.
Riley Wells is a senior at Grand Valley State University in Michigan, where he is majoring in vocal performance. They intend to pursue a master's degree after graduation, and a career in opera.
Ryder Emerson is a professional musical theater performer based in Ashland, Oregon.

Organization of the Book

This book is laid out in two major parts: Context and Praxis. Throughout this Introduction and the first two chapters, we provide a broad view of TGE persons by examining key questions about gender-sexual diversity. Chapter 1 introduces TGE persons—who they are and the kinds of things with which they deal in a society that assumes everyone is cisgender (read: not TGE). We discuss key terminology that will be used throughout the book and attempt to answer three main questions: why this book? why now? and why us? Chapter 2 depicts the realities that TGE youth face in schools. It is important that music educators understand how students navigate school environments that may or may not affirm their gender identities.

Part II, Praxis, lays out practical suggestions for implementation in music programs. We draw on ideas and best practices from LGBTQA studies and Culturally Responsive Pedagogy, in addition to our own experiences as teachers, researchers, and professional development leaders. Chapter 3 builds upon the previous two chapters by helping teachers understand how they can become *safe people* who provide *safe spaces* for TGE students. Chapter 4 provides practical advice for how music educators can make TGE students feel welcome and celebrated in their classrooms/programs. Chapter 5 explores how policy can influence the life of TGE persons in schools and what music educators can do to participate in the policy process. Because vocal/choral music has many uniquely "gendered" aspects, Chapter 6 provides guidance specific to choral settings. We conclude the book with Chapter 7, focusing almost entirely on the words of our collaborators. Each participant was asked to give advice to music educators about working with, and honoring, TGE students. We provide additional supporting resources through a series of appendices, including a glossary of gender- and sexuality-related terms. We hope this book is useful as you explore the wide-ranging and ever-evolving topic of gender diversity.

PART I
CONTEXT

This book is organized into two parts. Part I establishes context for learning how to honor TGE students in music education. We provide an overview of topics and vocabulary related to gender diversity, including a brief discussion of the role intersectionality played in learning from our collaborators. For individuals less familiar with the complexities of gender, we endeavor to provide foundational context that should be helpful throughout the book. In addition, our TGE collaborators share their experiences from school and school music program settings. Stories illustrating negative school climates contrast with narratives of resiliency, demonstrating that TGE persons are not monolithic, but beautifully individual. Having explored conceptual and situational foundations, readers should feel better prepared to engage with practical suggestions contained within Part II.

1

Starting a Conversation about Trans and Gender-Expansive Persons

Chapter Guide

DANA (she/her; female; white): My experience has taught me that there's so much more to being a woman (or man) that goes beyond observable physical gender, sex organs, physical appearance, voice, etc. There are intangible aspects of femininity and masculinity that are very subtle, and even genetic males and females don't always experience them because I think there's a mix of both genders in all of us and I still struggle with that. That said, my experience has taught me that we humans strongly need alignment between our perception of our internal and external gender identity in order to be at peace. When it's misaligned, we have a compulsory need to do something about it, else suffer profoundly.

Gender, American Society, and the Value of Music

Gender and sexuality landscapes continue to change rapidly in the United States. Legal cases appear with regularity in state and federal courts, and

Honoring Trans and Gender-Expansive Students in Music Education. Matthew L. Garrett and Joshua Palkki, Oxford University Press. © Oxford University Press 2021. DOI: 10.1093/oso/9780197506592.003.0002

members of the LGBTQA community celebrate forward progress and regroup after setbacks toward equity. These movements forward and backward resonate beyond social and political circles to communities, schools, and backyards of people throughout the country. Issues related to gender dominate news stories and have become a focal point for adults on the silver screen, as well as for youth in American schools. Across the country, transgender and gender-expansive (TGE) persons are coming out and speaking up to share their stories (e.g., Olson et al., 2015; Travers, 2018). We use *gender-expansive* as an umbrella term to describe a broader range of gender expressions and identities. TGE persons often feel that their gender can best be acknowledged as existing within a spectrum. As music educators, we have a responsibility to listen to such stories—the lived experiences—of our students. We also have a responsibility to make sure that all of the youth in our school music programs have meaningful music experiences in safe and encouraging learning environments. Researchers writing about gender in the areas of music and music education have primarily focused on the differences between men and women, which has reinforced gender roles and gender stereotypes in music education. Scholars writing on the topics of LGBTQA issues in education focus almost exclusively on lesbian, gay, and bisexual perspectives (DePalma, 2013; Elze, 2007; McCarthy, 2003), with little or no mention of transgender viewpoints. Gender discourse is important for all music educators because of the duration and strength of teacher–student relationships we develop over time. What we, as teachers, do and say matters, particularly for TGE persons who may not self-identify or "out" themselves to us, personally. For these reasons, all music educators can play an important role in being safe people for TGE students (e.g., Garrett & Spano, 2017; Palkki & Caldwell, 2018; Southerland, 2018; Taylor, 2018). As social norms and discourses surrounding gender change, so should the policies and routines of our music classrooms.

Trans and gender issues, in general, remain in the foreground of American social consciousness. In 2014, the country seemed to be at a "tipping point" regarding trans issues (Steinmetz, 2014a), as indicated by news media coverage (e.g., Bernstein, 2014; Schoenberg, 2015). The visibility and activism of celebrities and public figures like Chaz Bono, Laverne Cox, Janet Mock, Nicole Maines, and Caitlyn Jenner have ignited conversations about trans and gender issues. Heightened trans visibility and representation has been important to several of our collaborators. The Granger family describes a conversation that took place when their trans daughter, Gabriella (she/her; female; white), was in first grade:

GABRIELLA: First I heard about drag queens. And then, I figured out about transgender and I loved it, and I changed.

VICTORIA (SHE/HER; FEMALE; WHITE): So, what happened was we have a former student who was a drag queen, who is a drag queen. And so, Todd was posting pictures on Instagram and I said, Hey, Gabriella, you know Todd, and here's Todd as a drag queen. And, and her response to that was, "Oh, that's great, I think I'm a drag queen." And I was like, "Ooo, I'm not sure. I'm not sure if that's the direction exactly." So, we just happened on a book, at the library: a kid's book. I don't remember the name of it either . . . and it was a story where Nick becomes Hope and then her closet is full of dresses. And Gabriella read that book. It's not even published anymore, I don't think, 'cause we've looked for it. But she read that book and she was like, "Oh, well that's, that's me!" And I said, "well that's fine. You can, you could be called something else and live as a girl right now if you want." And she was like, "okay, let's do that." [The book is called] *Be who you are* by Jennifer Carr.

Similarly, JB (they/them; non-binary; white) recalls a moment when their life was impacted by print media:

> So, the "aha" moment did not really come until I read this book right here. This is the one, this is the book, I dunno if you know it [*Sissy: A Coming of Gender Story*]. So, I was just on the Daily Show Instagram page when I saw this person, Jacob Tobia, this non-binary person being interviewed. And what they were saying about how, "I don't see gender as neutral. I don't want everyone to have no gender. I want gender to be this amazing, colorful buffet where you can wake up and pick whatever gender you want and throw it on." And I was like, "this is what I need. This is what I want." So, I read their book immediately and I was like, "That's me."

As more TGE persons make their presence known through various media, we might expect to be made aware of more TGE students learning in our classrooms. School music teachers can create welcoming classrooms by signifying their respect for gender diversity.

Educators may be unfamiliar with or may not have considered gender diversity with relation to TGE youth. Teachers might not have had any training related to the inclusion of LGBTQA students in college, in continuing education settings, or through professional development opportunities (Garrett & Spano, 2017). Perhaps, due to a lack of training or familiarity, teachers might feel threatened or intimidated when working with students with whom they share little or no common lived experiences (Savin-Williams, 2018). Trans and/or gender-expansive students are present in all schools—yet they are often marginalized in school environments: "The number of transgender persons who participate in the education system is difficult to measure because the high level of societal transphobia ensures that many transgender individuals are not comfortable publicly acknowledging their identity" (Rands, 2009, p. 421). Furthermore, there can be a perceived generational gap related to educators understanding gender diversity:

> Many younger people indicate that they readily recognize and accept themselves as transgender. They can now see transgender images in popular culture, read about transgender issues in the mainstream media, and connect with other transgender youth through web pages, chat rooms, social networking sites, and other online venues. As a result, it seems that significantly fewer younger transgender people today lack information for an extended period of time or have a sense of prolonged confusion. (Beemyn & Rankin, 2011, p. 114)

In other words, TGE persons are "coming out," to themselves and to others, at a young age *because* they have a sense that there are more people with similar lived experiences, as portrayed in media formats. One of our collaborators, Phoebe (she/her or they/them; non-binary; white), speaks to a different perception of TGE persons, possibly related to generational differences:

> I think it's easier for people who are older to accept binary transgender people, "oh this person is switching," because they have a mindset and they don't have any problem with that because they're just like, "OK, I'm just going to let this person be the person they want to be." And there are people who have problems with that. My personal experience with people is: "I'm going to do my best" because—I'm mainly thinking about teachers—"I'm going to do my best to support this student." Whereas I think my generation (Gen Z) is more so "let people express themselves however they want to" and gender being a part of that so even if somebody is somewhat gender variant, they're understanding that this person can do what they want.

Differences in how we perceive others is likely influenced by our lived experiences, whether limited or broader in scope. Meaningful education and professional development for *all* music teachers can serve as a means to improve awareness of and celebrate gender diversity in school environments. A number of research studies have suggested that teacher training related to LGBTQA issues can have a positive impact on a teacher's ability to create opportunities for equal access to quality learning experiences (Garrett & Spano, 2017; Mayo, 2014; Ngo, 2003; Puchner & Klein, 2011; Szalacha, 2004). School music teachers, in particular, stand to benefit from gender education and training opportunities, given the high value young people place on music and the need for a safe learning environment in which students can express themselves (Garrett & Spano, 2017; McQueen, 2006).

Cultural and generational shifts have inspired emerging lines of scholarship on TGE issues in music education (e.g., Aguirre, 2018; Bartolome, 2016; Nichols, 2013; Palkki, 2020a; Sauerland, 2018; Silveira & Goff, 2016; Silveira, 2019). These authors have attempted to let the voices of trans/gender-variant persons, and those with whom they work, speak for themselves in the context of American music education. This scholarship coincided with a burgeoning conversation about trans choral singers on social media (e.g., Facebook) and choral bulletin boards (e.g., ChoralNet). Unfortunately, social media discourse often reveals a distinct lack of empathy and understanding about trans issues among music teachers. As an example, in December 2014, a concerned high-school choir teacher posted in a choral director group on Facebook about a trans boy in choir. The teacher explained that the student desired to sing tenor and had been "practicing low" and very much wanted to switch voice parts and wear a tux. This teacher's reaction is encouraging—she immediately was understanding and supportive about pronouns and concert dress, and she was trying to do the best thing for her student. What is not encouraging were some of the responses to this post, including the very first reply:

> Tell him there is such a thing as a boy-soprano. Then, tell him you didn't wake up one morning and decided [*sic*] to be a choir director; you went to college to learn the difference between a soprano and a tenor and that he has to sing soprano. (social media, December 2, 2014)

Likewise, in response to a similar request in the same Facebook group, one teacher wrote:

> Unpopular Opinion: I know this person identifies as a male, but that does not make them one. Their voice part is still the same. Shouldn't be in male choir. (social media, June 9, 2015)

If teachers value mutual respect in their classrooms, it is important to lead by example in actions and words. A commitment to lifelong learning, through a decision to teach young people, affords educators opportunities to reflect on their values and biases. While we, as teachers, do not necessarily need to agree with every new idea we discover or uncover, we can certainly agree to disagree or to reconsider our positions, based on our ability to learn and reflect on the impact of our actions on our students.

There are a number of ways that individuals express gender in music settings, from attire to instrument choice (Cates, 2019). This variety of expression is significant, because people often misunderstand the ways in which society constantly reinforces a gender binary—the notion that there are only two genders (man and woman; boy and girl), defined by tendencies toward masculinity and femininity. Increased attention to issues of gender in academic writings (e.g., educator magazines focused on professional development and research journals) can, and we believe should, inform the ways practicing teachers work to improve student learning. Further application of scholarship to the practices of music educators can help to ensure that TGE youth are afforded opportunities to develop, both musically and as individuals.

School music learning environments can afford young people with safe space (created by safe people) to explore their emotional intelligence and to develop a sense of individuality. The idea that school music experiences are important in adolescents' identity development has been supported by researchers for more than two decades (Campbell et al., 2007; Hylton, 1981). As students reaffirm or explore their identities and the expression of those identities, music teachers can serve as supportive allies and mentors to all students. TGE students who identify music teachers as supportive are more likely to participate in school music programs. The 2013 School Climate Survey published by GLSEN reports that about half of respondents "[participated] in band, orchestra, chorus, or choir (47.9%)" (Kosciw et al., 2014, p. 58). A strong sense of belonging accompanies participation in school music programs (e.g., Adderley et al., 2003; Morrison, 2001). Music teachers, therefore, bear an increased level of responsibility to ensure that all students, including those who have been historically marginalized, have equal access to school music experiences. In this book, we illustrate how music educators can become safe people for TGE youth in their schools. Before beginning our discussion in earnest, we define some important terms here that will be used throughout the book.

Key Terms

We understand that these gender- and identity-related terms can be confusing and even overwhelming. It's okay not to know what these things mean.

Everyone—including us as authors—is on a journey to become more aware of these terms and the ramifications of their use. We are fully aware that by the time this book goes to print, this list may be partially obsolete, as gender vernacular is a rapidly shifting field. A comprehensive glossary of gender-related vocabulary appears in Appendix A.

- **Gender identity**: a deeply held internal sense or feeling of being a particular gender or genders. For trans persons, their sex assigned at birth and their gender identity are not necessarily the same. People whose sex assigned at birth aligns with their gender identity are known as *cisgender*.
- **Gender expression**: the outward presentation of a person's femininity, masculinity, or other socially gendered traits, including choices of clothing, hairstyle, voice, and body language. Shared personal pronouns also serve as a means of expressing gender.
- **Gender-expansive**: an umbrella term that acknowledges the variety of gender identities and expressions in children, youth, and adults.
- **Intersectionality**: "People's lives and the organization of power in a given society are better understood as being shaped not by a single axis of social division, be it race or gender or class, but by many axes that work together and influence each other" (Collins & Bilge, 2016, p. 12).
- **Sexual orientation/sexuality**: emotional, romantic, or sexual feelings toward other people. Sexual behavior involves the choices one makes in acting on one's sexuality as part of the human condition. One's sexual activity does not define one's sexual orientation; typically, it is the attraction that helps determine orientation (Parents and Friends of Lesbians and Gays [PFLAG], 2019). We have chosen to use the term *sexual orientation* to denote the feelings (or lack thereof) one has toward another. For a deeper discussion on the use of the term, see Ahmed (2006).
- **Trans, transgender**: umbrella, or broadly encompassing term of many gender identities of those who do not identify or do not exclusively identify with their sex assigned at birth. The term *transgender* is not indicative of gender expression, sexual orientation, hormonal makeup, physical anatomy, or how one is perceived in daily life (Trans Student Educational Resources [TSER]).

Defining a few key terms will help establish common vocabulary for further conversation. We explore two of these terms, *transgender* and *gender-expansive*, later in this chapter.

Foundations for Further Conversation

Perception is reality for each one of us. Our perceptions vary, based on a number of factors, including age, ethnicity, socioeconomic status, race, geographical location, sexuality, gender, and lived experiences. The discourse surrounding gender can be fraught with assumptions and misunderstandings. Regardless of challenges caused by bias of perception or misinterpretation, foundational vocabulary is necessary to create a common starting place to hold conversations (Davis, 2009). Moving from larger concepts to more specific terms used within the LGBTQA community, we start the journey by attempting to disentangle the multifaceted concepts of sex, sexuality, and gender.

Intersections of Gender, Sex, and Sexuality

Gender and *sex* are not synonymous, although many people use them interchangeably in daily discourse. *Sex* historically has referred to the biological/genetic features that distinguish males and females, the product of three combined elements: genetics, anatomy, and hormones. Medical professionals use genetics to assign and classify sex based on a combination of X and Y chromosomes. While many people are born with chromosome combinations that easily classify them as male or female, some people are born *intersex*—with chromosomal combinations other than XY-male and XX-female. It is a common misconception that gender is a spectrum while sex is a binary. Anne Fausto-Sterling (2012), professor of biology and gender studies at Brown University and influential gender theorist, notes that at birth a baby has up to *five layers* of sex that "do not always agree with one another" (p. 5). For the purposes of this book, we refer to *sex* as features that distinguish male, female, and intersex individuals. Those people born with XX chromosomes often exhibit higher levels of estrogen, while XY-combination individuals often have more testosterone, although this is not always the case. Just as sex may be expressed beyond a binary of male and female, we can also consider gender as existing within a spectrum of possibilities.

Gender, on the other hand, is a set of socially constructed and context- and culture-dependent ideas and behaviors. Historically, gender categories, behaviors, and physical attributes have been considered as "masculine" or "feminine" (e.g., Airton, 2019; Bornstein, 1994; Järviluoma et al., 2003). Elements of *gender expression*, including hairstyles, clothing, gestures/gait, and posture, have traditionally related to gender norms within societies/

cultures. According to West and Zimmerman (1987), among others, biology does not create gender, but rather, we "do gender" via attributes such as the clothes we wear, the mannerisms we use, and the pitch of our voice—all attributes that play a role in musical experiences. Gender categories are culturally contextual attributes associated with the concepts of masculinity and femininity. A *gender binary* occurs when gender is reduced or oversimplified to two categories. For example, many people in the United States hold expectations that girls and women are feminine, and that men who exhibit feminine characteristics are not normal. Kim (they/them; genderqueer woman; white/Latinx) describes: "I . . . feel like as someone socialized a female—which some people [believe] that's not a thing, but I believe in my experience, that has been a thing—is that speaking up for myself isn't what I'm supposed to do." For the purposes of this book, we use the term *gender* to refer to a spectrum of gender identities and expressions, rather than to signify a man/male, woman/female binary.

Gender and *sexuality/sexual orientation* are distinctly separate concepts that are often confused as being the same (for a helpful analytical model, see Serano, 2013, pp. 152–155). People often conflate gender and sexuality because of assumptions made about someone's sexuality based on their adherence to or rejection of socially created gender norms (Butler, 1990; Schilt & Westbrook, 2009). For example, feminine men and masculine women are often assumed to be gay, based on stereotyped expectations, although conceptually, gender and sexuality are different. While it is important to understand the distinctions between these two concepts, *gender* and *sexuality/sexual orientation* do not exist alone; they also intersect with one another, but are not determined by one another (Stryker, 2008), as illustrated by our collaborator JB (they/them; non-binary; white) in a *Tablet* magazine article:

> Entering ninth grade in 2006, my daily application of eyeliner accompanied by a rainbow of plastic bead bracelets up my arm won me the label "emo" and assured that my sexuality was called into question by everyone I knew—including myself. In high school in the late 2000s, I didn't know about anywhere near as many label choices for queer identities as I do today. I never saw myself as a "gay man," because neither "gay" nor "man" ever felt like they really fit. (Levine, 2020, paras. 3–4)

This intersection of gender and sexuality is important when considering the multilayered experiences of TGE persons.

The LGBTQA acronym functions as an intersecting vernacular catch-all for queer persons. Likewise, alternate forms of this collection of letters, like LGBT and LGBTQ+, also can be used in an attempt to represent all members of queer communities. While this distinction is not inherently bad, the "T" is often forgotten or neglected in action. This exclusion, unintentional or otherwise, illustrates a larger quandary about how TGE persons fit into the larger queer community. Abby (they/them; non-binary; Black) shares their story of belonging:

> I used to say I was a gay, black man with a lot of sugar in their tank. But I was always a little bit too much extra for my gay friends, beyond just being a girl. It was like, "wow." So, I always fit there but didn't fit there and there was always something. And during that time, I had started doing a lot more within the trans community, especially with HRC, Human Rights Campaign. And more and more I was gravitating to all these trans men and women, gender nonconforming, gender nonbinary people. But at the time I didn't know they were trans or trans identified at all. I just looked at them like, "Oh, I found a new tribe." And through that, I found my voice again.

Similarly, MJ (she/her or they/them; trans woman; Black) describes how trans persons are a distinctive part of the larger LGBTQA community:

> I mean, and even in the gay community, you know, trans women are—it's like the trans community is its own community separate from the gay community. And most of my friends were gay men. And what if I, you know, all of a sudden decide to be my true self, would they accept me? Would they not run away?

Careful use of the LGBTQA acronym is needed, then, to avoid exclusion of intersecting components that people use to indicate who they are. Pressure to find and use the best label can be challenging due to preconceived ideas and expectations of gender.

Gender Categories, Stereotypes, and Expectations

Traditional gender norms are taught and learned from a very young age. As young as age two or three, children begin to comprehend gender categories through their perceptions of gender expression (Sullivan & Urraro, 2019a). More traditional boy and girl signifiers are present in textual form and color palette (blue signifying male and pink signifying female) in an endless variety of baby products. Commercial clothing designs begin to differentiate between boys (e.g., shorts) and girls (e.g., dresses) for infants and toddlers. Many of our collaborators speak of enacting their gender expression based on societal expectations to which they were expected to conform:

- MJ (she/her or they/them; trans woman; Black): I knew that I was an effeminate boy, B-O-I, when I was younger. And my parents always said to me, "don't walk like that. Don't talk like that. Don't move like that. Don't do anything that's feminine." [. . .] When I was around my parents, I acted a certain way. When I was around others, I acted a totally different way. And so, it was like I was playing two fields, and it was very traumatic because then once I got out of high school, going into college, I'm like, "I don't know who I am."
- Rex (they/them; non-binary; white): I would go home, and my parents started catching on to seeing what I was wearing [androgynous clothing]. And I remember distinctly them sitting me down one day at the kitchen table to have a conversation. And they were like, "you are not allowed to dress this way anymore. You can't wear men's pants." They hated that I was wearing studded belts. And they were like, "this is inappropriate. You need to be wearing appropriate clothes for a girl your age." And like, "you're going to go shopping with your mom from now on and she's going to pick things out for you." And so that was that experience of also being told, "you are not to express yourself this way."
- Michael (she/her; trans female; white): I remember growing up—this is something I haven't talked about in a long time, but this kind of is connected to what we're talking about. In high school, I made a concerted effort to learn how to talk like a male because I used very flowery adjectives and walk like a male. I did this because I wanted to fit in. I don't remember if I'd tried to drop my voice, but I do remember, the way I use language was something where I felt like I needed to change, to adapt to the males that were in high school. And the same thing with walking. I changed the gait of my walk after observing the way my male classmates carried themselves.
- Avery (he/him or they/them; agender; white): I was confused and annoyed when I entered puberty and people started boxing me in. Not only was my body changing in uncomfortable ways, but on top of that I also then had to navigate the minefield of sexism and stereotypical gender expectations that were imposed on me, being perceived as female. Suddenly my mannerisms, interests, and clothing style were under intense scrutiny, and I felt pressured to discard my "non-feminine" traits in order to fit in. It was hard.

Young children participating in day care, preschool, and kindergarten are sometimes grouped by boys and girls in a variety of ways, including division with regard to restroom facilities. This type of segregation can develop into unintended stereotypes associated with specific genders. According to Anne Fausto-Sterling,

> Even before the age of one, infants have assimilated the gendered connections that surround them. [. . .] As they enter their third year children's knowledge of culturally specific gender picks up steam, and kids start to express self-awareness of themselves as boys or girls. (2012, p. 54)

As TGE young persons grow and mature, they navigate educational systems that may or may not be prepared to honor their gender identities.

Schools are sites where gender roles are reinforced through a hidden curriculum, in which socially reinforced norms dictate what is acceptable, thereby reifying a *gender binary* (e.g., Apple, 2004; Pascoe, 2011; Thorne, 1993). As a manifestation of this binary, until very recently, most buildings in the United States had two restrooms only—men and women. *Gender*, however, is more complex than a simplistic binary construct, and further deconstruction into smaller components is helpful.

Visualizing Gender Identity and Gender Expression

To better understand the lived experiences of TGE individuals, it is important and helpful to illustrate the differences between gender identity, gender expression, sexuality, and emotional attraction, as these terms are frequently misused and are misunderstood to be similar or the same. A helpful tool for visualizing these concepts is the Gender Unicorn created by Trans Student Education Resources (http://www.transstudent.org/gender) (Figure 1.1).

Gender identity (the rainbow icon in the Unicorn's thought bubble) might be easily considered as a type of internal gender compass—how we experience gender through a variety of contexts. You'll note in the illustration that *gender identities* are possible as degrees of being female/woman/girl, or somewhere else along a continuum of possibilities. In Figure 1.1, the starting point is symbolized as small circles on the left side of a series of lines. Possibilities continue to extend through the arrowhead on the right side of the lines. As an example, if someone were charting their gender identity as entirely female on the Gender Unicorn graphic, they might place a dot on the arrowhead, closest to the text "Female/Woman/Girl." That same individual might place

Figure 1.1. The Gender Unicorn by Trans Student Educational Resources (TSER)

two other dots on the open circles to the far left of the arrowheads for the texts "Male/Man/Boy" and "Other Gender(s)." The underlying idea within each category and the descriptors within each category is that these labels exist on a spectrum or continuum. Just as gender is a socially constructed idea, *gender identity* is a construct that can help an individual define who they are. The use of multiple spectrums, then, can allow an individual to more accurately convey who they are to other people. TGE persons may identify with multiple spectrums (e.g., identify as female and male simultaneously).

Gender expression (represented by the small dots outlining the left side of the Unicorn's body, from horn to tail) refers to how someone exhibits their gender identity in and to the world around them. It is important to remember that *gender identity* and *gender expression* are socially constructed and that associations of behaviors to a spectrum of masculinity and femininity are culturally learned and reinforced behaviors. The ways in which some individuals express their gender can correspond to their gender identity, while for other individuals, gender identity and gender expression might be different. For example, someone may identify as male and sing using a higher voice (i.e., countertenor)—a behavior not traditionally associated with masculinity, through culturally reinforced ideals. In another instance, a self-identified male may express himself by growing a mustache and a beard—behavior more traditionally associated with masculinity. The importance of a continuum of *gender expression* might also be understood when working with a countertenor who has a full beard and mustache. As we discuss later in the book, some trans individuals do not consider their voices to be related to their *gender expression*. A trans woman may speak and sing in a lower vocal range and express herself by wearing a choir dress. In other words, there are many ways and a large spectrum of variation in the way people conceive of their own gender.

The concepts of *sexuality* or *sexual orientation* and *romantic* or *emotional attraction* (represented by the intertwined hearts on the Unicorn's chest) refer to how someone acts on or does not act on—in the case of aromantic or asexual people—their physical and/or emotional attractions. The distinction between *sexuality* and *emotional attraction* is important to understand in order to acknowledge the complexity of someone's individual identity. *Sexuality* (or *sexual orientation*) refers to sexual or physical attraction. An individual may experience (a) physical attraction to members of the same sex or gender (*homosexual*); (b) attraction to members of a sex or gender different from their own (*heterosexual*); (c) little to no sexual attraction to others (*asexual*); or (d) attraction to both men and women or other genders (*pansexual* or *bisexual*). *Emotional attraction* refers to a non-sexual bond of caring and compassion for another person. *Emotional attraction* and *physical* or *sexual attraction* can be interrelated or not. For example, a person might be emotionally attracted to women but sexually attracted to men; or, one might be emotionally attracted to lesbian women but sexually attracted to all genders. Human beings are complicated creatures when it comes to considering the ways in which we identify and express ourselves.

The frequently changing nature and complexity of concepts relating to gender, sex, and sexuality can be confusing and frustrating. Fear not. We can only know what we know, and we can continue to be lifelong learners on this front. This complexity further highlights the need for "generating trans informed knowledge and understandings" (Martino & Cumming-Potvin, 2018, p. 689). To help develop that knowledge, we share the lived experiences of our TGE collaborators throughout this book.

Learning about Gender Diversity from TGE Persons

Generational Perceptions of Gender Diversity

Our collaborators described how the gender landscape has changed in recent years and how the current generation of students in PK–12 schools differs from older age groups. Young children express gender identity more openly for self-expressed reasons that include how they perceive the world with a broader sense of gender, recognition of the shifting cultural zeitgeist, and increased visibility of TGE persons in media and popular culture. MJ (she/her or they/them; trans woman; Black) describes their perspective:

> Nowadays a lot of kids are smart. Like we, I had an eight year old, while I was in Colorado, come to me and tell me that they use pronouns they, them, theirs—that they identify not as binary—as an eight year old! I wish my eight year old self would hear that! And I wish I could go back in time and tell my eight year old self "identify as that forever!" Until you actually transition, which is going to happen when you're older, but you know, you are non-binary. And I wish someone would've told me that when I was eight years old, because I think, although yes, it was a journey for me, it would have been a lot easier for me. And I can handle things a lot easier growing up.

Michelle (she/her; transgender female; white), a 63-year-old, replied to a question whether or not she thought that society had changed since she was a child:

> They have it made, compared to what I couldn't go through. Because when I was growing up, there was nothing I could do about my feelings. [. . .] Society generally has become more accepting. So, the younger generation has a lot more going for them in their favor overall. There's still a long way to go, but in general, they have it much easier and it's more accepted. Society accepts it definitely as a whole.

Realizing Gender Identity

Each one of us develops at our own pace, and that journey can meander or remain constant. Reflecting back on lived experiences can help to pinpoint life moments that served to define our gender identity, or identities. Some of our collaborators had very early realizations about their gender identity, while others discovered it later in life. Dane (she/her; trans woman; Black [African, Cuban, Indigenous]) recalls an experience from a young age:

> When I was three years old, I had a doll. And my mother had given me this doll and it reminded me of my grandma, and some people in my family were like, "take that doll away, that's a boy not a girl." And I looked up at my mother and I said, "I'm a girl, I don't know what they're talking about."

Ryder (he/him; TransMan; not specified) recalls the atmosphere at his home, growing up:

> And all that time I was very much a tomboy growing up. Never really had any inkling that there was anything other. A bit of ignorance, a bit of, naivete, if you will. But also just the comfort of being at home. My parents and my friends and everybody were always fine with me being the most tomboy that I was. So, I never felt any sort of pull or desire to be anything different.

Likewise, Aaliyah (she/her; trans woman; Black) identifies her childhood recollections:

> I always knew since I was little, when I noticed that I was different. [. . .] That was so confusing but that's how I knew that I was supposed to be a woman.

Acknowledging gender identity, however, is a distinctly individual process, and some of the TGE persons we spoke with did not experience such early realizations. Emily (she/her; trans woman; white) says, "I was certainly not one of those kids who was saying, 'no, I'm a girl' at age five." Similarly, Avery (he/him or they/them; agender; white) notes: "Some people discover their gender identities early on, during childhood, but that didn't really happen for me. Growing up, I never felt like a boy or a girl, but that sentiment wasn't inherently distressing." Elliott (he/him; trans gay male; white) shares his experience, which was not clear to him until later in life:

> I had seen trans people [who] were like, "Oh yeah, I've known ever since I was a kid." And I'm just like, well, I wasn't sure. . . . I knew that I was a tomboy or something, but I didn't know that I was just a boy [*chuckles*]. I didn't understand where those feelings were coming from, I guess. So, I was just really confused because I was like, well, I didn't feel like a guy necessarily, but I definitely had some dysphoria from a young age. But I didn't know what it was. I thought it was just like something that a normal tomboy girl would go through.

What we say and do, as teachers, can impact identity formation, often in unseen ways and over long periods of time; hence, a framework is necessary for informing music educators' approaches to teaching with a distinctly intersectional and gender-expansive approach.

Self-Acceptance and Coming Out

Realizing and accepting one's own gender identity can be a complicated process if one identifies as trans or gender-expansive, often due to external pressures. This process is only as visible to others as an individual wishes for it to be. Wrestling and coming to terms with a true sense of self is celebrated internally. The coming out process is the more public acknowledgment of self-identifying as trans or gender-expansive. Accepting yourself and coming out are both processes that can be felt as freeing for some persons and distressing or extremely uncomfortable for others. This distress or discomfort associated with misalignment of assigned sex at birth and gender identity is known as *gender dysphoria*, and it may be expressed in many forms, as described by our collaborators.

- Avery (he/him or they/them; agender; white): In the middle of my sophomore year [of college], I was dealing with a lot of life challenges, in addition to intense gender dysphoria. I was hospitalized several times and was ultimately unable to finish school, but the support that people showed me throughout made things much more bearable. I wasn't able to start hormone replacement therapy until after I took medical leave and moved back home. After a long and slow period of stabilization and recovery, I started again as a brand-new person at a brand-new school. From day one, I was Avery. I think that helped make things easier for me, socially.
- Michael (she/her; trans female; white): When I reached puberty, I realized my body was changing in ways I wasn't really crazy about. For me personally, there were other elements adding to my gender dysphoria. I had a chronic illness and was traumatized by what was happening to my body as a result of this illness.

The stories from our collaborators highlight the varied experiences that TGE persons may have in regard to relationships, embodiment, and access to resources—three factors that can greatly influence self-acceptance and disclosure processes. TGE students may disclose their gender identity, or thoughts about their gender identity, to you as a music educator before other people in their lives. It is important, then, that we as music educators understand the processes of gender identity development.

Gender Identity Evolves over Time

Our collaborators consistently remarked how their gender identity is not static—that it evolves over time. That evolution can progress gradually for some persons, while others may experience a more rapid sense of change. These stories re-emphasize the fact that each TGE person has their own individual path to navigate.

- Jessica (she/her or they/them; transfeminine non-binary; white): In the trans community we call it being an egg. And when you go from your previous life into realizing that you're trans, it's like the egg cracking. So, I remember little moments as early as elementary school or middle school where these little cracks would form in the eggshell, where I would wonder, "Why couldn't I do these more feminine things? Why did I have to do these masculine things?" When it finally came to a head, though, was towards the end of my undergrad degree when my counselors and psychiatrist sort of posed the question to me. For the longest time before that I had always thought "Oh, I'd like to be Jessica, but that's impossible." Or "I'd like to be Jessica, but I don't know what my family is going to do"—or "I feel like Jessica, but that's not really a thing, is it?"

- Keizen (they/them; gender creative; Han Chinese): So, transition . . . I started to feel uncomfortable being "she'd" as early as college. And there was like some drama around gender and sexism that I was working through during college. But it wasn't until a couple of years after I graduated that I came out first as gender queer. And then you know, it took until I met someone who really was gender creative who had used testosterone to express that gender identity that he felt. And I was like, "Oh yeah, that's more like how I feel." So that's when I came out as male and started using male pronouns and transitioned hormonally [at age 23].
- JB (they/them; non-binary; white): The labels that would really say "I'm on some sort of gender journey" took shape at the beginning of last school year. [. . .] I just started questioning my gender. I just did. I just started dropping hints to friends. Things like "I'm not sure, I'm not saying I'm trans, I'm just saying, I don't know." "I'm not trans but—" I think what I said to my friend at one point, maybe really early on was like, "when I think about being a boy, I feel very kind of dull and kind of drab" and kind of like, "Oh, okay. I mean, I guess I could live that life. It sounds boring, but . . . I guess." And then when I think about living life in my feminine self, I was like, all of a sudden life feels like this amazing dance, this like joy-filled—like my soul can just be who it wants to be. Like my soul can dance. I wrote this one poem in which I said that your soul has permission to dance at all hours. And I think that's when I thought about, "if I were to just fully embrace my feminine side for whatever that meant, then I would feel like my soul has permission to dance at all hours." And I didn't know what to do with that.

Our collaborators' experiences illustrate the spectrum of gender journeys that TGE persons can experience. Music educators will want to keep in mind that this journey may or may not be difficult, and that support from a teacher can be invaluable to these students.

The Power of Language

Names and labels matter. For TGE individuals, labels can be extremely important in expressing their identity to others. Use of language to describe identities is a sensitive, delicate area of discourse because the words we choose can affirm those identities or nullify them. The infallibility of language falls short, however, in describing one's true essence and identity. Our collaborators speak about the importance of words and vocabulary in navigating their gender journeys:

- Abby (they/them; gender non-binary; Black): What's so funny is the gender journey, I realized, it was always there, what I didn't have was the vocabulary for it. So, I was okay when I was in my twenties and thirties. If I was performing in a show and they want me to play really androgynous or in drag or even just doing drag. But even with that for me, if I wanted to wear makeup, beat my face, wear a lip, wear nail polish or something like that. That is now part of my day to day. But back in the 80s, it was considered, something to be ashamed of because you are acting like a sissy. In the 90s it was "Oh, they're kind of edgy" or you know, they're "androgynous." We didn't have the vocabulary for nonconforming, non-binary, trans male, trans female. We didn't even say transgender back then or at least "I" didn't. We didn't. But I now realize for me, it was always there, right on the surface, just right there. And I'm so grateful that we do have this language now because it is a little vexing when you know that you're part of a "group" you know . . . LGB and end up the forgotten T, (non-binary). This is why I go by queer now. I knew I was in that "Q"—"queer"—spectrum.
- Sage (he/him; trans masculine non-binary; white/Latinx): I very much tried to stuff away any internal conversations about identity. I came out as a lesbian at 25, but around 27, one of my friends said, "There's a word for us, and it's 'trans.' Do you know what that is?" I had heard of trans women, but didn't really understand that there were lots of ways to be trans. I was very offended he thought I was trans. So, I honestly stopped talking to him because it was way too real for me to look at. A few years later, I heard the word non-binary and was like, "Oh my God, that's a thing. I totally get

> it. That's me." Over time, I've slowly figured out that I'm more trans masculine and I'm comfortable with the word trans now. I still don't identify as a man. I also don't identify as a woman. I say guy cause it's "man-light" or something. So, then I just started transitioning not that long ago.

As these shared stories illustrate, social norms about language for TGE persons can shift rapidly, further confounding an attempt to understand these complicated issues. Despite ongoing shifts, we argue the idea that labels are necessary in order to pursue a conversation about TGE students in music programs.

We draw a crucial distinction between *labels* and *labeling*. An important principle to keep in mind is to always honor the name/pronoun/word choices of TGE persons—even if they change. For example, a student may disclose their identity as being gender fluid but later identify as a trans woman. For example, Jessica (she/her or they/them; transfeminine non-binary; white) says, "I still identify very strongly as non-binary, but I'm way more comfortable with the transfeminine label than I am with a more neutral—or any other kind of more masculine-leaning identity." Similarly, a student may begin by using she/her/hers pronouns but later request that you use they/them/their. While this can be difficult, it is important that you honor these word choices. We all make mistakes in the process of working to celebrate and validate people's individual identities. Simply acknowledge the error, offer an apology, forgive yourself, and move on with your conversation. Based on our own experiences with TGE students and colleagues, we advocate for the idea that mistakes are going to happen in the process of learning, and they provide us with opportunities to grow and change to better serve our students. In that sense, our intentions can guide our actions and our gracious responses to critique.

Transgender

Transgender as a term and a concept has been understood in varying and sometimes contradictory ways. At the turn of the twentieth century, there was little to no vocabulary or understanding related to the concept that we now label *transgender*. There is considerable diversity within the trans community about words and terms used to express gender. For example, in gender scholars Genny Beemyn and Sue Rankin's (2011) study of 3,474 TGE persons, participants provided 603 unique descriptors for their gender identities. The most commonly understood usage of *transgender* (*trans*) is as a blanket or umbrella term to denote any kind of variance from, or opposition to, binary gender categories, though opinions about the use of this term vary widely (Davis, 2009; Elliot, 2010; Stryker, 2008). The norms surrounding language can fail when considering people who transition from one gender to another (e.g., male to female), some of whom no longer consider themselves trans (e.g., Beemyn & Rankin, 2011). The term *transgendered* generally is considered offensive and has fallen into disuse (Airton, 2019). Christina DiEdoardo, a trans person living in California, argued that what is perceived as a past-tense verb "makes it sound like 'something has been done to us,' as if they weren't the same person all along" (Steinmetz, 2014b). You may still be wondering, what exactly does *trans* or *transgender* mean? The terms essentially mean different things to different people, and these meanings can change based on a particular context. For the purposes of this text, *trans* denotes any person who defies the gender binary or identifies differently than their sex assigned at birth. We might also consider the meaning of trans through a question: Who is trans? The answer is: anyone who says that they are.

Medical Considerations

Persons who identify as trans or gender-expansive may choose to pursue medical care as a part of their transition, while others may not. Those who do pursue medical transitions approach their care in vastly different ways. Please note that it is inappropriate to ask a TGE person about their medical care unless you know them well (see Box 1.1, "Trans Etiquette," for additional information). Several of our collaborators discuss aspects of their medical care:

- Mari (she/her; transgender woman; Latina): So, in an ideal world, I would've been able to have access to hormone therapy as a college student because I had my conviction. And I either needed to be seeing a therapist who could evaluate me for medical transition or to be seeing somebody for medical transition. That impacted completely my choice to go to grad school immediately and my choice to apply to grad school only to schools on the West Coast.
- Mason (he/him; trans man; white): It was frightening for a while because I had to, you know, get my letter from the therapist and then go to a doctor to do everything by myself. And that took so long to get to the doctor part that I was like, I need to finish musicianship before I hit that, so I don't lose my singing ability and then fail my theory classes. So, I finished that out and started testosterone at the end of that, and it's been the best. I didn't even tell most people that I was going on testosterone. I told my close friends, but within the same month there were no physical changes, but every single person in my life stopped to tell me how much happier I was. You know, "what's going on? You are just a bundle of joy now!" And it was clearly emotionally different within a month.

Box 1.1 Trans Etiquette

Following are some of the most important principles for respectfully communicating to, and about, trans people. I have learned these principles by writings by Jacob Hale, Matt Kailey, and Riki Wilchins; videos by Calpernia Addams and Ethan Suniewick; and my participation in trans communities.

- *Remember* that you're not the expert on others' experiences. Everyone experiences gender differently. Exercise humility. Practice good listening skills.
- *Honor* others' self-definitions. For example, use others' chosen names and pronouns. If you don't know someone's pronouns, avoid pronouns or ask. If you make a mistake, don't turn it into a scene, and don't be too hard on yourself; discreetly apologize or just move on. [. . .]
- *Don't expect* others to serve as spokespeople or educators. No one can speak for every member of their group or community. Many trans people are happy to share their experiences. However, no one can be "on" as an educator 24/7. Take advantage of published resources. If you want to talk with a trans person about their experiences, wait until the topic comes up, or ask consent.
- *Don't "out"* others as trans. Even if someone is out to you, they may not be out in all areas of their life, such as family, work, and social media. Outing someone can have negative, even devastating, consequences.
- *Don't assume* that others' gender expression tells you something about their bodies, identities, or sexualities. For example, if someone looks to you like a woman, don't assume that person was assigned female at birth, self-identifies as a woman, or is sexually oriented toward men. [. . .]
- *Don't ask* invasive questions about others' bodies, identities, or sexualities. Often the first question that trans people are asked is, "Have you had the surgery?" Other questions are, "Are you a man or a woman?" and "Do you want to be with a man or a woman?" (As if "a man or a woman" were the only options.) A rule of thumb is: in a situation where it could be considered rude to ask a cis person a particular question, it is rude to ask a trans person.
- *Don't criticize* others' bodies, expressions, or sexualities for not aligning with the identities in a socially expected way. For example, if a trans man does not go on testosterone, don't make him feel like he is "not trans enough." Conversely, don't critique others' bodies, expressions, or sexualities for aligning with their identities in a socially expected way. [. . .] We are all enough.

Source: Cava (2014, pp. 125–126, italics in original).

Mari's and Mason's stories express not only their respective experiences, but also a level of comfort in sharing those experiences. TGE persons should be the initiators of these types of personal conversations.

Stealth and Passing

The language we use to describe other people can sometimes get lost in translation between the speaker and the receiver. Music teachers will want to take care when using less familiar terms in conversation with TGE persons. The next two terms will likely be perceived differently, depending on context and personal experience. PFLAG defines *stealth* as:

> A term used to describe transgender or gender-expansive individuals who do not disclose their transgender or gender-expansive status in their public or private lives (or certain aspects of their public and private lives). The term is increasingly considered offensive by some as it implies an element of deception. The phrase maintaining privacy is often used instead, though some individuals use both terms interchangeably. (PFLAG, 2020)

The term *passing* is also used to describe this phenomenon, though some trans persons find this term offensive. Camden: (he/him; trans man; white/Latinx) shares his experience with how other people have perceived him:

> The thing that's interesting to me is I feel, I'm kind of going back to when I came out to my parents, they were really nervous about how people would treat me. But at the same time, people don't "look trans." It's not something you could look at someone and assume "Oh, they're trans." So, I think that's the idea they had in their head, that I would somehow "look trans." So, I feel in that sense because I pass as male, I obviously have gained privilege, which is also a very weird thing that I have noticed.

Camden speaks to accurate perception of his gender identity in a positive context. Keep in mind this will not always be the case, as the context of passing is individualized and context-dependent.

Gender-Expansive

The idea that gender identity and expression can be considered on a spectrum necessitates a term that, for the purposes of our discussions, is simultaneously summative and inclusive. We have explored current terminology used in research and educational support materials in an effort to determine the most appropriate vocabulary for this text. Terms like *gender nonconforming*, *gender queer*, and *gender redefining* have been used as umbrella terms for individuals whose gender identity or expression is beyond the binary of male or female. In the attempt to label people who wished to interrupt the concept of gender, these terms, unfortunately, placed unwanted and undue emphasis on conformity. Conformity implies a norm which, in this case, is a cis-sexist reference to a male/female binary. LGBTQA scholars and community members, therefore, have felt that *gender nonconforming* generates a negative connotation and perhaps should no longer be used. *Gender variant* is another term used to reference people who identify somewhere(s) on the gender spectrum, possibly other than male or female. We struggled with the potential negative connotations of "variant," however, as once again referencing variation from a norm rooted in gender. In an effort to move from unwanted references "to" something, the concept of *gender creative* offers an interesting option. The idea of creating offers a sense of newness and individuality. *Gender creative* typically appears in discussions of gender identity and expression among young children (Ehrensaft, 2016). A successful term for young people, *gender creative*, may not apply as appropriately to adults. We use the term *gender-expansive* for the purposes of this book as an umbrella term that acknowledges the variety of gender identities and expressions in children, youth, and adults. The idea of expanding suggests growth in a positive and reaffirming way that can be associated with a variety of age groups.

By using appropriate vocabulary, we as authors hope to accurately describe people and the many aspects of our wonderfully complex identities. Our discussions of the terms *trans* and *gender-expansive* are offered, therefore, for two reasons. First, the remainder of this text will focus on persons whom we categorize as TGE, which means that an in-depth discussion of these terms should be helpful in building a foundational understanding for further conversation. Second, vocabulary used by, and in reference to, the LGBTQA community is constantly evolving to describe the individuals who claim those labels. Discussions within the LGBTQA community and among scholars continue to *queer*, or challenge, those labels. This brief primer of gender and sexual diversity will provide a foundation to consider how these issues manifest in society and in our classrooms. Understanding how gender identities play out in the music classroom is an important part of becoming a culturally responsive educator, focused on equal access to quality education for all students. The complexity and intersectionality of identities and behaviors makes intentional respect essential to ensure that people feel validated and included in the contexts of learning environments.

Intersectionality

Individuals are complex and multidimensional, with many facets and layers of identity. We consider gender from an intersectional perspective, because teachers engage with more than one aspect of their students' identity, even within the short time span of a single class. Patricia Hill Collins (distinguished professor of sociology at the University of Maryland, College Park) and Sirma Bilge (professor of sociology at Université de Montréal) write, "Intersectionality as an analytic tool gives people better access to the complexity of the world and of themselves" (2016, p. 12).

Rooted in racial justice and feminism, intersectionality can provide us with valuable perspective about our associations with the gender binary of masculine and feminine, and how our associations position us with regard to power, privilege, and oppression (Barker & Iantaffi, 2019). Author Andy Matzner (2001) writes about this power dynamic in the book *'O Au No Keia* by highlighting narratives of trans Hawaiians (known as *mahu*) so that the reader can empathize with "the feelings and thoughts of an often misunderstood segment of our society" and through this process, that "understanding and acceptance may blossom" (p. 20). We, as authors, recognize our need to claim and disclose our many layers of privilege as we engage in the delicate yet important work of honoring TGE students in music education (as disclosed in the Introduction). As trans filmmaker Kortney Ryan Ziegler and Naim Rasul, director of Student Support and Crisis Management at The New School (NYC), write:

> It is important to keep in mind that being an ally takes commitment and perseverance. Being an ally is not something that ever ends. Trans people of color will continue to struggle for the same rights and freedoms as white transgender and cisgender people. (2014, p. 38)

Lived experiences of a broad spectrum of trans individuals (e.g., Kruse, 2016) can illuminate journeys and experiences beyond white, middle-class, heteronormative, able-bodied, cisgender perspectives frequently highlighted in research discourses (de Vries, 2012). Our hope is that this book takes a step toward providing an intersectional focus among gender and additional components of an individual's identity. Trans persons face multiple layers of oppression from within an either/or binary only paradigm (Carter, 2014; Crenshaw, 1991; hooks, 2000). For Warner, "a different stereotype is elicited when considering gender and race together than when considering either race or gender alone" (2008, p. 457). Dane (she/her; trans woman; Black [African,

Cuban, Indigenous]) describes the importance of intersectionality in her education/experience:

> Growing up with [the National Great Blacks in Wax Museum] it really, really empowered me, just really learning how to love my Blackness. Learning how to understand what Kimberle Crenshaw identifies as "intersectionality." And just—it really fostered a love of history inside of me—that was really, really important for my aunt to gift to me . . . this love of history. And in being able to see Black people in particular before slavery. To see these Black and Brown bodies before they were brought to America and what our culture looked like before colonization.

The museum to which Dane refers presents "life-size, life-like wax figures highlighting historical and contemporary personalities of African ancestry" (National Great Blacks in Wax Museum, n.d.). Similarly, Mystic Rose (she/her or they/them; gender noncomforming; Latinx) explains how culture and gender identity intersect in her experience:

> So, I was born and raised in San Antonio, Texas, in 1996 near the westside-downtown area. [. . .] It's always felt kind of repressive in a way because I was always told as a kid, "boys can't do this, boys can't do this" or "you shouldn't like that." I describe myself as Latinx and in our culture, it's really machismo, really masculine oriented about how men/boys should present themselves in society.

Elements of identity including ability, religious identity, mental health status, and social class often are forgotten or left out of shared narratives. For example, one of our collaborators, Michael (she/her; trans female; white), speaking in the summer of 2020 in the wake of protests following the murder of George Floyd, says:

> I'm learning about assimilation and it's interesting that even though I was not intending to read for this purpose, I'm also learning about my own story as a trans person: the subconscious efforts of our society to assimilate fluid gender identities and non-binary gender identities into the binary. Also, as a person with chronic disability, even quite possibly even more so as a disabled person, this world is not set up to accommodate for disability. It feels like the desire is for disabled people to conform to an able body world.

As authors, we recognize and own the fact that we may misstep in this book. To mitigate such missteps, we have asked several TGE colleagues to proofread sections of the book prior to publication. We also consulted with TGE persons about specific language and we acknowledged errors when we said or wrote something that was inappropriate. Ultimately, despite inevitable missteps, we believe that this resource can be helpful in honoring TGE school music students.

Cultural and Historical Context

In the Age of Black Lives Matter and Renewed Advocacy for Racial Justice

At the time of this writing, the United States is in the midst of two crises: the Covid-19 pandemic and ongoing protests following the murder of George Floyd in Minneapolis. Protests have taken place in over 60 countries and on every continent except Antarctica. Calls for racial justice reverberate more intensely, and increased attention has been focused on the often underplayed murder of trans women—especially trans women of color (Demby & Meraji, 2020)—part of a persistent pattern of violence against TGE persons (e.g., Human Rights Campaign, n.d.; Kaleem, 2019). Trans persons' experiences are surfacing in the present context, as exemplified by the All Black Lives Matter protest in Los Angeles in June 2020 (Branson-Potts & Stiles, 2020). Human Rights Campaign maintains a website that tracks violence against trans persons (see Appendix B): In 2019, advocates tracked at least 27 deaths of transgender or gender nonconforming persons in the United States due to fatal violence, the majority of whom were Black transgender women (Human Rights Campaign, n.d.). One of our collaborators, MJ (she/her or they/them; trans woman; Black), speaks of potential solutions to violence against trans youth and trans women of color:

> There's a little company, they're mostly run by trans women, especially trans women of color. I think it will be interesting if we can partner up with them and maybe we can do a little something and we can bring a lot of trans youth into this program and help them out. And instead of kicking people out on the streets, why don't we help people out? Why don't we just literally give them programs and resources to help them out? Especially our young trans women of color. [. . .] There's other programs, especially here in Chicago, like Howard Brown, the center for youth. [. . .] They're really trying to help out trans women of color because there have been a lot of us dying over the past few years, just a lot of us dying and we need to do all we can to help them. And I wish that the gay community would step

> up. And that's where I feel like I need to kind of be like a Marsha P. Johnson of everything and get people to rally up and help out our trans women of color, help them out because we are dying. We are dying.

In 2015, trans woman of color, performer, playwright, and advocate Dane Figueroa Edidi wrote:

> Now we are in 2015 and five Transwomen of color (Twoc) are dead already—that is one for every week of the new year. [. . .] When the media speaks, although Transwomen are quoted, I have yet to see these same Transwomen honored for the work they have already been doing around fighting structural oppression. The Trans community has already been unpacking and fighting the webs of oppression which become manifest in the silence around Twoc deaths, and the oppressive structures that continue to tighten nooses around the necks of many living Trans persons of color. (para. 3)

Lady Dane's poignant words once again remind us of the importance of an intersectional approach to justice for marginalized minorities like trans women of color (Paz & Astor, 2020). In the midst of the unrest of 2020, an important legal ruling was released that has changed the lives of many persons in LGBTQA communities.

In the Age of the June 2020 Supreme Court Ruling

On June 15, 2020, the US Supreme Court (*Bostock v. Clayton County*) ruled that gay, lesbian, bisexual, and transgender persons are protected from workplace discrimination under the 1964 Civil Rights Act.

> That opinion and two dissents, spanning 168 pages, touched on a host of flash points in the culture wars involving the L.G.B.T. community—bathrooms, locker rooms, sports, pronouns and religious objections to same-sex marriage. The decision, the first major case on transgender rights, came amid widespread demonstrations, some protesting violence aimed at transgender people of color. Until Monday's decision, it was legal in more than half of the [United States] to fire workers for being gay, bisexual or transgender. (Liptak, 2020, para. 3–4)

This important ruling impacted two subsequent court cases. The Court of Appeals for the Eleventh Circuit ruled on a prior court decision in which a Florida school district refused to permit a trans boy student to use the boy's restroom at school. The appellate court ruling concluded with statements referencing the recent Supreme Court ruling, noting,

> Bostock confirmed that workplace discrimination against transgender people is contrary to law. Neither should this discrimination be tolerated in schools. [. . .] A public school may not punish its students for gender nonconformity. Neither may a public school harm transgender students by establishing arbitrary, separate rules for their restroom use. (*Adams ex rel. Kasper v. School Board of St. Johns Co.*, 2020)

A second appellate court case also ruled in favor of a trans man's right to use the school restroom congruent with his gender identity. The Court of Appeals for the Fourth Circuit began the majority opinion by stating,

> At the heart of this appeal is whether equal protection and Title IX can protect transgender students from school bathroom policies that prohibit them from affirming their gender. We join a growing consensus of courts in holding that the answer is resoundingly yes. (*Grimm v. Gloucester Co. School Board*, 2020)

The recent court rulings illustrate how quickly the rights of TGE persons can change. The latter appellate court ruling serves as an example of how rapidly federal law can impact local policy, and how music teachers might honor their TGE students by improving school climate.

TGE Issues: Essential, Not "Controversial"

Honoring gender diversity in schools is often avoided because it is regarded as immaterial or controversial (e.g., Blair & Deckman, 2019). Rutgers University education professor Melinda Mangin (2020) describes: "The expectation that school leaders should be focused on students' needs may seem intuitive; however, transgender people's needs are often portrayed as being at odds with the interests of larger society" (p. 266). TGE students in rural areas may face additional difficulties. As psychologist Lyndsey Hampton writes, "On the whole, transgender youth perceive there to be few safe environments in which to express their authentic gender identity . . . [and] this is even more likely in rural communities founded on conservative values" (2014, p. 178).

While issues of equity for TGE students are essential to social, emotional, and academic success of young persons, this view is not held by everyone. In recent years, anti-LGBTQA sentiment has increased in school settings (Kosciw et al., 2018, 2020). As Joshua writes with his colleague William Sauerland, assistant professor of music at Purdue University–Fort Wayne: "Cultural shifts, which may influence government policy, also indicate less acceptance of . . . LGBTQA people. [. . .] Since schools exist within historical and socio-political contexts, these recent developments may put trans students at risk" (2019, p. 75). In 2017, the conservative-leaning Heritage Foundation released a policy document arguing for *less* protection of trans students (Kim, 2017). University of North Texas music education professor Donald Taylor discusses the notion of how music educators can navigate these potentially turbulent situations:

> One of the easiest default positions is to *agree to disagree* on issues. While this strategy allows for a truce of sorts, this approach is limited and often results in communication shutdown. Fearing confrontation, people may just avoid each other. Avoidance may then foster cliques and polarization that is antithetical to a cooperative learning environment. To move beyond avoidance, teachers can seek a more practical alternative by practicing and teaching empathy. (2018, p. 56, emphasis in original)

Music teachers seeking to educate students about empathy may consider the tenets of social emotional learning (SEL) as a means to accomplish this goal (Edgar, 2017). The five elements of SEL are self-awareness, self-management, social awareness, relationship skills, and responsible decision-making. Social awareness is particularly important: "the ability to take the perspective of and empathize with others from diverse backgrounds and cultures" (CASEL, 2021). We, as authors, advocate that TGE identities are essential to a paradigm of inclusivity. Music teachers have the opportunity to serve as people who respect, protect, and love the TGE students in our classrooms.

Recap

This chapter provides contextual knowledge about gender and sexual diversity, and the norms and practices related to these ideas. The content and experiences shared in Chapters 1 and 2 help to lay a foundation upon which practical suggestions will be explored throughout the latter Praxis section of the text (Chapters 3–7). The voices of TGE persons are highlighted throughout this book, in an effort to provide music educators with practical tools and suggestions for making their classrooms positive and safe environments for students. Our collaborators' stories illustrate how gender issues manifest in various music education settings, and we offer suggestions to honor TGE students in school music classrooms (Chapters 3–6). The stories of TGE youth and the music teachers who work with them can humanize seemingly abstract gender diversity issues and concepts (Chapter 7 is dedicated exclusively to the voices of our TGE collaborators). Through these narratives, we strive to honor the experiences of those in the diverse TGE community. In the next chapter, we explore the realities of TGE students in public schools.

Reflect/Remember

1. Consider your own elementary and secondary school learning experiences. Reflect on how schools can be gendered. List ways you perceive that the gender binary is reinforced in school environments. Next, think about music classrooms and generate another list. Are there any items on your lists you had not previously considered? How might you alter some of those gendered spaces?
2. In this chapter we discussed *labels* and *labeling*. Create a list of labels to describe your various *intersectional* identities (e.g., sexuality, gender, race, socioeconomic status). How important are these labels to you? In what ways might someone mislabeling you cause you distress?
3. Examining your own biases is an important step toward being able to honor TGE persons. Have you met persons who were "out" as trans or gender expansive? If so, what was your initial reaction? Why do you think you felt that way? How do you think your lived experiences influence your feelings or reactions?

2

Understanding School Climate for Trans and Gender-Expansive Persons

Chapter Guide

ANDY (he/him; FTM transgender; white): I think in general, just realizing high school's so temporary, like it's going to go by so fast and you know, it sucks. Like, I don't think anyone who is queer has a fun high school experience. I mean, there's fun parts of it of course, but like overall it's not going to be great. And realizing that it's not like the pinnacle of your life, that you know, you're going to go to college and meet a lot more like minded people and you're going to go out and have a professional life and you know, you're going to be able to choose the people that you surround yourself with, which is something you can't really do in high school.

MARI (she/her; transgender woman; Latina): Just the fact that there's an openly trans student at the high school is a complete change from when I was in high school. Last year, I had a non-binary student and a trans student. And for that to be normal or expected or not uncommon in Texas where I grew up in 2019 or 2020, even 2018, it's just way different. . . . Things have already evolved. You can't put the cat back inside the bag. You can't. It would be impractical.

Honoring Trans and Gender-Expansive Students in Music Education. Matthew L. Garrett and Joshua Palkki, Oxford University Press. © Oxford University Press 2021. DOI: 10.1093/oso/9780197506592.003.0003

Why Consider Gender Diversity in Schools?

Schools reflect the dominant cultural values of the communities in which they operate. These cultural values include a community's understanding about, and perception of, gender. Just as communities are composed of people from a variety of backgrounds, having different lived experiences, the cultural and personal values held by community members will echo these individualized perspectives. Some commonalities, however, likely find their way into the foundations of communal institutions, like schools in which "LGBT students, teachers, and the school site administrators have found themselves at the eye of the proverbial storm as school communities confront the rapidly changing realities in this area" (Biegel, 2010, pp. xvi–xvii).

For instance, from a sociological perspective, schools often are regarded as places for young people to learn respect for themselves and for others, so they can work together regardless of their individual differences. One teacher educator advocates, "an all positive and welcoming school climate will help everyone and hurt no one" (Biegel, 2010, p. 119). The question becomes, how can teachers navigate facilitating equity in a "gendered" environment?

Students encounter perceptions of gender throughout the school day. Gender binary stereotypes persist in school environments via a "trickle-down system": societal norms influence schools, which in turn affect programs within schools. School music programs introduce complex curricular, co-curricular, and extracurricular situations. Navigating gendered spaces can be particularly difficult for students in these types of classroom/ensemble settings, where students are working together toward common goals (Adderley et al., 2003; Morrison, 2001). Young people can explore interests and ideas and learn about gender diversity as an integral part of their educational experience. In order to demonstrate a value for diversity present in community settings, teachers can address issues of love, family, and relationships with their students (Meyer, 2010). All school personnel share responsibility for modeling behaviors that allow students to understand differences and maintain commonly held values like respect for one another (Sullivan & Urraro, 2019a, 2019b). Teachers play a role in empowering students, especially considering the amount of contact time with students (Fisher & Komosa-Hawkins, 2013). As a result, it is important for teachers to understand and acknowledge their own values and how those values might manifest in classroom settings.

Teachers bring their own experiences with and perceptions of gender to classrooms. These ideas of gender may or may not align with those of the school community or the ideas of individual students or groups of students. When teachers take time to reflect on and acknowledge their own biases associated with gender, they may better understand the impact gender norms/stereotypes play in school settings. Teacher and university administrator Elizabeth Meyer (2010) suggested that teachers' knowledge of gender diversity is important in creating a positive learning environment for all students. This type of inclusive approach to serving students can lead to more positive associations with school and psychological well-being, particularly for young people seeking greater acceptance of gender diversity.

Child gender therapist Diane Ehrensaft notes, "When working with gender-expansive children there is no action or lack of action without an associated impact and a consequence" (Ehrensaft et al., 2018, p. 262). Understanding the action–consequence framework of gender inclusivity can assist teachers in determining what values they bring with them into school settings and, consequently, how they reinforce a communally shared value of respect. For example, as we will discuss in the next chapter, simply including your pronouns in an email signature or verbal introduction can send a clear signal to TGE students that you are supportive and understanding.

Similarities exist among approaches to inclusive teaching. Music teachers working with TGE youth can transfer ideas from instructional frameworks like culturally responsive pedagogy. School officials, in general, can benefit from understanding the importance and the limitations of these approaches. Expanded connections among and between diversities present in classrooms provide additional strength to the need for gender-diversity education in school systems (Garrett, 2012). In their book *The Trans Generation: How Trans Kids (and Their Parents) Are Creating a Gender Revolution*, Ann Travers (2018) writes:

> Schools are essential sites where children bump up against an environment built around naturalized but falsely universal abilities: including but not limited to those related to gender and sexual conformity, English language proficiency, neurotypical learning styles, the "able body," and white, middle-class standards of living and cultural norms. (pp. 48–49)

Educational researcher Jenny Muñiz (2019) identifies a model of eight competencies for culturally responsive teaching which supports ties to gender diversity. They describe culturally responsive teaching as an approach that challenges educators to recognize students' cultural differences as strengths, rather than deficits. Muñiz notes that these strengths "should be leveraged to make learning experiences more relevant to and effective for [students]" (2019, p. 6). As a specific example from their model, Muñiz suggested that culturally responsive educators should work to reflect on their own cultural lens, through which they perceive the world around them. An application of this model might be realized by teachers critically reflecting on their own values and biases that they bring into school classroom settings (we explore additional suggestions for transfer from Muñiz's model to music classrooms in Chapter 3). Teachers who develop a foundational understanding of gender diversity may be better equipped to establish, maintain, and champion student experiences that include and move beyond the gender binary (McQuillan & Leininger, 2020).

How Does the Gender Binary Manifest in School Music Programs?

Ideas associated with the female/male gender binary are taught and reinforced by multiple sources. These binary influences permeate school music programs as a result of community and institutional ties. Psychology professor Susan Basow (2004) notes that children come to school after years of gleaning gender messages from their families, surroundings, and the mass media. Parents, healthcare workers, and community members begin to model and teach gender concepts quickly after childbirth. Color choices for clothing, toys, and furniture may be selected to reinforce traditional gender-stereotyped colors (e.g., blue for boys, pink for girls). Pronouns are selected that most appropriately represent sex assigned at birth. Within schools, reinforcement of this gender binary continues with classroom language (e.g., "boys and girls . . .") and access to restrooms and locker room facilities. Consider how school physical spaces (e.g., public restrooms, locker rooms) inadvertently pressure students to choose between "boy" and "girl," even if those two options differ from what students internally feel (Sullivan & Urraro, 2019a, 2019b). TGE individuals are pressured to adapt to traditional binary roles of male or female, in order to fit into a narrowly constructed binary system. Education researcher Barrie Thorne describes specific examples of reinforcing the gender binary in an ethnographic study of two elementary schools: "Gender [was] threaded through the routines of lining up, waiting and moving in a queue, and dispersing in a new place" (1993, p. 39). These broader examples of teachers reinforcing the gender binary through directions such as "boys in one line and girls in another line" often are paralleled in school music programs.

School music teachers make conscious and unconscious decisions that emphasize the gender binary. These types of decisions manifest in classroom language, student access to restrooms and changing rooms in performing arts facilities, choices associated with performance attire, and instrument choice/

selection. To illustrate one way in which the gender binary manifests in music programs, consider a brief retrieval exercise. Take a moment to recall a school band, choir, or orchestra concert that you attended and think about what students wore in that performance. You may find yourself visualizing two performance attire options: girls in dresses and boys in suits or tuxedos. In another example, think about the last instrumental performance you experienced and try to recall who was playing the different types of instruments. How many people who presented as male were playing the flute? How many persons who presented as women were playing the trombone? Your memories may align with ideas of music instrument gender stereotyping. Music education researchers have examined the notion that students and teachers perceive some instruments (e.g., flute and harp) as feminine and other instruments (e.g., trombone and double bass) as masculine (Abeles & Porter, 1978; Abeles, 2009; Conway, 2000; Hallam et al., 2008; Wych, 2012). It seems that this type of gender binary association is more closely associated with student perceptions than with music teacher bias (Johnson & Stewart, 2004, 2005). The idea, however, that people may associate an instrument more strongly with one side of the gender binary further reinforces the need for instrumental music teachers to seek ways to de-emphasize these biases. To counteract this, rather than restricting instrument choice or selection based on sex or gender, instrumental music educators can encourage students to choose the instrument that speaks to their interest.

The gender binary system works for many, but not all, students who participate in school music programs. If teachers value the idea of access/equity for school music education, then it may be productive to expand the relevant and narrow concept of the gender binary. Teachers can consider invisible or hidden ways that the gender binary is reinforced as a means to disrupt an either/or paradigm, replacing it with a both/and ideology that would expand access equity to a greater number of students. A simple example is, when lining up elementary music students to enter or leave class, finding ways other than "boys and girls" to divide them. Rather, line them up by some non-gendered trait such as birthday month or clothing colors.

A hidden curriculum exists in school classrooms, hallways, playgrounds, and cafeterias that includes often unspoken lessons about societal norms around social issues, including gender (Apple, 2004; Basow, 2004; Pascoe, 2011; Roberts et al., 2007; Thorne, 1993). In this context, "hidden" is not meant to be equated with deceitful or dubious, but rather something that is not overtly stated or referenced. Students glean messages from this hidden curriculum by encountering school and program expectations and routines during their elementary and secondary school experiences (Apple, 2004).

Susan Basow referenced gender as a part of this hidden curriculum: "Students learn about gender both directly, through instructional material, and indirectly, through observation and differential treatment" (2004, p. 117). Music teachers can consider how instructional materials may illustrate gender to students in order to ensure broader representation to diverse student populations.

Concepts of gender are evident in school curricular materials and in student behaviors demonstrated during co-curricular activities such as marching band. Anthropologist Kimberly Marshall (2009) reports that color guard and baton twirlers/majorettes were generally coded as "feminine" roles, while drum major is considered "masculine," in a study of two university marching bands. Further expanding this concept of gender in schools, music education scholar Patricia O'Toole writes, "Teachers are not immune from society's notions of gender . . . their pedagogy is laden with subtle messages about who is important in the classroom" (1998, p. 13). While these tacit implications of gender bias may not be intentional, students and teachers can learn to recognize how they are perceived and internalized. In a 2017 national school climate survey of 23,001 LGBTQ youth between the ages of 13 and 21, approximately two-thirds of respondents reported observable gender bias (Kosciw et al., 2018). The survey research team notes, "Students most commonly reported practices related to school athletics and music activities, such as chorus, band, or orchestra" (p. 40). School music programs may wish to include a "both/and" approach in an effort to create a welcoming learning environment for all students who may participate in classes, as well as co-curricular and extracurricular music activities. In Part II of this book, we will discuss practices that you can enact in your own setting to counteract this hidden gender curriculum.

Understanding how the gender binary can impact students' ability to fully participate in school music programs can lead teachers to consider how to best disrupt and/or expand this barrier. All types of music educators need resources and ideas grounded in research and best practices to honor their TGE students. An emerging line of research indicates that music teachers can be influential in supporting LGBTQA youth in schools (Garrett & Spano, 2017; Palkki & Caldwell, 2018; Silveira & Goff, 2016). While these studies indicate that music teachers are, in general, supportive of LGBTQA students, there is a distinct lack of training among pre- and in-service teachers on this topic (Garrett & Spano, 2017; Palkki & Caldwell, 2018). School music teachers have the ability to create positive and inclusive learning environments that, in turn, can afford students the opportunity to experience deep connections with music (Salvador et al., 2020). Exploring opportunities beyond the gender binary can provide insight into ways we can help celebrate the authentic lives of our TGE students.

Learning beyond the Binary: Gender-Expansive Students

The gender binary system is both relevant (many people identify as either female or male) and narrow (gender-expansive individuals necessitate flexibility beyond two points on a spectrum of possibilities). One team of educators and researchers notes, "The both/and is not doing away with binaries or discarding them from our lived experiences, rather it is advocating for a more complex and contextually grounded engagement with the binary" (Green et al., 2020, p. 42). In other words, the gender binary serves a purpose and, at the same time, requires additional exploration and conversation to discover how additional options are necessary to honor gender diversity among students in twenty-first-century schools. To explore this idea of how gender binary is relevant to a conversation about school music programs, it is important to note that some individuals who identify as members of the trans community use a binary label to indicate their gender identity. Knowing that the gender binary can be useful for some, but limiting for others, how can we as teachers work to create a more expansive, and thus inclusive concept of gender identity in school environments?

Either/or vs. *Both/and*

Spectrums exist in many facets of life to help us understand complex situations that we regularly encounter. For example, even though most people think of only two major political parties in the United States, others do exist on a spectrum from far left to far right. Concepts and issues often require expansion beyond two poles of right or wrong, good or bad, or yes or no. Gender diversity perceived across a spectrum can allow TGE persons the flexibility they need to thrive. The gender binary is reinforced by presenting gender identity and expression as *either/or* phenomena: namely, an individual is either male/masculine or female/feminine, as agreed upon by societal norms. Considering positions between and among two or more points allows for *both/and* possibilities. As an example, an individual might identify politically as socially moderate and fiscally conservative. Applying simply one or the other label to this person would not accurately describe the complexity of their personal political ideology. Similarly, a public-school band teacher who grew up singing in choirs might not be accurately labeled as solely a vocalist or an instrumentalist; their lived experience reveals a more nuanced musical life that supersedes labels. When we as teachers are unable to think beyond binary terms, we limit our ability to acknowledge the expansive spectrum of identities and expressions that are personified by the students in our classrooms.

As educators, we make a commitment to educating all of the students who enter our classrooms. Mission and vision statements printed on school letterhead and painted on school walls often appear to be aligned in a goal toward educating young persons in positive and constructive learning environments. As ideas about gender diversity develop, this commitment to work with all students will continue to include TGE young persons. Learning how to honor and celebrate the gender identity and gender expression of individual students can foster opportunities for trusting relationships between teachers and students. Educators seeking to learn about or broaden their understanding of TGE persons may benefit from a holistic approach as misconceptions and generalizations complicate the relationships among body, identity, and expression (Gender Spectrum, 2019b). For the purposes of this book, we have chosen three foundational concepts to help frame an understanding of learning beyond the binary.

Gender-Complex Approach

Teaching students to examine and acknowledge gender diversity in classroom settings is a core component to a *Gender-Complex* approach to working with students. Educator Kathleen Rands (2009) proposed the idea of a Gender-Complex approach to classroom instruction as a way to disrupt the limitations of the gender binary. This approach incorporates four components to help teachers and students explore gender diversity:

1. Reflect on ways that gender operates in classroom situations;
2. Respect the idea of gender diversity in spectrums;
3. Analyze how gender is represented in classroom situations;
4. Create gender equity for all students.

Imagine a class piano setting in which students question why the majority of repertoire that they are playing has been composed by cisgender male musicians. Using a Gender-Complex approach to facilitate appropriate curricular discussion, the teacher might acknowledge the historical gender bias evident in the data about whose music has been published, then begin a conversation about the context of male, female, and TGE composers over time. By expanding a learning opportunity beyond the limitations of gender-binary male/female composers, within the context of musical composers of piano literature, teachers and students can work through the identified components of a Gender-Complex approach, focusing on gender equity for all. This type of conversation could be easily modified to multiple age groups and music education settings (e.g., elementary general music, secondary instrumental, secondary choral, modern band).

Gender Affirmative Model

The Gender Affirmative Model (GAM) can also be useful in learning beyond the binary. Educators and psychologists Colt Keo-Meier and Diane Ehrensaft developed this model seeking "to reevaluate our social constructs of gender and sexuality within our cultural context and the positions we impose on children" (2018, p. 15). Recalling the idea mentioned earlier in this chapter, that teachers bring their own experiences with and perceptions of gender to classrooms, the GAM supports recognition of how our values as educators manifest through everyday interactions with students. Four tenets of the GAM with potential connections to school settings include:

1. Focus on resilience, coping, and wellness of young persons;
2. Respect for all gender identities, expressions, and presentations;
3. Respect for a TGE person's identity whatever it may be at a given point in time;
4. Reinforcement of gender equity and disapproval/disruption of gender inequity.

Music teachers often seek to introduce students to a particular music instrument, historical genre, or to convey different styles of music via exposure to, and interaction with, professional musicians. Integrating the GAM, teachers might ensure that these musicians reinforce ideas of gender equity, potentially disrupting unfortunate stereotypes (e.g., only women play the violin, or only men play percussion). We discuss specific suggestions for elementary and instrumental music teachers to disrupt gender stereotypes in Chapter 4, and ideas for vocal music teachers are explored in Chapter 6. With thoughtful long-range planning, school music teachers can incorporate these tenets of the GAM and help to broaden students' understanding of gender diversity, including introducing them to TGE musicians.

Transgender Theory

The third foundational concept provides more specific context to celebrate and honor transgender students. Transgender theory is a relatively recent tool that can help to conceptually challenge and expand the idea of the gender binary by including members of the TGE community with gender fluid identities, identities beyond an either/or, and gender binary identities. Professors Julie L. Nagoshi and Stephanie Brzuzy (2010) define the principal tenets of the theory:

> Transgender theory encompasses and transcends feminist and queer theory by explicitly incorporating ideas of the fluidly embodied, socially constructed, and self-constructed aspects of social identity, along with the dynamic interaction and integration of these aspects of identity within the *narratives of lived experiences*. (p. 433, emphasis added)

In other words, while previous theories about gender have attempted to be prescriptive in nature, Transgender theory recognizes the power of the experiences of transgender persons in society as a tool to reclaim stories from which others may be able to learn. The framework of transgender theory prioritizes the lived experiences of trans individuals, and this approach is foundational to *Honoring Trans and Gender-Expansive Students in Music Education*. The vignettes featured throughout this book and concentrated in Chapter 7, then, are examples of transgender theory in action. Stories of empowerment provide teachers with clarity as to how positive experiences can be reinforced and potentially repeated. Learning how moments of gender discrimination can impact the perceptions and lived experiences of TGE individuals may likewise provide insight to teachers who want to improve school climate for their students.

School Climate for TGE Students

Students in US schools frequently experience acts of discrimination and harassment with regard to elements of their identity and how these identities are expressed. A group of California teachers note that bias-based bullying includes any number of issues faced by children and youth: "languages spoken, gender, racial and ethnic identity, perceived sexual orientation, national identity, immigration and documentation status, and family diversity" (Chappell et al., 2018, p. 2). It is important to acknowledge the discrimination of these young persons while, at the same time, recognizing that children and youth in schools also demonstrate a great deal of resilience and are not simply helpless victims. Teachers gain a more complete image of participants in school classrooms when they see and acknowledge the resiliency of these young persons. We will first examine the challenges faced by TGE youth in schools and then consider stories of resilience from the students' perspective.

National School Climate Studies

TGE youth are particularly vulnerable in school settings, compared with students who identify as lesbian, gay, bisexual, and/or queer (Kosciw et al., 2018, 2020; Palkki & Caldwell, 2018). From navigating restroom use and school uniform policies to having their birth name printed on school rosters, TGE youth face many issues that their cisgender peers do not. How do we really know, from the students' perspectives, what goes on in US schools after the first tardy bell rings? Who is documenting the experiences of TGE youth in school settings? To answer these questions, we examine research data collected by national education and social justice organizations, as well as data from researchers studying general education and those studying music education.

For over two decades, GLSEN has captured snapshots of what it is like to be an LGBTQ student in US schools. Founded by a group of teachers in 1990, GLSEN has conducted a national school climate survey every two years to raise awareness of the challenges faced by LGBTQ students and to advocate for institutional change on their behalf. In the most recent iteration of the study, the GLSEN research team collected information from a sample of 16,713 self-identifying LGBTQ students between the ages of 13 and 21 in 2019 (Kosciw et al., 2020). Results from the study indicated that trans students faced the most hostile school climate of any LGBTQ group (pp. 93–106). These young persons were more likely to miss school due to fears of personal safety and discomfort, and trans students were four times more likely than cisgender LGBQ and gender-expansive students to consider dropping out of high school due to negative school climate. While trans students were identified as the group experiencing the highest percentage of discrimination and harassment, gender-expansive students also reported higher levels of school-related hostility than cisgender LGBQ students. Issues of poor school climate for TGE youth correlate with absent or unsupportive school policies that specifically target these individuals. The GLSEN research team documented that 44.5% of trans students from their study were prevented by school policy from using their real name or pronouns and over 58% of these students reported that they were required to use restroom and locker room facilities that aligned with their assigned or legally recognized sex (p. 100). In addition to reporting what types of harassment were experienced by TGE students and how school policies played a role in creating poor school environments, the research team also indicated five effect categories of hostile school climates for these young persons:

1. Lower educational aspirations;
2. Lower grade point averages;
3. Higher absenteeism from classes and school;
4. Higher percentages of experiencing school discipline;
5. Negative impacts on students' mental health and self-esteem (pp. 45–54).

The biennial GLSEN National School Climate Survey illustrates how lived experiences, school policies, and interpersonal interactions between teachers, students, and staff can impact TGE youth. School environments have, however, changed over time.

School environments for LGBTQ youth generally have improved since 2001 as education efforts and institutional supports have continued to expand. As an example, the percentage of LGBTQ-supportive teachers in US school systems increased from 2001 to 2015, with no change in the two years preceding 2017. In 2019, survey participants reported the highest percentage of LGBTQ supportive educators to date (Kosciw et al., 2020, p. 139). Similarly, results indicated a small increase in the quantity of comprehensive school policies (statements written to protect students from sexual-orientation and gender-identity/expression discrimination), with the rate remaining consistent from 2017 to 2019 (p. 139). A closer examination of the GLSEN report also reveals more recent stagnations or reversals in support and related student perceptions of school climate. Researchers documented an overall decrease in verbal harassment since 2001, and limited fluctuation in negative remarks about gender expression from students and school staff, including teachers, since 2015 (p. 134). While school climate improvements over time for TGE youth offer hope for the future, GLSEN research team members express caution: "although we do not see an overall trend that schools are becoming appreciably safer for LGBTQ students, we do not see that they have become significantly worse" (p. 136). Harassment of even a few TGE students within a school system should cause concern among teachers and community members.

The National Center for Transgender Equality (NCTE) reported the educational experiences of transgender persons in the United States in a pair of reports (Grant et al., 2011; James et al., 2016). For both the GLSEN and NCTE reports, researchers collected data from a large number of participants in all fifty US states, the District of Columbia, and five US territories. The organizations spaced the timing of their surveys, which allowed for the documentation of changes from one report to another. The NCTE report differs, however, in that the 27,715 respondents from their 2015 study all identify as "transgender, trans, genderqueer, non-binary, and other identities on the transgender spectrum" (James et al., 2016, p. 23). The NCTE study, then, provides a closer look at TGE individuals' lived experiences in a broad range of areas, including family life, health, income and employment status, civic participation, and experiences at school. The research team was able to isolate K–12 educational experiences to individuals who self-identified or were perceived as transgender at any point during that time frame in their lives. A majority of respondents, 77%, indicated they had experienced some form of mistreatment in school because people thought that they were transgender (p. 11). Just over half of survey participants, 54%, reported instances of verbal harassment, and 24% reported acts of physical violence in school settings; some individuals (17%) even left a K–12 school because of severe discrimination. From the time of the original study with which NCTE was involved (Grant et al., 2011) and this 2015 follow-up study (James et al., 2016), researchers noted that school environments had improved for transgender students by 2015, although negative experiences were documented by more than three-quarters of respondents (p. 137). The data from the NCTE and GLSEN reports provide a small snapshot of the types of school experiences TGE students continue to face on a daily basis. In addition to the large quantitative data set analyzed in studies by national organizations, individual narratives provide insight on a different scale.

From Our Collaborators: Bullying/Harassment

Many of the collaborators that we interviewed for this book spoke of the harassment that they experienced during their schooling, as illustrated in the following scenarios. Keizen (they/them; gender creative; Han Chinese) describes their cumulative school experiences:

> K through 12 was horrible for me, so I can't even—I don't know what to say. It would be really hard for me to teach anyone from that age group. Cause as a student, there was so much going on for me, you know, I'd say even worse than sexism was racism for me. I am traumatized from the chronic stress of navigating racism and culture clash between home and school. And you know, where I grew up at that time, I was the only Asian often—I was often the only Asian in the room. And I was the only East Asian until college. I knew one other person in a different class. So, we never even had classes together. And I had no resources to figure that out and deal with that until I was an adult and even after transition. So, you see someone, I don't know—I would imagine seeing a student having trouble or, who just has a problem—we all have problems. And sometimes it's really obvious for some students or some people that they have problems and we can't know what the rainbow of problems that they're experiencing is.

Keizen's story illuminates the concept of *intersectionality* described in Chapter 1. Elliott (he/him; trans gay male; white) and his mother Tavia (she/her; Cis-het woman; white) describe an interaction with school administrators who seemed to misunderstand LGBTQA students:

TAVIA: At one point during one of the more heated discussions one of our building administrators was saying," Oh, well we saw him hugging like romantically with a boy, so that must mean he's not trans." And we're like "not how it works! [*laughs*] So there was, there was some education that had to happen.

ELLIOTT: They just sort of thought that gay trans people did not exist. They were like, "Oh yeah. Well if you like a guy, you're obviously a girl."

Common misunderstandings about how sexuality and gender identity interact can perpetuate poor school climates (Bornstein, 1994; Butler, 1990; Pascoe, 2011). Remember, TGE persons may claim any sexuality (e.g., straight, gay, bisexual, pansexual, asexual) as a part of who they are.

It may surprise you to learn that mistreatment of TGE individuals sometimes comes from teachers, as Emily's (she/her; trans woman; white) experience being misgendered by a professor in graduate school as a conducting major illustrates:

> There's something really uniquely miserable about the experience of getting misgendered at the podium. Everyone's eyes are on you and everybody is watching you and perceiving you and that already feels bad cause you're wondering whether they're really perceiving you as a woman or not—and then you get explicitly called a man in front of everybody. It's especially hard when the person

> who misgenders you is someone who's in a position of authority, like faculty in grad school. That made grad school really hard. It made it hard to learn. It made it hard to focus on gesture while I was at the podium because I was constantly anxious, constantly on guard, bracing for that to happen. It was a real problem in conducting lessons, too.

This illustrates how small word slip-ups can have a negative impact on TGE persons. Similarly, Camden (he/him; trans man; Latinx/white) notes:

> I was also pretty nervous to come out to, or to be outed to my classmates because there were a lot of freshmen in that choir who would use "gay" as an insult and say other things in a derogatory manner.

Words matter. Camden's teacher intervened on his behalf, illustrating the larger point that meaningful student–teacher actions can make a positive impact for TGE youth, as discussed in the next section.

From Our Collaborators: Supportive People, Policies, etc.

We, as authors, heard many stories of supportive teachers and school staff who helped our TGE collaborators navigate their gender journeys at school. For example, the following vignette from the Granger family describes a supportive teacher.

JOSHUA (HE/HIM; CIS MAN; WHITE): So, did all of the teachers at school, were they very nice and supportive right away when you were in second grade?

GABRIELLA (SHE/HER; FEMALE; WHITE): Mhmm . . . [*affirmative sound*] I think so.

VICTORIA (SHE/HER; FEMALE; WHITE): Her teacher now would walk through fire for her. She's like a supportive bulldog type, like "don't you mess with Gabriella," right? And her and her second grade teacher too worked really hard because there were some things that we just didn't—we didn't see coming. Her name wasn't changed in the school computer system basically until—it took a little pushing because they were like, "well, if it's not a legal name change then we can't change it." And, we were getting mixed messages about that. And as staff members [in the district], we kind of pushed a little bit more like, "Hey, we've known each other for a long time. I really think there's probably a way to change this so that she doesn't have Gabriel

> written on everything that comes across her desk." It took a little bit of pushing and they made it happen before her legal name change.

Similarly, Percy (they/them; nonbinary; Asian-American) describes the open, welcoming "vibe" of their urban performing arts high school:

> Renaissance is a very open environment. It's a public arts school, but it's very small. Look at the size of the campus. It's incredibly small compared to [two larger district high schools], but we don't have uniforms. So, everyone is very self-expressive with the way they dress, the way they do their makeup, the way they style their hair. Everyone dresses in a sort of way that compiles all of their personality traits together into their outer appearance. Some people don't, some people do. But no matter what, there's just a sprinkle of everybody into everything that everyone does.

We also spoke with some teachers that identify as TGE persons. For example, JB (they/them; non-binary; white) describes their process of requesting to come out as non-binary in their job as a high-school choral teacher.

> The week before I left for the summer, I started telling a few friends that I'm going to start going by JB and start using the pronouns they/them and we're going to see how it works. And they said, "Okay, great. Good for you. Cool," and then I left. But before I left, I talked to my associate principal. I said "I'm going to begin some kind of transition. I identify with JB, I identify with they/them. I identify this way and I want to dress on all sides of the dress code. I want to put they/them in my email signature. I want to assert this as a thing—I want to wear a button that says they/them. And if a student says, 'what's that?' I want to be able to say, 'Oh, those are my pronouns. I use they/them as my pronouns, you know?' " And my administrator, this Black man, this ex-Marine, said, "that's cool. That's great. That sounds wonderful. I support you, totally. Let's figure out how to talk to the principal." I had to wait until I got back from summer to talk to the principal, but I did, I was able to do it literally the day—I think it was the day after I got back, which was stressful. But we went and sat and talked to the principal, the two of us. [. . .] I started telling her what I want and pretty quickly she said, "I want you to know that personally, I completely support you."

The experiences of our collaborators echo themes that have been uncovered in education and music education research.

School Climate in Education Research

Just as larger studies can illustrate school experiences of TGE youth on a national scale, smaller studies focusing on specific populations can yield results in more specific contextual settings. For example, Shannon E. Wyss (2004), a community activist in Washington, DC, conducted a qualitative study chronicling the experiences of nine adults who were "out" as trans in high school. Nearly all relayed stories of taunting, shoving, inappropriate touching, and even rape—both in and out of school. Wyss reports that five of the nine participants in her study dropped out of high school. Similarly, researcher Lydia A. Sausa (2005) interviewed 24 trans youth in the hope of formulating recommendations for schools on how to better support TGE students. Echoing themes of a team of researchers who "found that school harassment due to transgender identity was pervasive, and this harassment was negatively associated with feelings of safety" (McGuire et al., 2010, p. 1175), 96% of the participants in Sausa's study reported verbal harassment at school and 83% reported physical attacks. In most cases their concerns were "ignored by administrators, teachers, and staff" (p. 20). As education professors Ashley L. Sullivan and Laurie L. Urraro (2019a, p. 29) note,

> Transgender students in particular, report that teachers do not respond to their requests for help and appear indifferent toward any bias or bullying directed at them. They also cite lack of teacher intervention when trans students are being assaulted (Case & Meier, 2014). In addition, educators will often blame trans students when they attempt to bring their concerns to teachers, suggesting that their "violation of gender norms" legitimated the harassment or bullying (Case & Meier, 2014). (p. 29)

Researchers Laura J. Wernick, Alex Kulick, and M. H. Inglehart conducted a study exploring reactions to transphobic language use. They discovered that peer interaction may be more impactful than intervention by a faculty or staff member: "youth-led interventions in peer networks might be effective in diminishing transphobic bullying and supporting the healthy development of transgender young people" (2014, p. 927). Effective methods of reinforcing appropriate classroom behavior may convey faculty expectations of respect and trust among students.

These studies on the harassment of trans students evoke bell hooks's (2000) definition of oppression: "Being oppressed means the *absence of choices*. It is the primary point of contact between the oppressed and the oppressor" (p. 5, emphasis in original). TGE youth face an educational system that may not be fully prepared to honor their gender identity and expression. How does all of this translate from broader school contexts to school music classrooms? For a closer look at how instances of mistreatment manifest in school music settings, we turn to the work of music education researchers.

School Climate in Music Education Research

School music programs exemplify the concept of a community within a community. Students work together in large and small performing ensembles, create new music cooperatively in theory/composition classes, or synthesize music with assistance from music technology. These within-group bonds are not always as strong as they might seem. Bullying persists for music students, even with a close sense of within-group community (Rawlings, 2016; Rawlings & Espelage, 2020; Rawlings & Young, 2020). Music education professors Kenneth Elpus and Bruce Carter (2016) analyze "nationally representative data from five waves (2005–2013) of the biannual School Crime Supplement to the National Crime Victimization Survey" (p. 322) and the results of their study "showed that music ensemble and theatre students were significantly more likely to be victimized by in-person bullying than their non-arts peers" (p. 322). This finding was similar to results from a study that Joshua undertook with colleague Paul Caldwell in which they discovered that 1,123 self-identified LGBTQ collegiate singers (22% of study participants) had encountered bullying and/or harassment from other choral students in school music classrooms or during co-curricular events, including music festivals and all-state choir (Palkki & Caldwell, 2018). Music classes and ensembles succeed, in part, due to the closeness of the participants and their ability to work together cohesively. Music education research helps researchers and teachers to understand where and how group dynamics may weaken, due to harassment and inappropriate behaviors.

Music education scholars have offered guidance and advice for music teachers in confronting bullying and harassment in the music classroom (Carter, 2011; Hendricks et al., 2014; Taylor, 2011). These articles share a common suggestion in challenging music teachers to create safe spaces for their students. We discuss specific ideas for creating positive and productive music classrooms in Chapter 3. Music education researcher Bruce Carter (2011) notes that music teachers are in a unique position to be advocates for safe spaces:

> Legally and ethically, we must work to stop harassment against children and teens on the basis of race, religion, gender, sexual orientation, language of origin, or physical or mental abilities. When students observe teachers making a stand against bullying and harassment, they recognize your intention for a safe classroom. *When students feel safe, they are more likely to ask questions and engage in your class in dynamic and meaningful ways—both musically and nonmusically.* (p. 32, emphasis added)

We as music educators, similar to our school staff and administrative colleagues, are responsible for the physical and mental well-being of students in our classroom and related learning environments. One practice that educators could easily adopt in school settings is: *see something, say something*. Contingent reinforcement of appropriate behavior includes disapproval of inappropriate behavior (Madsen & Madsen, 2016). An application of this principle might occur when a teacher hears a student use an inappropriate slur like "faggot" or "tranny" (an offensive term used against trans women). Upon witnessing the incident, the teacher should address the issue with a disapproval, inquire as to why the inappropriate slur was used, and, if necessary, document the incident and follow up with the appropriate school administrators and parents/guardians. This hypothetical scenario assumes that music teachers are actively engaged in the school culture—that we avoid getting "siloed" in the music classroom. Music education professor Donald Taylor (2011) queries music teachers about ways they might develop community within a school system:

> How frequently do we leave our classrooms to engage with other teachers? Do we make an effort to have a campus presence with all students, or do we focus only on the individuals who come to us? Do we attempt to get to know the parents of students who are not in our classes, or do we show interest only in parents willing to help meet our needs? How accessible do we make ourselves and our work to the community around us? Many people may not relate to our musical interests and may feel they have little in common with us, thus perpetuating the idea of musicians as "outsiders." What are we doing to reach out to meet their musical interests? The effort required to build relationships can pay off in ways that not only strengthen community engagement but may also advance our own programs. (p. 43)

Music teachers who are actively engaged in developing and maintaining interconnected productive school learning environments can expand the idea of safe spaces by creating a network of safe persons who support gender diversity.

As Yale University professor James Comer (1995) notes, "No significant learning occurs without a significant relationship." The time and energy that we spend in relationship building with our students and other stakeholders in our school communities will almost inevitably bear fruit. The goal is to really *see* our students for who they truly are—and to recognize all parts of their intersectional identities. And while it is important for music educators to be realistic about the victimization of TGE youth in schools, we must learn to see beyond this paradigm and take action if we wish to view trans youth as resilient.

TGE Youth Resiliency

TGE youth must simultaneously navigate familial, societal, and policy norms that may not honor their identities. Individuals who develop strategies to cope with, and potentially recover from, discriminatory actions exhibit resilience. The American Psychological Association defines resilience as "the process of adapting well in the face of adversity, trauma, tragedy, threats or significant sources of stress" (Palmiter et al., 2012). Mystic Rose (she/her or they/them; gender nonconforming; Latinx) gives advice for resilient living in saying:

> Dye your hair purple. You know, you only live once. Make sure you're safe first of all but remember that we are only given one life that we know of. So, enjoy it. Don't hold yourself back because of what people may think. Enjoy wearing what you want to wear. Have fun. Society puts us in boxes and makes us restrictive of what we want to do with our lives. So never let society tell you what you should be. You tell society who you are and live your truth.

Similarly, Brendan (he/him; transgender male; white) comments about an incremental and significant step in his life:

> I think the defining moment was the summer before my senior year when I was finally willing to recognize that something was wrong. My junior year was kind of a mess, but I remember thinking to myself at the time, "something's really off and I've got to address something here. I think it's related to my gender." But I knew that if I named it, I'd have to address it and at the time, I didn't want to address it. Anyway, I went to work at an arts camp that summer and I started to go by gender neutral pronouns there because I wasn't ready to transition to male fully quite yet. But this was at least a small step I needed to take for myself and I continued this into my senior year of college.

These narratives indicate how resilient TGE youth can be in the face of societal and school environments that may not understand or accept them.

School personnel who have dealt with stressful situations may empathize more easily with students who struggle with discriminatory actions. Teachers with an understanding of TGE youth resiliency may be better equipped to support the health and well-being of these students (Elze, 2007). TGE individuals seeking ways to process discrimination and other forms of stress often speak of the idea of empowerment. As Abby (they/them; Gender non-binary; Black) says,

> I did find my voice through that chorus [Trans Chorus of LA] again. But now mine is changing the trans narrative from victim to victorious. So, moving even further, moving that needle, just inching it up little by little musically. And that's what we do.

TGE youth can live truthfully and resiliently through empowerment. In other words, teachers can empower students' identity development by establishing and maintaining learning environments that celebrate gender diversity. A team of researchers interviewed 55 trans youth between the ages of 15 and 21 to learn about the role of resiliency in their development as individuals (Grossman et al., 2011). Study participants indicated that three sources of resiliency were particularly beneficial in promoting positive mental health outcomes: a stronger sense of self-esteem, a stronger sense of having personal control in decision-making processes, and a greater degree of perceived social support. Teachers can provide TGE students with both academic and social support, which may lead to increased self-efficacy. When school personnel honor a student's name and pronouns on official school documents, including class rosters, those students have a higher level of control in an important decision process, and better mental health outcomes (Pollitt et al., 2021). Another team of researchers explored strategies of resilience of 21 trans individuals between the ages of 19 and 52 (Singh et al., 2011). Findings from this study indicate five resiliency themes common to these individuals; they:

1. Define their own gender identity;
2. Embrace a strong sense of self-worth;
3. Identify negative societal messages as forms of trans oppression;
4. Develop a community of supportive people;
5. Cultivate hope for the future (pp. 23–24).

Singh and colleagues (2011) also note that a majority of their 21 study participants engaged in some form of social activism and sought careers that allowed them to help others. Both of these ideas exemplify the construct of empowerment, whether through engaging with educational or legislative systems for positive change or actively working to improve quality of life for others. Some of the suggestions from the studies mentioned here would also empower TGE youth to thrive and succeed in school settings.

Teachers who employ the use of TGE students' real names and pronouns signal a value for respect and establish a safe and supportive community to celebrate and honor gender diversity. Enumerated classroom guidelines and school policies (discussed further in Chapter 5) help to identify spaces in which oppressive acts of discrimination will not be tolerated. When we, as teachers, begin to consider the complex, multilayered issues of gender identity and gender expression, TGE students stand to benefit from teachers' reflections. The culminating effects of these types of actions can help TGE youth develop a sense of hope for the future, even if that sense of hope develops over a longer period of time.

Students bring their multilayered, sometimes complicated identities with them into music classrooms. These wonderful complexities relate back to our discussion of *intersectionality* in Chapter 1. TGE students do not lose their identities as they walk down school hallways moving from one classroom or another. In fact, some identities may even exacerbate discriminatory practices. According to the 2019 GLSEN School Climate Survey:

> Black students were more likely to feel unsafe about their race/ethnicity than AAPI, Latinx, Native and Indigenous, multiracial, and White students [and] Native and Indigenous LGBTQ students were generally more likely than other racial/ethnic groups to experience anti-LGBTQ victimization and discrimination. (Kosciw et al., 2020, p. xxvii)

Students proceed through their school day, perceiving peer and faculty interactions through the lens of their intersectional identities. Music educator William Southerland observes, "students recognize that gender and sexuality are part of their school experience whether teachers address them or not" (2018, p. 44). Considering the reality of this statement from a student's perspective, teachers will want to seek ways to create music-learning environments and music-making experiences that are respectful and safe for all students. For those young persons in our classrooms who are more vulnerable to discrimination and harassment, these efforts may help to provide a positive sense of hope for their future, as highlighted in the following narratives from some of our participants about what schooling and school music was like for them.

Stories of Resilience

The collaborators whom we interviewed shared many stories of resilience. These lived experiences provide a glimpse of positive self-efficacy, demonstrating that TGE youth are more than victims. Brendan (he/him; transgender male; white) describes the experience of searching for a school teaching position as a person whose name and ID gender marker do not match.

> I have been pretty upset for a while because I have other friends and colleagues out of college who got jobs and I was thinking, "They got a job and I didn't?" You know? So, I think that has a lot to do with why I didn't get asked back for another interview. But there's no way to know for sure. I didn't make it past the second round or even make it past the first round in a lot of interviews. But I will say that when I was applying to schools within [a Western US metropolitan school system], they had a space where I could put preferred names and legal name, so it didn't matter. And then, I put my legal name on things, but then I still get all the emails to Brendan and not the other name. The principal knew that she was talking to Brendan and I was like, "Thank you!" It just made it all so easy. And I was thinking the whole time with this district, "This is easy. This is how it should be done."

This experience is similar to that of Melanie, as described in other publications (Bartolome, 2016; Bartolome & Stanford, 2017). Melanie (she/her; Transgender female; white) now has a new teaching position and describes "coming out" as trans at her new teacher training:

> Yesterday, we did our last day of new teacher training and we had a couple of sessions at this conference. I remember one of the ones that I did was about restorative justice and it was about doing a circle, right? The restorative circles. And we're sitting in this circle and we started off and she had us write down a value. And we had done a similar restorative justice thing on Tuesday, where we talked about values and stuff. I didn't disclose who I was then, but yesterday, I don't know. I felt like I could. I was in a circle [at new teacher training] and we're kind of sharing and being vulnerable. Just a couple of people went before me and I wrote my value of acceptance and I felt safe to share who I was and to share my identity. And so, I remember yesterday just sitting in that circle and having my little paper plate or whatever we wrote them on, an index card, I think. I wrote "acceptance" and they said, "okay, well, what was your value? And who instilled that in you?" And I said something along the lines of, "I chose acceptance. And it really wasn't because somebody instilled it in me. It was because I know what it's like to not have that from everybody else because I'm trans." And I outed myself and said, "I know what it's

> like to be that person that is ostracized or marginalized or isn't included because of who they are or is disliked because of who they are." And I think one of my biggest drives is that I don't want people to feel like that. And that's something that I've really tried to, you know, I think ever since back in my sophomore year of high school, when I attempted suicide because of being trans. That was something where it's like, I don't want people to feel the way that I feel about myself. And so, when I talk about acceptance and I said, "you know, this is what has really shaped me and is what I try [to] model." I finished talking and I passed the little talking piece over and a couple of people are crying and I'm like, Oh God, you know. My friend is sitting next to me and she texted me. She's like, "I'm proud of you."

Finally, Lu (he/him; transgender man; white) describes the process of his voice masculinization through hormone replacement therapy—a topic we discuss further in Chapter 6—the semester of his senior voice recital in college:

> I really took my time and I was singing alto, not really liking it, but it was kind of just what I had. And then over the summer I started hormones and I auditioned in the fall for choir and I was like, "nothing's really happened yet." Cause it had only been like six weeks or something. And so, I was like, "I can sing alto or I can sing tenor." And I ended up singing tenor and it was fine until like October and then it was really not fine anymore. And just as the year progressed, I just like moved down the line from being literally on the highest end of the tenors to sitting on the border between the baritones and the basses. Just cause as things progressed, it was like, "Oh no." I did a recital in April and that was quite the journey. Basically, I had picked my rep from juries past and I assembled a team of friends who could help me out and we just transposed my entire recital down from even from a month before my recital, I had the final one was like, okay, down another whole step, just cause I didn't want to worry about is this note going to be there today? What is going to happen on the day? But you know, it went well. I did it, I was happy with it. It was definitely a moment of triumph in my journey.

The good news is that we as music educators can create the type of acceptance that these collaborators so beautifully describe.

Recap

In this chapter we have explored the schooling experiences of TGE persons in an effort to provide perspective and context for more detailed practical suggestions. In the following *Praxis* chapters of the book, we share specific ideas to honor gender diversity in school music settings. As you read, remember that TGE persons are not monolithic and that the stories and lived experiences shared in this book are not meant to speak for, or apply to, all TGE persons. School climates vary from harmful to celebratory, and TGE youth can overcome challenges in school settings with a sense of personal resilience. Music teachers have the ability to foster opportunities for resilience through words and actions (Chapters 3 and 4), inclusive policies (Chapter 5), and choral environments that acknowledge and honor gender diversity (Chapter 6). In the next chapter, we explore specific ideas as to how music teachers can become safe people creating safe space for TGE students.

Reflect/Remember

1. Think about your own experiences as a student in elementary, middle/junior high, and high school. Do you remember any instances in which LGBTQA students were bullied in your school(s)? If so, how did the faculty/staff/administration react? How did you react? If you were unable to recall any instances of LGBTQA bullying, do you think that it was not prevalent in your school? Is it possible that you might not have noticed the bullying because it did not directly affect you?
2. Think about the myriad instances every day that involve gender. For example, how you styled your hair this morning, what you wore, the barista at the coffee shop calling you "sir" or "ma'am," or your boss using the phrase "ladies and gentlemen." Now, think of what it must be like for a gender-expansive person to navigate those experiences. Perhaps try this for an entire day as a thought experiment. Do you operate in the world differently or make different choices as a result of your heightened awareness? How might this thought experiment influence teaching interactions with your own students?
3. Understanding that school climates can be difficult for TGE youth, how might you create opportunities for students to experience moments of personal resilience? What small changes could you make in your school music classroom that would signal to TGE students that you are working to create a supportive and safe environment in which they can thrive?

PART II
PRAXIS

Part II focuses on praxis, or the application of strategies, techniques, and pedagogy to honor trans and gender-expansive (TGE) students. Our TGE collaborators share stories of the importance of establishing and developing trust in teacher-student relationships. We consider how school policies can positively impact TGE student life on a daily basis. Listening again to the lived experiences of TGE persons and their music teachers, we curate suggestions to honor gender diversity in music classrooms through student-teacher interactions (verbal and written) and thoughtful selection of curricular materials. We also provide recommendations for music educators to thoughtfully engage in equity-minded policy work at district, state, and national levels. Based on stories from our TGE collaborators, vocal and choral music classrooms can be particularly gendered spaces within music education communities. As we share those stories, we also provide practical ideas for celebrating TGE singers in choral classrooms. The book concludes with a focus on TGE voices. As authors, we step back from discourse to highlight suggestions and advice from our TGE collaborators to help music educators reimagine ways to honor and celebrate the individuals we teach.

3
Safe People Creating Safe Spaces

Chapter Guide

MASON (he/him; Trans Man; white): I think one of the reasons I liked my high school so much was that even though they were my teachers, there was always at least one faculty member every student felt like at any time of the day they could email—anytime they could go to—for anything. And, just that, even though it's not trans specific, it opens that way up of "I have an adult I can talk to about anything." And my parents weren't—you know, my dad was overseas a lot and my mom worked a lot when I grew up. So, everything I had value-wise pretty much came from teachers and they were who I spent most of my life growing up with. So, just having that kind of parental figure or just friend that is an adult that you can go to for anything opens it up immediately. And when you're going through something like that, you want to go to your band teacher or your orchestra teacher because that's the class you want to go to—the person you want to see and that you look up to in general.

ELIZABETH (she/her; cis female; white): I think that every kid just wants to feel safe and they want to be who they are. And they don't want to have to hide. And high school and middle school are rough places to be. So, if you can just be their safe place and honor what they want. . . . That's what everybody wants.

VICTORIA (she/her; female; white): I would say that every student is a new opportunity to learn about something that you thought maybe you knew more

Honoring Trans and Gender-Expansive Students in Music Education. Matthew L. Garrett and Joshua Palkki, Oxford University Press. © Oxford University Press 2021. DOI: 10.1093/oso/9780197506592.003.0004

about and you still don't. And I even feel like, as a parent of a transgender student, that I should have it all figured out. And I still don't, even with my high school students, so we just still keep sitting down and talking and I just keep opening that door. Like, "I'm doing my best here."

Creating Safe Spaces for Music Learning

Celebrating the young people that we teach involves honoring their individual identities and wishes regarding gender identity and expression. Students place a great deal of trust in teachers, staff, and administrators with whom they choose to disclose their gender identity. In order for students to disclose such a personal detail about themselves in school, they must feel safe. Teachers have a great deal of privilege in student–teacher interactions, and working to mitigate that privilege in order to facilitate conversation and action is pivotal to our work. The quote from Victoria illustrates one way to start building trust with students from the first day of the school year, which is what we discuss in this chapter. We begin with broad considerations for music teachers seeking to build and maintain trust with trans and gender-expansive (TGE) students. We continue the chapter by exploring broad issues of policy and how they can influence TGE students in music settings, then end by reflecting on the notion that the *why* of inclusion informs *how* we empower our students to learn.

Building Trust

A safe space is not safe because someone says that it is safe. Safe spaces are actively created by safe *people*. Scholars have written about safe spaces for LGBTQA students in schools (Hunter, 2008; Kitchen & Bellini, 2012; Peters, 2003; Poynter & Tubbs, 2008; Rom, 1998; Woolley, 2017) and in music education (Southerland, 2018). Taylor (2018) notes that while music educators are not expected to be counselors, "what is in music teachers' job descriptions is establishing a supportive environment where students can learn without hindrance" (p. 56). Just as Mason's music teachers were intentional about creating safety for students (as illuminated in the opening quotes to this chapter), music teachers can take time to consider how to establish safe spaces for students. Jason Nichols (2016), lecturer in African American Studies at the University of Maryland, writes in the *Maryland Political Review*,

> In some cases, an open exchange of ideas can be uncomfortable, but leads to the creation of safe people rather than safe spaces. Safe spaces are stationary and stagnant. The classroom safe space stays within the walls of the ivory tower of academia. *Safe people travel, carrying the message of justice.* (para. 2, emphasis added)

Stated simply: safe space is created through a series of reiterative words and actions taken by individuals who strive to make students feel safe and supported, as illustrated by Mari (she/her; transgender woman; Latina):

> It wasn't obvious to me that my professors were safe. It needs to be blatantly obvious, for especially in the closet trans people to even feel okay to trust a professor or even a friend, another student, with you know, stuff that happens or things that you need.

From Mari's words, merely thinking that we, as teachers, are safe people is not sufficient. Students look to peers and adults for signals that they will be safe, respected, cared for, and empowered to learn. Aaliyah (she/her; trans woman; Black) uses the notion of a "safe Haven" to describe this construct:

> I think there should be a safe Haven—a teacher that has a safe Haven room that trans people can get access to in case they're getting attacked from somebody—you know how there's hotlines and stuff, or like a teacher that talks to them if something's happening, cause I don't know if the schools have that.

Rex (they/them; non-binary; white) speaks about creating safe spaces through teacher self-awareness and education:

> I feel like the only way to be seen by others is through education. And that's when I can then be seen by people. It's not through changing anything about myself. It's by helping other people understand how they've been socialized to view gender with very specific lenses. And to help educate them about what gender diversity truly looks like in order to help break away from that.

Roger (he/him; cis male; white), a parent of a trans child, used the phrase "safe zone" when speaking of his son's school music experience:

> I think the fact that [my trans son] Ryder found a home [in high school choir], a safe zone, is just everything. It's critical and it is the role that I think we collectively take on as music educators. Just be ready because you will be that quasi-parent.

From the accounts of our collaborators, creating safe learning spaces can positively impact TGE students' daily lives. How, then, can teachers develop the trust needed for students to acknowledge our efforts?

TGE youth may enter school settings with a trust deficit generated by negative perceptions and social stereotypes. Because a majority of the population identifies as heterosexual, *heteronormative* male–female relationships have become accepted as "normal" and thus anything outside that paradigm is often considered abnormal (Rogers et al., 2013). Likewise, cisgender people comprise the vast majority of the population, resulting in *cisnormativity*, the idea that all people have a gender identity that matches their assigned sex at birth. To help teachers avoid reinforcing hetero- and cis-normative classroom environments, college professors Ashley L. Sullivan and Laurie L. Urraro (2019b) suggest guidelines based on their research with trans students in early childhood settings: "(a) allow children to be themselves, (b) abandon assumptions, (c) eliminate gender segregation, (d) involve parents, (e) create a safe environment, and (f) support and protect transgender children" (p. 201). Teachers can consider their students' backgrounds and vantage points as they navigate interactions in schools: "Every opportunity to see the world through your student's lens will bring you closer to understanding what it is that has captured their imagination or is impacting them in ways that either worry or scare you" (DiCaro, 2017, p. 13). While the visibility of TGE persons continues to increase, they are still considered by some as being outside of the mainstream, or what we might consider as members of a marginalized group. It is important, then, that adults in schools send clear messages to marginalized populations that they are safe and protected on campus.

Actions that teachers take to support TGE youth—especially open and mutually vulnerable dialogues—may not always be easy. It may feel terrifying to engage in this kind of discourse, and yet teachers need courage to engage students in supportive dialogue. As music education professor Karen Salvador (2019) notes, "Risking change can be emotional labor, but like other kinds of labor, it can bear fruit—in this case, the possibility of a more just and equitable world" (p. 62). Recall that teachers have a great deal of privilege in student–teacher interactions, and an open exchange of ideas between a student and a teacher requires both parties to be vulnerable so that privilege does not prevent the development of trust and respect. A quote from bestselling author and vulnerability/shame researcher Brené Brown's 2019 Netflix special captures this point beautifully:

> To not have the conversations because they make you feel uncomfortable is the definition of privilege. Your comfort is not at the center of this discussion. That is

not how this works. *Of course* you're going to get your ass handed to you in these conversations. And the whiter, straighter, Christian, majority culture you are, the more mistakes you're going to make. It's not a question about whether you have a bias or not, it's about which biases do you have and how many and how bad and how deep. That's going to happen. That's what we sign up for when we have these conversations—that's how it works. And you listen and you learn, and you don't hold the people accountable—you know, the people who are targeted by racism and homophobia and heterosexism and gender bias are not responsible for initiating these conversations and building the tables where they should be happening—that's not how this works. We *have* to be able to choose courage over comfort, and we have to say, "Look, I don't know that I'm going to nail this, but I'm going to try, because what I'm sure as hell not going to do is to stay quiet." That's what we can't do. And so, yeah, you're going to make a lot of mistakes, yeah, it's going to be uncomfortable. Yeah, you're going to learn about blind spots you didn't even know you had. And then you're going to be grateful for that moment and take learning in it into your own hands—not make other people responsible for teaching it. And that's how we move forward. But if you think there's going to be real conversations in this country or in companies or organizations around equity and diversity and inclusivity while you remain comfortable, that is not going to happen. And it shouldn't happen (58:58–1:00:58).

Music teachers encourage students to express their own emotions through music-making experiences. For many students, expressing emotion can be an uncomfortable experience. If we, as teachers, expect our students to step into spaces of vulnerability to engage more deeply with music, then we ourselves should be willing to enter uncomfortable spaces in an effort to engage with the often difficult work of equity and inclusion for TGE students.

When it comes to empowering students, teachers can use the power of privilege for good. Imagine for a moment that your favorite music teachers are superheroes (we, the authors, think of *our* music teachers as superheroes). It is probably fairly easy to recall a situation in which those teachers did something to make you feel good about how you were engaging with music. Now, start brainstorming ways that you might make an indelible impression on the lives of your students who hold less privilege. In the words of education researchers Graciela Slesaransky-Poe, Lisa Ruzzi, Connie Dimedio, and Jeanne Stanley, "Recognize how the work you are doing now will help other [students] in the future. . . . You must be willing to spend the time and effort, and know you are making a difference" (2013, p. 40). We, as educators, can be a tremendous force for good (or evil) in the lives of our TGE students. Middle-school instrumental teacher Max (he/him; trans man; white) talks about understanding challenges faced by marginalized student populations:

> There's so much stuff that well-meaning people try to do that just makes everything worse, because they just don't know. And it sucks for the kids that are marginalized because that's basically the problem of marginalized people: everyone means well, but everyone is starting so at the beginning that the marginalized people just have to deal with the same stupid stuff every time. It just gets exhausting. And so, if we can get more beginning teachers and more teachers in general to understand the basic struggles of marginalized people, and actually get them to a point where they can actually start treading new ground with their students, I feel like even that could be so meaningful. Like—the kids already in middle school [are] so used to being mistreated—already . . . and experiencing microaggressions constantly. As far as they know, that's just what life is like and they don't get anything better. And so, to have someone even know the basics would be so valuable in their lives.

Max raises the conundrum of "stuff that well-meaning people try to do that just makes everything worse." This quote is not meant to frighten you or cause you to disengage from doing anything at all. As authors, rather, we encourage you to consider how your teaching and community environments intersect with your well-intentioned efforts and how both of those contexts allow you to consider inclusive possibilities for TGE students. After reflection, you may wish to deepen, change, or discontinue certain practices. We encourage you to allow appropriate time and space to explore what might work best for you and for your students.

Once teachers more clearly perceive challenges faced by marginalized students, they can take steps to change classrooms and other learning spaces to lessen or eliminate the impact of those challenges. Jessica (she/her or they/them; transfeminine nonbinary; white) shares how her college band director honored TGE students:

> I had known the director of bands for a long time. I'd been in the wind symphony for the last few years of my undergrad. He learned my old name. [. . .] When I transitioned, it took him about a semester. He never had used my old name. I think he was being extremely careful so as not to use my old name. So, he kind of reverted back to saying, you know, "tubas do this" for a little while, but it didn't take him too long, more than a semester, to start using my real name again.

A process of developing productive student–teacher relationships can begin after students perceive they are in a safe learning space.

Developing Relationships

Music teachers should thoughtfully consider how to reinforce values of respect and trust, beyond the first day or week of class. The safe school environments discussed by Elizabeth, Mason, and Victoria at the beginning of this chapter can be reinforced through written and verbal communication with students (we discuss these ideas in more detail in Chapter 4). Music teachers may consider several guidelines in order to make informed ethical decisions about how best to honor a student's individual rights and wishes, including:

1. Put the student first and engage in open communication.
2. Involve other adults as appropriate—remember to do this with the consent of the student.
3. Learn about the legal rights and protections of TGE students (discussed further in Chapter 5).

Jaqui (she/her; cis female; white), a private voice instructor, describes how she attempted to engage a new TGE student through open communication:

> So, when I started with Ty, I just sat him down and we did a lot of talking and relationship building. I mean, my general approach to all lessons is relationship building; students aren't going to open up and really experiment with their instrument if they don't trust who they're with. So, I sat down with Ty and I said, "Okay, I want to know about you. Obviously male pronouns. Yes, talk to me." So, I asked a million questions such as, "When did you come out and how does your family react?" And then I also interspersed my opinions because I do want to affirm him just so that he knows that I'm not going to disapprove of or judge what he tells me. I think that trans and nonbinary people in general are extremely cautious—rightfully—about the people that they provide information to because they don't know who they can trust. And they don't know what people are going to weaponize it. And I just want to go straight away into the affirmation.

For Jaqui, engaging with students through conversation was a way to develop trust. Remember that the process of relationship building is unique to the individuals seeking to establish respect and trust. Teachers may wish to consider limiting their questions at first, to allow the student to take the lead in what they wish to disclose and at what pace they wish to develop a teacher-student relationship. The process, much like the persons involved, is not monolithic, and care is needed to determine appropriate contexts for communication (for further guidance, see Box 1.1, *Trans Etiquette*).

Avery (he/him or they/them; agender; white) recalls how an intuitive choral conductor-teacher validated his gender identity in an audition, quickly establishing a sense of trust:

> Just a couple of weeks after starting T, I decided to audition for a local community college choir. Being an instrumentalist, I was more accustomed to blind auditions, so I was actually pretty nervous to be "seen." I knew that I would have to disclose being trans to the director when I met her at the audition, but I had no idea how she would react. It turned out to be an amazing experience that I'll never forget. She had little slips of paper for everyone to write their names and voice part, and on mine I wrote: "Hey, I just started testosterone. I'm not sure how fast it will change, and this is my first time in choir, so I don't know what part I am." She was very nice and respectful about it. After she heard me sing, she said, "well, you land somewhere between an alto and a tenor right now. What do you want to be?" She actually gave me a choice, which blew my mind. I wanted to be in a section that was not associated with females, because I didn't want people to misgender me. I was too shy to say it, but I wanted to be a tenor so badly. I think she could tell, though, because the next day she posted the audition results and my chosen name was at the top of the tenor list. I was beaming the whole rest of the day.

TGE teachers need support and understanding, particularly as they join the teaching profession. Quality mentoring experiences by accepting colleagues can ease the stress of starting a new teaching position. Brendan (he/him; transgender male; white), a music teacher relatively new to the profession, describes a situation from his student teaching in which he found a mentor and advocate:

> Part of the reason the one school in particular was pretty great was because of my middle school band cooperating teacher. He is actually a gay man and he has a partner. And he was just so with it. And I think honestly, his experiences as a gay man made it so much easier for me to connect with him and him with me. We still keep in touch and he's one of the best mentors that I've had.

As these quotes from our collaborators indicate, when music teachers consciously create learning environments that honor and celebrate the identities of TGE persons, safe spaces become a part of a quality learning experience. In the next section of this chapter, we explore specific ways that music educators can establish and maintain safe learning spaces for TGE youth.

Maintaining Trust

When teachers establish classroom guidelines, the majority of those statements likely refer back to one central value: respect. Respect is earned, maintained, and measured by actions over time. Much of the respect between TGE students and their teachers also is associated with respecting the confidentiality of student–teacher conversations. *Teachers should never make assumptions about to whom TGE students are "out,"* as illustrated by high-school choral teacher (and mother of a trans daughter) Victoria (she/her; cis female; white):

> These are uncharted waters in a lot of cases. And [they] just keep coming to me—keep coming to my office. . . . You know, I still don't know what to do sometimes. How to help those kids that are stuck in homes that are unsupportive, where I'm the only one that knows that they're trans besides all their friends. And I just—I feel sort of ineffective in those situations too. Like I want to be able to help them on their journey, but they can't journey anywhere right now. They're just stuck at home.

If a student comes to you and asks you to use a different name and pronouns than appear on school records, you should *definitely* ask the student if they are "out" to their parents or guardians before making a phone call home with an inquiry about this change. Middle-school instrumental educator Tavia (she/her; Cis-het female; white) says that part of supporting trans students

> is knowing what their situation is and what their situation is at home if they've come out to you. One of the conversations that I'll always have with students like that, "okay, you want me to address you as this? Should I do that in communications home? Is that how you want [it] in the program?" That kind of thing. Cause some kids are like, "yeah, I'm supported." And others like, "no, please don't. I will get kicked out of my house." And you know—oh my goodness—people will start arguing about it and the Band Directors Facebook group is the worst about this, where they'll just start arguing about it and like, "you have to do what the parents want." I'm like, "Nope, Nope." That is a hill I'm willing to die on.

If a queer student "comes out" to you, that most likely means that they trust you and feel comfortable with you. Teachers will want to honor that trust by not inadvertently sharing that information with other students, teachers, administrators, or parents without the student's express permission. Maintenance of confidentiality is a crucial part of ethical teacher practice. Queer people are in charge of their own identity disclosure as they "negotiate the closet door" (Jackson, 2007; Palkki, 2015b). Teachers able to maintain trusting relationships with their TGE students are often remembered fondly because of their efforts. Marshall (he/him; trans male; Asian-American) recalls a supportive music teacher from his school music experience:

> Yeah, my choir teacher will definitely, she makes sure that you respect other people but especially her LGBT students cause she cares about her students a lot. But especially for her LGBT students cause she wants everyone to have a safe and loving environment and a place to be themselves.

Students can more easily make music with a sense of emotional openness when they feel that they are in a safe environment, and we as educators can work with our students to develop plans to ensure respect and safety.

Work with Students to Develop a Plan

Music teachers begin the journey of earning students' respect by building working relationships based on listening and trust. When, to whom, and whether a student reveals their gender identity to a teacher or other school employee is the *student's* decision. When possible, other family members may be involved in the decision to disclose, potentially creating a stronger support system for the student. Personal disclosures to teachers must be treated with confidentiality, so as not to violate a school's compliance with the Family Educational Rights and Privacy Act (FERPA) guidelines, which protect the privacy of student academic records, and which are overseen by parents until the student turns 18. Some students will choose to disclose to family members first, while others may decide to speak initially with a teacher (Grossman & D'Augelli, 2006). The best way to learn how to honor a student's wishes surrounding disclosure is simply to *discuss the matter with the student*. Privacy and confidentiality also are essential when students do not have supportive families at home and disclosure to family members may place the student in a potentially dangerous situation. Developing a plan of action helps to create opportunities for student success and helps ensure students' safety in and out of school. Fortunately, a number of LGBTQA-supportive organizations have developed best practices and guidelines for working with students who disclose that they plan to transition or that they wish to acknowledge their gender identity at school (e.g., Orr & Baum, 2015; Gender Spectrum, 2019b; GLSEN and NCTE, 2018; Wells et al., 2012). We continue with a discussion of some principles and policy areas that we as music educators might consider.

We may be able to help TGE students feel safe if we have a common understanding and vocabulary, which may be clarified by gender-related resources with which they are consulting.

Online Resources for TGE Youth

TGE youth growing up today have a wealth of resources at their fingertips on the internet. There are myriad web resources—websites, social media platforms, video repositories, and message boards—dedicated to TGE-related content. Research indicates that online research and connection are common among TGE teens (e.g., Beemyn & Rankin, 2011; Palkki, 2016; Singh, 2013). As researchers Genny Beemyn and Sue Rankin (2011) write, "The importance of the Internet in the lives of many of the participants was reflected in how they first met other transgender people" (p. 58). Young people now have opportunities to be seen and heard through the forums of social media. Opportunities now exist for TGE students to create virtual communities where physical communities are not possible (this became especially apparent during the Covid-19 pandemic). Mari (she/her; transgender woman; Latina) mentions YouTube as a resource:

> YouTube is an encyclopedia for trans people or what it is to be transgender because you can find medical things, you can find stories, you can find all kinds of things online in writing. But as far as firsthand accounts, there's a lot of it now on YouTube. Back then, there was just a handful, and that summer I started questioning my gender identity because—and this was the main thing—I didn't even know that it was scientifically, medically, or legally possible to transition. And I didn't even know the word transgender until then.

Appendix B contains a curated list of print and online resources for teacher and student reference. Additionally, there are vocal-specific resources online to which choral conductor-teachers can refer their students (we expand on resources for choral classrooms in Chapter 6).

When a teacher is able to build and maintain trusting relationships with their students, they may be regarded as a *safe person* who works to create *safe spaces* for students—someone who values mutual respect. From another perspective, as the safe teacher moves throughout the school, the safe space may be transported along with them. This demonstrated value for respect translates easily to guidelines, or policies, that follow the teacher: "respect for all, all of the time." While this seven-word phrase may not seem like the same thing as a school or district policy, it still functions like a policy created by a safe person. Music teachers who take the opportunity to reflect on ethical decision-making, influenced by demonstrating individually held values, can more easily consider and create policies that will positively impact TGE students. Sincere effort to engage with policy work, then, marks progress along the journey to honor all students in school music programs (P. Schmidt, 2019).

Engaging with Policy to Support TGE Students

Who Writes Policy? Whom Does Policy Affect?

Some organizations have very unique policies. For example, there is a company that forbids their employees from eating meat at work: "Matt and Nat, a Canadian handbag company, allows its employees to eat whatever they want during lunch breaks, as long as it never had eyes or a mother" (Larkin, 2018, para. 17). Imagine working for this company that mandates a vegetarian diet. If you're a vegetarian working for this company, you may not give a second thought to this policy. However, if you have a medical condition that requires you to eat meat, then this policy could seriously affect your health. As odd as this analogy may seem at first glance, it illuminates the principle that policies often influence people who have less privilege (Iverson, 2007). While reviewing recent literature on the secondary-school experiences of trans youth, education researcher Ruari-Santiago McBride (2021) notes that

> only a minority of schools have the resources in place to ensure gender diversity is valued [. . .]. However, the majority of the research suggests that schools are hostile environments for trans youth and that trans youth's educational lives are shaped by institutional macroaggressions, interpersonal microaggressions, and cisnormative violence. (p. 112)

It is this disconnect that necessitates more attention to policy as it relates to trans youth.

Legislation, laws, and policies are influenced by those who write them (e.g., Carbonara et al., 2008; P. Schmidt, 2019). The same is true of policies for school districts, schools, and music education organizations. The truism "all politics is local" may be applicable here, as the cultural norms of a given region or community can also influence educational policies (e.g., Meyer & Keenan, 2018; Taylor, 2007). For example, at the time of this writing, US states have differing policies regarding trans persons changing a "gender marker" on documents such as birth certificates. For example, Tennessee Code Ann. § 68-3-203(d) (2006) states:

> The sex of an individual will not be changed on the original certificate of birth as a result of sex change surgery. . . . This is the only state that has a statute specifically forbidding the correction of sex designations on birth certificates for transgender people. (Lambda Legal, 2018)

This policy stands in great contrast to state laws in California, namely Cal. Health & Safety Code §103426 (2018):

> California will issue a new birth certificate when an applicant submits to the State Registrar an affidavit that, pursuant to Cal. Health & Safety Code §103430(a), contains substantially the following "I, (petitioner's full name), hereby attest under penalty of perjury that the request for a change in gender to (female, male, or non-binary) is to confirm my legal gender to my gender identity and is not for any fraudulent purpose." There is a $23 fee for a new birth certificate, pursuant to Cal. Health & Safety Code 103725. (Lambda Legal, 2018)

This disparity in policy illustrates the notion that the experiences of a trans person can vary greatly depending on the state in which they live.

Policies shape the day-to-day experiences of TGE students in tangible ways (Pascoe, 2011; Woolley, 2017). For example, which restroom will they use? Which dressing room will they use during the school musical production? With whom will they room on school field trips? Policies are not simply words in a handbook or online document for TGE students—they have real implications for real lives and real school experiences. It is possible that schools may not have policies in place to support trans/gender-expansive students, causing further confusion among the very adults who are meant to protect and mentor them (e.g., Leonardi & Staley, 2018; Meyer, 2010, 2014; Meyer & Leonardi, 2018; Wells et al., 2012; Woolley, 2019). Education professor and nonbinary advocate Lee Airton (2018) discusses the importance of centering the *audience* of a specific policy (those who carry it out) while still maintaining respect for the *beneficiary* of said policy (those whom the policy is meant to protect): "Micropolitically, gender-expansive policies and practices may succeed based on whether they can change how (mostly) cisgender institutional actors *feel about and narrate* their own involvement in the institutional commitments demanded by law and policy, in everyday life" (p. 806, emphasis in original). It is important, then, that PK–12 music educators understand gender-laden music (education) policies and the context and history surrounding them, as well as how policies at various levels might be changed.

Music education professor Patrick Schmidt (2019) argues that policy need not be seen as something for those in district offices and legislative chambers—that policy is embedded in the daily work of music educators, should we choose to speak up and get involved: "policy outcomes and processes will be affected depending on who is around the table" (p. 29). Just as printed sheet music means nothing without musicians who bring the music to life, policy is a "living, breathing, deeply human endeavor" (P. Schmidt, 2019, p. 81). We continue with a short primer on how federal law and policy can influence trans students in American schools.

Impact of Federal Law on School Policy

Legal guidance for TGE students exists in various forms at the federal, state, and local levels of government. At the time of this writing, there were no federal laws that specifically protect TGE students from discrimination in the United States, but legal foundations do exist that provide for equal protection under federal law. The Equal Protection Clause of the Fourteenth Amendment (1868) "prohibits a school district or individual employees of a school or district from treating students differently based on personal characteristics, such as race, sex, and disability" (Orr & Komosa-Hawkins, 2013, p. 93). Under the Equal Protection Clause, school districts and school employees must apply policies consistently for all students and must seriously attend to student complaints of unequal treatment. As a specific example, schools must address incidents of harassment reported by TGE students if school policy mandates investigation of harassment reported by non-TGE students. Understanding how the court system views the broad wording of the Fourteenth Amendment can help teachers recognize potentially discriminatory school and district policies.

The First Amendment to the US Constitution (1791) protects students' rights to freedom of speech and expression. As the National Center for Transgender Equality (2016) notes on their website, "that includes the right to dress according to your gender identity, talk about being transgender openly, and express your gender in other ways." Case law citing First Amendment rights was used to secure students' rights to discuss their sexual orientation in school (Lambda Legal, 2002). The court's decision also could apply to TGE students' expression of their gender identities (Meyer, 2014). As case law supporting LGBTQA students continues to develop and expand, teachers and school systems need to be aware of these changes if they wish to support equal access for all students.

Title IX of the Education Amendments of 1972 broadly prohibits sex discrimination in schools and education programs receiving federal financial assistance. The latter qualifier applies to all schools, K–12 and colleges, that receive federal funding. Case law dating from 2000 (*Montgomery v. Independent School District No. 709*) provides legal relief for students who are harassed because of their gender expression. In May 2016, the Federal Office for Civil Rights issued additional support for transgender students in the form of a "Dear Colleague" letter:

> Title IX of the Education Amendments of 1972 (Title IX) and its implementing regulations prohibit sex discrimination in educational programs and activities operated by recipients of Federal financial assistance. This prohibition encompasses discrimination based on a student's gender identity, including discrimination based on a student's transgender status. (Lhamon & Gupta, 2016, p. 1)

The guidance afforded to TGE students in 2016 quickly was withdrawn less than one year later, with a change in US presidential administration (Peters et al., 2017). While the US Department of Justice, Civil Rights Division, and the Department of Education Office for Civil Rights formally withdrew clarification that Title IX protects TGE students from discrimination, the actual language and meaning of Title IX remains intact. GLSEN indicates, "even after the guidance document was rolled back, courts have continued to affirm that anti-transgender discrimination is banned under Title IX" (2018, p. 3). The importance of the Obama administration guidelines being rescinded should not be taken lightly, because the decision has direct implications for TGE youth. The National Association for Music Education (NAfME) released a statement on February 24, 2017, denouncing this decision by the 45th presidential administration: "We believe that removing these guidelines impedes that mission by potentially making it more difficult for transgender students to receive a quality well-rounded education, including music" (Odegard & Blakeslee, 2017, para. 2).

The absence of specific federal laws protecting TGE students from discrimination in schools has prompted a number of state governments to craft legislation to that effect. The National Center for Transgender Equality (2020) maintains an active list of states with guidelines for the rights of trans students. At the time of this writing, California, Connecticut, Hawaii, Illinois, Maine, Maryland, Massachusetts, Michigan, Minnesota, New Jersey, New York,

Oregon, Rhode Island, Vermont, Washington, and the District of Columbia had detailed guidance in place that prohibits discrimination against trans students. In addition to these state laws, over 200 cities and counties have enacted non-discrimination policies that include gender. LGBTQA advocacy groups, like the Human Rights Campaign (2018), track the creation of these protections and provide frequent updates through their websites. It is important to note that some state constitutions limit the ability of cities and counties to create policies and statutes to extend legal protections to TGE persons. As of 2019, "More than 40% of American public-school students already attend a school that protects transgender students from discrimination" (Elias, 2019, p. 9). Navigating the rapidly changing and frequently complicated legal landscape surrounding gender diversity can seem daunting. If we, as teachers, value equal access to learning, then we can find ways to inform ourselves of our students' rights in our own town, city, or state.

What Happens in the Absence of Policy?

When you think about policies at your workplace or in your school environment, consider also what might happen if they were not observed, effectively rendering them absent. Joshua recalls a situation in which he implemented a gender-inclusive policy in an honor ensemble setting that was not observed consistently (see Box 3.1). If you are a music teacher, think about policies that you enforce every day but may not think twice about. Did any policies come to

Box 3.1 Author Aside: Joshua

In the fall of 2019, I had the privilege of conducting a regional high school SSAA honor choir (the organization sponsoring the event used SSAA, TTBB, and SATB as labels for the three ensembles). I worked hard all weekend to use gender-inclusive language, and I knew that we had more than one "out" trans student in the choir, including one trans male. The day of the concert, a local high-school teacher came to help the students file off of the stage to where they would be sitting during the concert. As soon as this teacher began to speak to the students, she began to refer to them as "ladies." While my use of gender-inclusive language was not a formal policy (far from it), this is an illustration that if not all policy implementers are on board with a policy (or even aware of the policy), they can disavow the gender identities of many students with one or two seemingly harmless words.

mind? If yes, you may find yourself thinking something like the adage, "with great power comes great responsibility."

It is not always clear who is responsible for enforcing policy. If your school has a specific dress code policy, but teachers have never been explicitly told to enforce it, they may assume that an administrator or other school official will take up that responsibility. This confusion may lead to well-meaning policies that do not achieve their desired effect. Patrick Schmidt (2019) notes, "Implementation is a theoretically neat but practically messy process" (p. 58) and, "narrow views of implementation can create significant waste, while failing to help those on the ground" (p. 59). This can be especially true for important documents like passports, drivers licenses, and state ID cards: "The paradigm of permanence is strongly implied in most U.S. laws by the requirement that individuals' decision to change their sex marker on an official identity document be medically authorized" (Davis, 2017, p. 43). Ryder (he/him; TransMan; *not specified*) shares his story about applying for a driver's license as a result of a legal name change that illustrates this point:

> The birth certificate, I believe, was the hardest part. The driver's license was actually the easiest part. And I don't know if it was just the time, but I recall that I only had to—I just went in and marked male instead of female when I asked for a replacement. And at the time they didn't ask questions. The lady was like, "Oh, okay. Yeah, sure."

The gracious actions of a state motor vehicle agency employee honoring Ryder's truth saved him from a potentially awkward/difficult line of questioning. In a related story, Melanie (she/her; Transgender female; white) describes an experience with a difference in gender markers on personal and official documents:

> One of the things that I found going into the teaching sphere, at least for the elementary job, was that my gender pronouns were pulled from my applicant file. On the website, for every school in the district, it was "Mr. So and So," or "Ms. So and So," and because my gender marker on my applicant file was male, the website listed me as Mr. Melanie Stapleton, which obviously had a disconnect.
>
> So, when the HR director had come in and asked . . . "How can I help you in any way? I'm here for you, etc.," which was great, I said, "Well, the website is a problem." So the district HR director got my prefix on the school website fixed for me, but it was definitely something that I recognized going into the field and going into any new teaching jobs, this mismatch between my gender marker and my identity, which is going to happen for a lot of people across the US. Because, depending

> on your state's policy, that might not even be a possibility. To file in Texas for the gender marker change, it was $300, let alone any kind of legal fees or preparation.
>
> So, when I applied with my second school district, I was honest. I put male because in Texas, when you do any kind of teaching application, you're required to do a background check and that background check specifically asks you for your sex, not your gender. And it doesn't have an "Other" option. Sometimes the district might provide a "decline to identify" option, but typically not. So, you're forced with the binary of male or female. So, I would choose what's on my driver's license, which was in direct conflict with my feminine name, or with how anybody spoke about me. In this school district, I ended up running into issues with insurance and paperwork because somewhere along the way, I guess an HR person maybe thought that was a mistake and "fixed" it for me.

An important element in both Ryan's and Melanie's stories is that of considering the people potentially impacted by narrow policies. This humanistic approach to engaging with policy may help identify policy issues that need to be changed in order to provide access equity for TGE persons.

School officials need to understand how and why policies may positively impact the daily school experiences of TGE students. Without awareness and training, school officials may feel "justified by the logic that trans* students do not exist in their presence [. . .] and do not need inclusion or access to K–12 schooling" (Woolley, 2019, p. 31). In some cases, districts have policies, but they are not carried out as planned. A disconnect between policy creation and implementation is illustrated in a study examining trans-inclusive policies of the New York City Department of Education (DoE). Education professor Susan W. Woolley (2019) remarks: "I observed, as well as discussed, with principals, deans, teachers, and staff various practices in their schools that conflicted with the NYC DoE's guidelines" (p. 34). Additionally, "some teachers were aware of, but refused to adhere to and implement the NYC DoE's guidelines" (p. 35), with one teacher remarking that "I don't want to get involved in your politics" (p. 36).

This latter statement indicates an impasse. We as authors believe that teachers should act in the most inclusive manner possible, especially when policies exist at various levels to honor the gender identities of TGE youth. If we can make the lives of a marginalized population more better, we should consider it ethically responsible to do so. The important message is that *policies require implementation at the most local level.* Even federal- and state-level policies about education have the most impact when they are ethically implemented at the classroom level. Schmidt (2015, 2017, 2019) suggests that this is an integral part of our work as teachers. As we look more closely at the role teachers play in policy work, we need to consider the role of specific, enumerated policies for TGE youth.

The Importance of Enumerated Policies

It is important that schools and school districts draft and enact an *enumerated* policy for TGE youth—one that specifically states which groups of people are protected. In a survey study with 1,123 LGBTQ-identified collegiate choral singers, Joshua and choral conductor-teacher Paul Caldwell (2018) stated,

> These survey data also indicate that policies surrounding bullying and hate speech should enumerate specific groups that are protected by such a policy. The following is an example policy statement from choral music educator Tim Estberg from New Trier High School in Illinois:
>
> *If any student feels that our classroom is in any way uncomfortable, he or she is strongly encouraged to speak with me as soon as possible. Together, we will create an environment in which each of us can grow and learn in a safe place for everyone, regardless of gender, gender identity, race, religion, sexual orientation, class, level, or physical or mental ability*. (p. 42)

Similarly, the District of Columbia Public Schools (2015) designed an enumerated policy for the entire school district:

> DCPS does not discriminate or tolerate discrimination against employees, applicants for employment, or students on the basis of actual or perceived race, color, religion, national origin, sex (including pregnancy), age, marital status, personal appearance, *sexual orientation, gender identity or expression*, family status, family responsibilities, matriculation, political affiliation, genetic information, disability, source of income, status as a victim of an interfamily offense, or place of residence or business. (p. 22, emphasis added)

Enumerated policies are important for LGBTQA students because they indicate that a group, school, program, or adult is safe and supportive. Because we live in a cis-sexist society (one in which everyone is assumed to be cisgender and that cisgender is "normal"), TGE students may assume, without a clear indication, that a music teacher is not a safe person who will support them. Knowing that TGE students need clear, supportive communication to ensure their safety in school learning environments, teachers must consider what may be perceived as bold steps to truly celebrate all of the students we teach.

In Chapter 5, we provide a more in-depth discussion of policies that may influence TGE students and what we as music educators can do to influence policy processes.

Recap

Being safe people in music education classrooms can inform how we as music teachers empower students to learn. As revealed in the opening quotes from Elizabeth, Mason, and Victoria, teachers can make the decision to act on their values of inclusion and to guide students to show respect for one another. Teachers regarded as safe people will engender the idea of safe spaces in which students can engage with music in deeply meaningful ways. As music teachers, we know that emotional security is paramount to learning how art informs, impacts, and illustrates the way we feel in a given moment. Inclusive language used in the classroom and in policies that affect students' lives can empower young people to live, and to make music, as their authentic selves.

Throughout the next three chapters, we continue our focus on *praxis*, or practical application to assist music teachers and music teacher educators to honor and celebrate gender diversity. In Chapter 4, we explore ways to celebrate gender diversity in elementary, general, and instrumental music classrooms. We further consider ideas for engaging with inclusive policies for TGE students in Chapter 5. In Chapter 6, we focus on specific challenges music teachers may experience in vocal music settings. Throughout these *praxis* chapters, we elevate the voices of TGE students and their teachers. Learning from and with TGE persons will hopefully aid readers in understanding how inclusive practices are essential to ensuring quality musical experiences for students.

Reflect/Remember

1. Think about teachers in your PK–12 school experience that you trusted and with whom you felt a bond of mutual respect. What did that teacher do to create that sense of trust? How did that teacher convey an atmosphere of mutual respect, perhaps through things they said and by their actions? How could you create a school music environment that honors TGE students?
2. Do you have TGE-supportive policies in your district or in your school? How do those policies or the lack of any enumerated policies impact

your ability to honor TGE students in your classroom? With whom might you start a conversation that could help you improve access equity for TGE students by actively engaging in policy work?

3. What has been your role in policy creation and enforcement at the classroom, school building, and district levels? How might you view yourself as a policy actor in the future with regard to TGE students in your district?

4

Honoring Gender Diversity in Music Classrooms

Chapter Guide

TRAVIS (he/him; male; white) Good teaching is good teaching. Good teaching is aware teaching. Good teaching allows you to leave your ignorance at the door to have your students teach you.

Creating Safe Music Classrooms through Words and Actions

Music teachers seeking ways to create safe classrooms and musical experiences for TGE students make continuous choices to celebrate and honor gender diversity. In other words, teachers establish and maintain safe spaces through practical, reiterative processes, including written and nonverbal communication. Phoebe (she/her; non-binary; white) speaks of the supportive power

Honoring Trans and Gender-Expansive Students in Music Education. Matthew L. Garrett and Joshua Palkki, Oxford University Press. © Oxford University Press 2021. DOI: 10.1093/oso/9780197506592.003.0005

of her collegiate orchestra director as student and teacher had an open discussion:

> My current orchestra director asked me, he said—he was telling me, "I can't imagine going through a transition like you are going through right now and not feeling stressed and worried and anxious all the time, but you seem like you are thriving this semester." I remember saying just, "I'm no longer burdened by a false presentation. I no longer have the burden of expressing a false identity."

Avery (he/him or they/them; agender; white) had a similar experience while coming out to music professors in college who they had predicted may be less than accepting:

> I was missing weeks to months of school at a time due to being in and out of the hospital, so my professors already knew something was up. I think it was a pretty inevitable conversation of, "okay, what's been going on for you?" Based on the way I dressed and acted though, I felt like most of my professors already had an idea that there was something LGBT-related going on. I was surprised, but they all took it really well. One of the faculty members did have trouble with the new name and pronouns at first, but it wasn't intentional. It was more of a—just trying to change their gestalt, I guess—of me as a person. And they've since come around.

Similarly, Camden (he/him; trans man; Latinx/white) also describes a positive experience in which he felt honored by his high-school choral teacher:

> [He] was the only teacher that I was "out" to my junior year in 2017. I sent him an email and was saying, "Oh, I go by this now. Can you call me this?" [. . .] He also had mentioned to me individually that when I told him I was changing my name, he would practice in his head over and over so he wouldn't say the wrong one, which meant a lot to me. He also wanted to make sure that the concert attire that people were wearing was what they felt most comfortable in. And he tried to also use they/them pronouns for everyone, which was really nice. And ever since he had learned about using more gender-neutral terms, he would always correct himself, which was really such an affirming experience. I also had other trans friends in class as well, and they felt the same way.

Notice here that Camden's teacher took time to *rehearse* his new name and made conscious, deliberate efforts to avoid *dead-naming* (using the name that a TGE student was given at birth). We as educators can take these intentional steps as we reflect on the environment that we work to create in our classrooms. As we move to a discussion of specific ways to support TGE youth, it is important to acknowledge that teachers and students are fallible humans, and that we all make mistakes. Students likely will be able to distinguish mistakes made with good intentions, so if some or all of the following ideas are new to you, just remember to start by putting one foot in front of the other, treating students like the fascinating individuals that they are while being kind to yourself.

Names, Pronouns, and Titles

Our names, pronouns, and titles can represent the essence of who we are. Take a moment to reflect on how many times a day you or someone else uses your name. How many times do you answer when someone calls you or when you get a notification on your smartphone that someone has reached out to you through social media? Now, imagine that one day, people started calling you by a different name—a name that represents a part of your past that you do not want to relive, and a name that causes you discomfort. *Words matter*. What we say in our classrooms carries a great deal of weight. Additionally, *how* we use our words can influence the experiences of our students (e.g., Kelly, 2020). Because language carries great weight, particularly when discussing gender (Beemyn & Rankin, 2011; Davis, 2009; Järviluoma et al., 2003; Valentine, 2007), music educators seeking to honor gender diversity can choose classroom language carefully. The point here is that we can *normalize the sharing of pronouns as a part of our classroom culture and procedures*, thus reducing stigma for TGE students. For example, Marshall (he/him; trans male; Asian-American) describes:

> When it comes to her trans students, [my high-school choir teacher] makes sure people respect us and our names and our pronouns. What's great is that even if you aren't trans, she normalizes people who wish to go by a different name or nickname.

For TGE youth, the use of their real name is a vital part of honoring and respecting them. In a study about the use of chosen names for trans youth, researchers report that:

> regardless of whether or not schools have LGBTQ anti-bullying policies, it is critical that schoolteachers and staff engage in activities that create safe climates for transgender youth in order for them to feel safe using their chosen names. Youth reported higher self-esteem, lower depressive symptoms, and less negative suicidal

ideation when they were able to use their chosen name in more contexts. Our results suggest that support and *validation of transgender youths' chosen name buffer negative mental health outcomes*. (Pollitt et al., 2021, pp. 334–335, emphasis added)

Sharing pronouns with students will seem innocuous to most people, though this practice is becoming more common (Airton, 2018). This simple act, however, can identify a music teacher as a safe person for a TGE student who may or may not have identified themselves to their peers or to other adults.

Email Signature and Video Communication Name

What we include in our email signature and in our videoconferencing title can send a subtle yet powerful message to recipients, as illustrated by choral teacher Susan (she/her; cis; white):

> Kids are pretty clear about [my support for LGBTQ people]. I think mostly because of the interaction that I have with all of the performing arts kids, I've changed my language in rehearsal. I don't use he/she binaries. It's always soprano, alto, tenor, bass, you, they. I've just tried to get out of the binary world as much as possible with my language. You will see in my emails that I include my pronouns, they/them/their and she/her/hers so they can refer to me either way. Whatever they feel comfortable with.

Considering the volume of email that music educators process on a daily basis, an email signature may carry more weight than you might think. Figure 4.1 illustrates how you might share your pronouns with every email you send.

At the time of this writing, many US music educators have experienced a school year involving some type of hybrid or virtual teaching. For those

Mx. Riley Madison
pronouns: *they/them/their*
Instrumental Music Teacher
Canyon Heights Middle School

Figure 4.1. Email signature with pronouns.

teachers using the Zoom video communication platform for synchronous teaching activities, changing your Zoom display name to include pronouns is another way to show support for TGE students. Especially if you identify as cisgender, these seemingly simple adaptations to electronic correspondence could give a clear signal that you are a safe person.

Classroom Guidelines or Posters

Adding visual pronoun cues to classroom guidelines or posters can help TGE youth understand that adults recognize the power of name and pronoun use and that they are willing to demonstrate that support publicly, as shown in Figure 4.2.

Depending on grade level or the type of music classroom, similar examples might include classroom posters, handbooks/syllabi, and handouts. These simple cues can make a major difference in signaling your support for TGE youth.

Welcome to the Freedom Middle School Orchestra Room
Room 24

Mr. Calvin Terrier, director
pronouns: *he/him/his*

Class Guidelines:

- Come to class prepared to work together productively.
- Place your backpack, case and personal belongings in the designated storage area (please do not bring unnecessary materials to your seat).
- Bring your instrument to your seat and put your music in rehearsal order.
- Remember to rosin your bow if needed BEFORE class begins.
- Most importantly, respect yourself and others in our class.

Figure 4.2. Classroom poster with pronouns.

Sharing Names and Pronouns in Verbal Communication

Navigating the appropriate use of a student's name and pronouns likely will require open communication between student and teacher. Teachers easily can begin a conversation by demonstrating an openness to a spectrum of gender identities and gender expressions. An example of teacher-to-student verbal interaction might be: "My name is Mx. Lopez, my pronouns are they/them, and this is concert band" (we will discuss the use of pronouns and titles that exist on a more expansive spectrum, like the "Mx." title, later in this chapter). Once a teacher begins this type of conversation, any response from an individual student may need to take place privately, away from the eyes and ears of other students.

Roll Call

In addition to identifying your own pronouns, it is important that you provide students with the option to privately identify their name and pronouns at the beginning of each term. Figure 4.3 illustrates a practical and easy way of doing this. For example, you might ask for a student's name and pronouns, height (for ensemble sitting or standing position), instrument/voice part, favorite genre or style of music, and a little-known fact about them on an index card or digital form. In this way, music teachers engage students while collecting information that allows for more individualized instruction. Collecting this type of information privately reinforces the important idea that intention must match action. Students questioning their gender identity should not be put in a position in which they must publicly share their pronouns or name. In other words, sharing pronouns is meant to be an *inclusive* strategy that welcomes students, not a forced mandate that may create discomfort or potentially "out" someone. We advise repeating this exercise every quarter (or perhaps every semester) as students' identities shift, as new students enter your class/school, or as TGE students become more comfortable in their identities.

Important: Any face-to-face conversations about names/pronouns should be conducted privately so that students who are not "out" yet are not forced to disclose their gender identity in front of the whole class. If you do not get the opportunity to speak with students in advance of your first classroom interactions, you could call roll using the student's last names only. You can begin the process by stating, "If anyone uses a different first name than appears on my roster, please let me know in any way you're comfortable, like after class

Back-To-School Student Information Card
Ms. Travis [she/her]

Last Name:

____

First Name (on the roster):

____

The name I like to be called is:

____

The name my parents call me at home is:

____

My pronouns are:

____

My email address is:

____

In order for me to be successful in the class,
I need you to know that:

____

Figure 4.3. Back-to-school student information card.

or in an email." Teachers concerned with singling out any unidentified TGE students should keep in mind that this idea also may apply to students who prefer a shorter version of their name, like Sam vs. Samantha. Following a process like this will avoid unnecessary embarrassment and discomfort for any student who has changed their name but whose birth (dead) name still appears in school system records. In the following quote, middle-school instrumental teacher Max (he/him; trans man; white) discusses his process with using the proper name and pronouns of a non-binary student.

> And so, they [a non-binary student] told me their pronouns and their name. And I think I might be one of the only people—unfortunately, they've told a lot of people—that actually addresses them correctly. They're in high school now, but on the last day of eighth grade, they gave me a hug and they were like, "thank you so much, because you're the only teacher that actually calls me my name."

This story illuminates how powerful it can be for a PK–12 student who has yet to turn 18, and thus cannot legally change their name without parental consent, to be addressed properly by a teacher. We discuss policy implications for students who are not able to complete name changes in Chapter 5.

Pronouns on an Identity Spectrum

An increasing number of TGE persons use pronouns that exist outside the gender binary of he/him and she/her (Wayne, 2005). It is important that teachers understand the use of alternative pronouns such as they/them and ze/hir (pronounced "zee" and "here"). Some educators dislike the grammatical use of "they" when referring to one person. The use of the singular they has been adopted by widely used dictionaries. In fact, "they" was the *Merriam-Webster Dictionary* word of the year in 2019:

> Much has been written on they, and we aren't going to attempt to cover it here. We will note that they has been in consistent use as a singular pronoun since the late 1300s; that the development of singular they mirrors the development of the singular you from the plural you, yet we don't complain that singular you is ungrammatical; and that regardless of what detractors say, nearly everyone uses the singular they in casual conversation and often in formal writing. (Merriam-Webster, n.d.)

Figure 4.4 identifies gender-expansive pronoun possibilities. Some TGE individuals might refer to options like the singular *they* as gender-neutral pronouns. As you consider these possibilities, remember that there are a nearly indefinite number of pronouns now in use. The most important thing is that you *ask* a person what pronouns they use.

Gender Pronouns

Please note that these are not the only pronouns. There are an infinite number of pronouns as new ones emerge in our language. Always ask someone for their pronouns.

Subjective	Objective	Possessive	Reflexive	Example
She	Her	Hers	Herself	She is speaking. I listened to her. The backpack is hers.
He	Him	His	Himself	He is speaking. I listened to him. The backpack is his.
They	Them	Theirs	Themself	They are speaking. I listened to them. The backpack is theirs.
Ze	Hir/Zir	Hirs/Zirs	Hirself/ Zirself	Ze is speaking. I listened to hir. The backpack is zirs.

Design by Landyn Pan

transstudent.tumblr.com
facebook.com/transstudent
twitter.com/transstudent

For more information, go to transstudent.org/graphics

TSER
Trans Student Educational Resources

Figure 4.4. Gender pronouns by Trans Student Educational Resources (TSER).

Gender Pronoun Possibilities

As with pronoun possibilities, some TGE persons choose to use an alternative honorific (something other than Mr., Mrs., or Ms.); some nonbinary or nonconforming persons choose the prefix "Mx." (pronounced "mix"). This honorific has now been adopted by major dictionaries including the *Oxford English Dictionary* (McDonald, 2015). For TGE college students completing pre-service field work or student teaching, using gender-expansive pronouns or titles can be complicated (Bartolome et al., 2017). Music teacher educators should engage students in candid conversations to learn about student choices and to consider possibilities when using less familiar pronouns or honorific titles. Pronouns will not necessarily match outward appearance (Airton, 2018). One can identify as nonbinary but present as male; for example, *Queer Eye*'s Jonathan Van Ness identifies as nonbinary but primarily uses he/him pronouns and often wears a beard (S. Schmidt, 2019). It is likely that many people have never interacted with an openly nonbinary person, as JB (they/them; non-binary; white) notes:

> I'm not trying to be a trailblazer per se for non-binary and genderqueer music educators, but also, I don't know any non-binary and genderqueer music educators. I want people to know it's possible. I don't just want to give teachers tools for teaching their students. I also want to give future music educators and current music educators permission and visibility and I want to let them know it can be done. That they can be genderqueer and music educators even in a public school in (my home state) Texas. Here's how I did it, here's my experience and you can do it, too.

One of the simple-in-theory but complex-in-practice items regarding honoring TGE youth is use of their name and pronouns.

Pronoun and Name Changes in School Records

Students deserve the right to be called by the name with which they identify. This right, unfortunately, is not always recognized on official school records, including class rosters and student directories. As trans activist and scholar Genny Beemyn (they/them) (2005) wrote,

> Being able to alter their records and documents, though, is personally and legally important for many trans students. Not only does having the appropriate name and gender listed reflect and validate their identity, but it can also protect trans students from constantly having to explain why they use a name different from their birth name and why their appearance does not match a photo or gender designation on an identification card. Moreover, updated records and documents can ensure that trans students will not be outed and will help protect them from discrimination when they apply for jobs, seek admission to graduate and professional schools, and at any other time that they must show a college document. (p. 83)

Teachers should be familiar with school or district policies regarding the use of a student's name and pronouns. We will discuss policies that impact TGE students in Chapter 5; however, school records are worth mentioning briefly here. Based on our experiences with TGE students, their parents, and music educators who teach these individuals, we posit that many individual school districts do not have specific policies for chosen or claimed names or personal pronouns. Teachers who learn that enumerated policies do exist can reinforce the implementation of those policies to celebrate and honor TGE students in school record systems. Similarly, teachers can privately inquire about the status of a TGE student's legal name change. There may be instances in which the student is "out" at school but not at home, or a student may not have parents who support use of their new name in public. The process of changing one's name can be complicated, as illuminated by some of our collaborators. Mason (he/him; Trans Man; white) describes the complications that come along with having a legal name change:

> Most applications, even for just regular jobs, say, "have you gone by any other legal name?" And I used to be Madison, which is a feminine name. And so, it's a very obvious not-random change to Mason kind of thing. It's not like, "Oh, my name's Sam and you could really do anything." It's kind of obviously like, "Oh, you didn't change it because you're getting away from something legally. You changed it cause you're that way."

Mason mentions the name "Sam" as potentially applicable as a masculine or a feminine name, from his perspective. The difficulty of navigating a job search without having one's name legally changed illuminates one aspect of cisgender privilege, as cisgender people likely will never experience this discomfort.

Music teachers can take intentional steps to inquire about which pronouns TGE students use at school vs. what they use at home, as illuminated in Figure 4.3. For example, JB (they/them; Non-binary; white), a high-school choir teacher at the time of the interview, says:

> I know it can get tricky with parents. But I have a colleague who says, "well, if the parent doesn't call him that, then I'm not calling him that." And I don't subscribe to that. I go with what the student tells me to call them. Period. End of story. And then when I talk about the student to the parent, I will probably use the name that the parent knows. I'll just do what's best for the kid. If it's about gender, then I'm not going to say, "well, the parent tells me to do this, I'm going to do this." It is more important to me that I validate a student where they are right now than it is for me to do what their parents tell me to do. It just is.

Similarly, Percy (they/them; Nonbinary; Asian-American) describes an inclusive process undertaken by all teachers at their high school:

> During the beginning of the year every teacher has you fill out this little information card. It's your name, your preferred name, your preferred pronouns, what they're supposed to call you at home—pronouns, name and everything—and everything that you prefer to be called while you're at school versus while you're at home. So, they keep that in mind every time they see you, and every time they contact home for official things.

Understanding that the infrastructure of large school systems can be imperfect may help us appreciate the value of correcting errors and mistakes. Most school districts will not provide modified class lists that acknowledge the correct name and pronouns for TGE student who are not yet 18 and have not had their names legally changed. From this perspective, failure in using the correct name and/or pronouns may be considered a learning experience. When guest teachers or substitutes are present, you may wish to create an alternative roll sheet, especially if a TGE student's name has not been changed within the school record system (more on that in Chapter 5). We believe that our job as teachers is to always do what is best for our students. This may mean using a student's name and pronouns in class even if they are not used at home. The use of the correct name and pronouns for a student can make a *huge* difference in their schooling experience and can even reduce their likelihood of self-harm. Based on data from a quantitative study with 129 TGE youth, researchers Andrea Pollitt and their colleagues (2021) note that:

> [TGE] Youth reported higher self-esteem, lower depressive symptoms, and less negative suicidal ideation when they were able to use their chosen name in more contexts. Our results suggest that support and validation of transgender youths' chosen name buffer negative mental health outcomes. Our study extends previous research to show that chosen name is a behavior that is associated with better mental health because it affirms one's gender identity through reducing the discrepancy between one's identity and presentation. We found that chosen name use appeared to be a stronger buffer of negative mental health rather than a promoter of positive well-being. (p. 335)

Stated more simply, the "capacity to use one's chosen name was associated with better mental health" (p. 336). Because schools can be unsafe spaces for TGE youth, it is important that educators make a concerted effort to practice the use of TGE students' proper name and pronouns.

Practicing and Making Mistakes

Teachers may need time and repetition (rehearsal) to avoid using outdated gendered language. Similarly, using new pronouns for a person you've known for a while can be difficult and requires effort:

> Using someone's (visually) unlikely she/her or he/him pronoun or changing pronouns for someone is not effortless. It is intensive. It can be a demand to make

> an effort without understanding why: to think, practice and be corrected about the pronouns we apply to others. It can feel like too much to ask: to see *that* body but say *those* words. It feels like too much because in this instance, using a person's correct gender pronoun does not feel like doing nothing; it takes effort. (Airton, 2018, p. 799, emphasis in original)

Some veteran teachers may be trying to retrain themselves after more than 20 years in the classroom. Time and repetition, coincidentally, are the same parameters teacher educators advise pre-service teachers to use as they develop professional behaviors—and are bedrock principles of rehearsal technique. In other words, teachers new or experienced can learn new ways of thinking and doing, with sufficient practice. College professor Lee Airton (2019) offers suggestions for practicing pronouns, particularly when a pronoun is challenging in everyday conversation:

1. Use singular "they" all the time as a way to develop a new habit.
2. Practice saying the pronoun out loud with someone else who also needs practice.
3. Take a pause in conversation, before responding to someone.
4. Make better mistakes—say a quick sorry and move on with conversation.
5. Offer gentle correction to others (e.g., "Remember, Lee uses *they*, not *she* or *he*").
6. Be real about your own challenges by leaning into mistakes and revisiting them later.
7. Embrace the awkwardness. You'll get better over time. (2019, pp. 114–118, emphasis in original)

When a TGE person shifts to use of a new pronoun, they may have been contemplating that change for weeks or months. The teacher encountering the pronoun change, however, is reacting in real time. This is one reason that mistakes (understandably) happen.

Many teachers misstep as they attempt to change their vocabulary. *Making mistakes is perfectly all right provided that the mistakes are acknowledged.* Mistakes with good intentions are all right, as Avery (he/him or they/them; agender; white) illustrates:

> One of the faculty members did have trouble with the new name and pronouns at first, but it wasn't intentional. It was more of a, just trying to change their gestalt, I guess, of me as a person. And they've since come around.

Amplifying a mistake may not help TGE persons feel better—it can make them feel worse. For example, Andy (he/him; FTM transgender; white) shares:

> I find sometimes I'll have teachers who want to be supportive, but it feels more like they're singling me out and, you know, treating me differently than other people, which is not really what I want. I just want to, you know, live, I guess. Especially with pronouns. I think like in classroom situations that if a teacher messes up sometimes, they just like, apologize a little too much and you're like, you know, "just correct yourself and move on." Sometimes it feels like people walk on eggshells around me just 'cause it makes them frightened of getting in trouble and, yeah, that just makes you feel weird.

Teachers can easily model mistakes as learning experiences, fix them, and move on. It's the effort that counts. And, with caring educators, TGE students likely will notice the effort.

Selecting Inclusive Classroom Curricular Materials

We all learn from experience, and our daily experiences shape who we become. Curricular materials selected for use in music classrooms may impact student learning in ways teachers may not always consider (e.g., Hawkins, 2007; Shaffer & Shevitz, 2001). Imagine that you were just hired to teach elementary-school general music in central Florida, and you are starting to take stock of the resources available to you in your new classroom. You find Boomwhackers, a set of quality Orff instruments, a functional SMART Board, and a set of old music textbooks from the late 1990s. Just about the time you think that you have what you need to get started, you take a closer look at the music texts and realize that most of the photographs portray white and Black cisnormative students engaged in music-making activities. You quickly recognize that the students in your largely Latinx community will not see young people like themselves in those images, and there is no representation of TGE youth. Acknowledging that these dated text materials will not provide the types of experiences that you want to create for your community of students, you begin to reach out to new colleagues in the area for assistance about more inclusive materials and where to locate them. Another simple way to counteract this is to feature diverse representation in slide presentation images. Considering what students might learn from the images and texts we use in music classes—that music making is for privileged white, cisgender, straight people—takes on a high level of importance in this particular example.

Scholars of children's literature have described two paradigms that music teachers may find helpful in reviewing classroom curricular materials. Professor Emerita Rudine Sims Bishop (1990) originated the idea that books serve as windows, mirrors, and sliding glass doors:

> When children cannot find themselves reflected in the books they read, or when the images they see are distorted, negative, or laughable, they learn a powerful lesson about how they are devalued in the society of which they are a part. (p. x)

Music classroom materials, from this perspective, should allow students to see themselves represented in illustrations and stories and to imagine future possibilities beyond their current experience. As an exercise, music teachers might reflect on aspects of their identities that were not represented in the music materials they used when they were younger.

A second, related paradigm to consider the level of diversity in music materials involves the idea of single stories. Nigerian novelist Chimamanda Adichie spoke about the danger of the single story in a 2009 TedGlobal conference, saying, "The single story creates stereotypes, and the problem with stereotypes is not that they are untrue, but that they are incomplete. They make one story become the only story" (12:55). When students learn only one possibility for TGE youth, that can become the only possibility they know or might imagine. Music teachers can avoid single stories by planning for a wider variety of cultural experiences, including the spectrums between and among masculinity and femininity. So how might music teachers avoid unnecessary bias in the curricular materials they provide for students?

Reviewing Classroom Materials for Bias

Music teachers selecting a curricular textbook series or investing in a methods-based approach to learning likely will be required to evaluate those materials for bias. Even if a formal requirement does not exist, this type of thoughtful review can help identify inequities related to gender identity and gender expression, as well as other aspects of identity such as race, in learning materials. Music educators and researchers indicate that gender bias and inequity have existed in music curricular materials (Koza, 1991, 1992, 1993a, 1994; McBride & Palkki, 2020) and in professional journals (Koza, 1993b; Kruse et al., 2015) for decades. Images of males predominate in quantity and in stereotypically masculine roles of leadership or assertiveness. Early childhood educators Louise Derman-Sparks and Julie Edwards note, "Differences do not create bias. Children learn prejudice from prejudice—not from learning about human diversity" (2019, p. 7). Individual states or districts may have systematic evaluation tools for use with curricular materials. If anti-bias evaluations are not available in your particular area, you may wish to consider the questions listed in Figure 4.5, modified from the Washington state models for the evaluation of bias content (2009).

Eight Ideas to Evaluate Curricular Materials for Gender Bias and Sexism
1. Check illustrations for stereotypes, tokenism, and to identify the roles being portrayed.
2. Check the stories and examples provided, considering portrayals of individuals who present as feminine or masculine. Could these stories and examples be valid if gender presentation were reversed?
3. Analyze the quantity and quality of gender diversity in text and images. Are TGE individuals identified? Are they represented appropriately, in relation to cisnormative or gender binary individuals?
4. Consider the impact of the material on a student's self-image. Is the material telling a "single story?" What might be the effect on students who identify or express themselves in more feminine ways if they see femininity portrayed as subservient to or lesser than portrayals of masculinity? Will curricular examples allow students to see themselves reflected positively or will they be excluded altogether?
5. Consider the author's/editor's/illustrator's background. Learn about the biographical backgrounds of the creators of the work. How are they associated with gender diversity or how does their work help qualify them to speak for/about/with the TGE community?
6. What is the author's perspective? Consider how the author approaches gender diversity and how they include the stories or experiences of TGE individuals.
7. Examine the text for "loaded words." Look for sexist language and adjectives that exclude feminine individuals or for instances in which masculine pronouns are used to refer to multiple gender identities.
8. Consider the copyright date. Copyright date can be a clue as to sociocultural perspectives in place at the time the materials were created. This information might be a starting point before a more thorough review of the curricular material.

Figure 4.5. Curricular materials evaluation adapted from original materials provided by the Washington Office of Superintendent of Public Instruction. Original materials may be accessed for free on the OSPI website.

A sample evaluation form that expands on the eight ideas in Figure 4.5 is available on the Washington Office of Superintendent of Public Instruction website (n.d.) With these ideas as a starting point, consider the following example of a stereotype that might appear in curricular materials and a contrasting alternative. A teacher might discover that images of males in materials designed for children are frequently depicted as more active than images of females, who are seen as passive, or simply watching the action. A more appropriate text, conversely, would portray individuals presenting as more masculine or more feminine, as independent/dependent, active/passive, and caring for others regardless of gender identity or expression.

Gender Diversity in Elementary Music Materials

The pieces that we choose to utilize in the classroom may contain gendered connotations. For example, lyrics describing interpersonal relationships are most often illustrated through heterosexual examples and context: "Regardless of genre, from opera to commercial country songs, declarations of love usually assume opposite-gender partners" (Taylor, 2018, p. 56). Music educators can consider ways to move beyond examples that solely reinforce heterosexual relationships and cisnormativity when discussing teaching repertoire. Many of the nursery rhymes and folk songs that were used in elementary classrooms well into the 1980s reflect outdated social norms and sensibilities. For example, the nursery rhyme "Peter Peter Pumpkin Eater" contains the following lyrics:

Peter Peter pumpkin eater
Had a wife and couldn't keep her
He put her in a pumpkin shell
And there he kept her very well!

This rhyme focuses on an interesting domestic situation, with the implication that the wife is being "kept" by the husband. With other song texts available for teaching, music teachers might consider avoiding the gender bias and the complicated domestic situation inherent in this innocent-looking tale. With the wealth of nursery rhymes available for use in elementary music classrooms, it is possible to select songs and chants that avoid gender bias. Equipped with a computer or similar technology device and web access, music teachers can quickly search for background information on folk songs and nursery rhymes. A small amount of time and effort can assist music teachers in avoiding gender stereotyping and the danger of the single story in songs and activities.

Elementary teachers also might consider the idea of themes to assist with the selection of teaching songs. An elementary colleague in Ohio described how she had to let go of the folk song–driven curriculum that had been used at her school for many years prior to her arrival. Teaching in a multi-racial community, the teacher found that the majority of the folk songs were no longer culturally relevant to the students in her community. In other words, she felt there was not enough mirroring between the students in her classroom and the curricular materials that had been used in the past. To help move beyond that barrier, she decided to work with students to choose thematic ideas for different parts of the year. Ideas like "United, we are stronger" and "Keep our planet green" may help to provide focal points for a selection process that honors the gender diversity of the school community. Working with students to identify themes can help empower young people to make decisions about how they engage in musical activities.

Avoiding Gender Stereotypes in Instrumental Settings

Instrumental music teachers carry a great deal of responsibility as students choose instruments. Students likely have some idea of what instrument(s) they might like to learn, and those initial thoughts may or may not have been influenced by family members or financial concerns. Students also can, unfortunately, perceive that certain instruments are more closely associated with being masculine or feminine, and this can unduly influence their initial choices.

Band and orchestra teachers can and should avoid stereotypical labeling of instruments as masculine or feminine and be ready to hear and respond to student comments like "my mom/dad/brother says that's a girl instrument." Socially reinforced gender stereotypes have persisted for decades, despite research that has carefully documented this issue (e.g., Abeles & Porter, 1978; Abeles, 2009). TGE musicians, however, may associate their instrument with an aspect of their queerness. For example, Phoebe (she/her; non-binary; white) describes a unique "queer" connotation of her instrument.

> I was just talking about switching from violin to viola—saying like the viola felt more connected to me. Maybe some people don't share this but for me personally I feel like viola is very representative—as an instrument, as it fits into orchestras and stuff—I refer to it in conversations with friends as a queer instrument and how that fits with my sense of queer identity. And I've met a lot of people who share some sense of LGBTQ identity in viola sections, a lot more so than in violin sections, which I think is really interesting. And, so, deciding to play it as my primary instrument in

> college, I think, was an important decision that perhaps lent itself to feeling that I could form my identity.

Phoebe's quote suggests that for some TGE instrumentalists, their instrument choice may play a role in their gender identity development, providing a sense of freedom and flexibility within a gender spectrum.

Music education researchers have described how many young people regard certain instruments as more masculine and certain instruments as more feminine (e.g., Abeles, 2009). In the twenty-first century, PK–12 instrumental music programs can work to change the trend of gender/sex stereotyping of musical instruments. Instrumental music educators can help disrupt instrument gender bias through conversation with students and parents during the instrument-selection process. Teachers can use music-specific language to describe the mechanical aspects of instruments or timbre produced by specific instruments. By focusing on the physical aspects of the instrument, and carefully listening to the wishes of the students and parents, instrumental music teachers can place emphasis on the selection process, not on gendered stereotypes. Figure 4.6 is from a study by Australian professor Scott Harrison, who asked 98 male-identifying university students to "read the alphabetical list and circle the number (1–10) that applied to their perception of whether the instrument was associated with masculine or feminine attributes, 1 being most feminine" (2007, p. 272). The results are reminiscent of previous research (e.g., Abeles & Porter, 1978), which did not include the voice as an instrument.

Now compare this to the continua we can use to describe gender expression, showing a spectrum of masculinities—an alternative to *toxic masculinity*, "a loosely interrelated collection of norms, beliefs, and behaviors associated with masculinity, which are harmful to women, men, children, and society more broadly" (Sculos, 2017, para. 2). Figure 4.7 demonstrates that both femininity and masculinity are not set in stone—there is a range of expression in both categories that exists fluidly within a spectrum.

Music educators actively can disrupt a student's learned instrumental gender bias by approaching the instrument-selection process with a focus

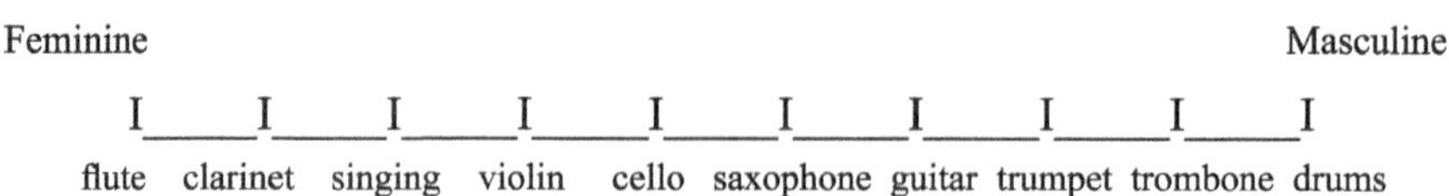

Figure 4.6. Masculine–feminine continuum of instrument choice.
Source: Harrison (2007, p. 273).

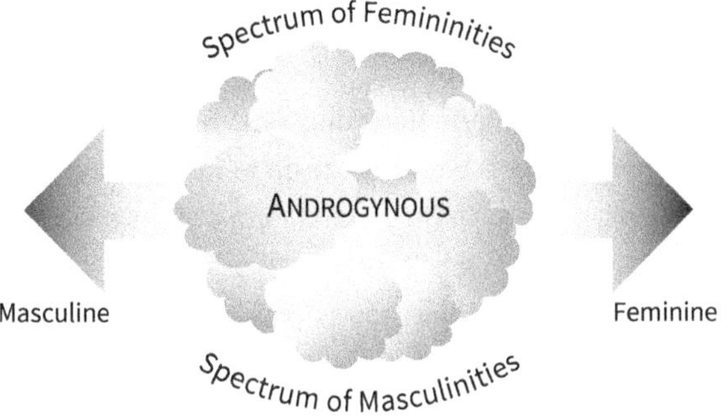

Figure 4.7. Spectrum of femininities and masculinities.

on student preference and intentional modeling for students and families. Instrumental music teachers who serve as facilitators during the instrument-selection process can design a process that is focused on a combination of student interest and timbre preference, thus avoiding the application of gender stereotypes (Abeles & Porter, 1978; Millican, 2017). Teachers who discover resistance from families wanting their children to play specific instruments, whether from a gender-biased perspective, sentimentality (e.g., Aunt Lolita's trumpet as a family heirloom), or for perceived financial reasons (e.g., affordability and feasibility of a tuba versus a saxophone), can offer guidance based on a combination of student interest and student achievement on a particular instrument or family of instruments. Music teachers might also consider a "tryout" opportunity for students to play individual instruments and receive feedback about the tone quality, for example, that the student was able to produce after picking up the instrument for the first time. Music teachers with larger programs could invite local private instructors or a music store vendor to assist in this listening and feedback process. In these facilitator roles, with perhaps a bit of negotiation, instrumental teachers can preemptively shift focus from any preconceived gender bias to a more music-specific approach that incorporates student wishes and student ability. As Max (he/him; trans man; white), a middle-school instrumental teacher, notes:

> I won't even tell instrument jokes to my beginners [. . .] because I feel like it starts gendering things. Like, who gets to be arrogant in our society? Do girls really get to be arrogant? No, that's totally a boy stereotype.

Similarly, college student Avery (he/him or they/them; agender; white) describes their experience with the trumpet:

> The trumpet was traditionally a "masculine" instrument, and today women are still underrepresented in most trumpet sections, so being a trumpet player who was perceived as female was an interesting dynamic. After nearly every performance, well-meaning strangers would come up to me and say, "trumpet girls are awesome" and things like that. Or they would gush over how they were "surprised that a tiny girl could make so much noise." And those comments were okay at first, because I appreciated the attention. But as time went on, those comments kept coming and they started making me feel really bad. Each one was a reminder that society didn't really see me the way I was. It was frustrating, too. I didn't understand why people had to make such a big deal about gender when it didn't have anything to do with the music I was creating.

Instrumental music teachers might consider creative ideas when it comes to the initial modeling of instruments for students and their families (Cooper & Burns, 2019). A middle-school band colleague observed that much of the gender bias associated with instrument choice in her community was coming from parents. To help disrupt these ideas, and to ensure better instrument distribution in school ensembles, the teacher decided to model all of the instruments herself during a demonstration fair. Similarly, teachers can have TGE students model instruments. Elementary students and their parents in that community experienced a female band director modeling each instrument before students began trying things out for themselves. Instrumental educators may choose to actively disrupt stereotypes by encouraging a variety of students or adult colleagues to model instruments that may carry a particular bias in their community setting. For example, instrumental music education professor Stephanie Prichard advises:

> Work together with colleagues to disrupt stereotypes as you are able. As a cis female band teacher, I worked with a cis male colleague to model anti-stereotype examples (e.g., me playing tuba and him playing clarinet, or us playing a trombone duet). Alternatively, ask older students to model, and be deliberate about who you choose. Teachers should also be mindful of who ends up on what instrument. Even from an assigned sex standpoint, it's easier to be one of two girls in the trumpet section than to be the only one. Teachers need to prioritize student needs and inclinations over the "ideal" instrumentation. (S. Prichard, personal communication, July 29, 2020)

This type of intentional modeling procedure is a small but important step in being more gender-inclusive in our music practices. Instrumental music teachers can help frame the instrument selection process as discovery, feedback, and listening. The latter component of listening is important, as communication with students and parents can be essential to long-term student success. In addition to the things that we *do* as music educators, what we *say* is significant.

Using Thoughtful Language in Music Classes

Teacher preparation programs frequently advocate for students to use appropriate music-specific language in classroom settings. As we discussed earlier, the words that we use in conversation and in our written materials as teachers can carry great emotional weight. Music teachers may consider teacher-tested ideas from non-music classrooms when approaching the topics of gender identity and gender equity language (Woolley & Airton, 2020). As our understanding and use of the gender spectrum expand, we as music teachers will want to examine the ways in which speech influences and impacts students—especially those who identify as TGE. In discussing the experiences of her eight-year-old trans daughter Gabriella at school, high-school choral teacher Victoria (she/her; female; white) gives advice to elementary educators regarding avoiding the gender binary:

> Well, I would say in the elementary setting, there's a tendency to sometimes go binary. Like, when you're dividing for groups you know, like "all the girls do this, and all the boys raise your hand." And I know that before she transitioned, that was especially confusing. Like if you say, "girls on this side and boys on this side . . ." [Gabriella may think] ". . . well I don't really want to be with the boys" but you know, that makes it confusing." So, you know [try] people who are wearing red and blue can go over here and people who are—[*changing course*] And I would say gosh—I mean they're just kids. So once, you know, once you know what to call a kid and what their pronouns are and. . . . And of course, we're all trying to use as few gendered kinds of words as possible.

Another way to separate students would be through birthday month (January–June on one side and July–December on the other).

Age-Appropriate Interactions with Young Students

In light of an increasing number of young people who identify outside of the gender binary, teachers may want to consider language and potential interactions with students that avoid reinforcing the gender binary and open possibilities to honor gender diversity. As an example, "boys and girls" can easily be replaced with "friends," "students," or "musicians" ("y'all" is also a good gender neutral option). As Tavia (she/her; Cis-het female; white), a middle-school band teacher, says:

> I was always supportive and sensitive, but it's been magnified, you know, at this point where, you know, I don't say "ladies and gentlemen" anymore and that kind of thing, [I say] "Oh, good morning friends"—that kind of thing. And I pick up on it pretty quickly with the kids too. And I think the fact that they know that I'm open and supportive and they—a lot of [queer students] will come up to me too.

Tavia's shift away from binary language is an example of modeling preferred behavior in her classroom. When students follow their teacher's lead, that behavior can be reinforced so that students understand the importance of inclusive communication. What might a teacher do if a student offers statements that primarily reinforce gender binary language? Gender Spectrum (2019a) provides educators and parents with tools and resources to "create gender sensitive and inclusive environments for all children and teens." The organization's online presence offers easy steps for teachers to help honor TGE students with inclusive, age-appropriate language and activities. The following ideas are specific classroom applications from Gender Spectrum's "Tips for your Classroom" (2019c).

Counter-narratives provide an opportunity for teachers and students to uncover meaning through communication. For example, if a student were to offer the comment "Only girls can have long hair and earrings," the teacher might respond by asking, "Can you tell me a little more about that?" The adult response is neither an approval nor a disapproval of the student's behavior, but an invitation to engage in further discussion to learn how the student arrived at that comment. Other possible responses might include: "Do all boys have only short hair and no earrings?" or "I think I know a few people with long hair and earrings who are not girls, so I might see it differently than you do." Again, both of these responses encourage student reflection without shutting down dialogue. The longer a conversation continues, the more opportunity for reflection on, and reconsideration of, future comments that reinforce the gender binary.

Music teachers have opportunities to mix gender portrayals, either through pre-selected curricular materials or examples chosen to enrich the curriculum. Gender language could be altered when singing songs, to help avoid telling a single story. For example, the lyrics to B-I-N-G-O easily can be altered for greater inclusivity:

> *There was a farmer, had a dog, and Bingo was his name-o.*
> *B-I-N-G-O, B-I-N-G-O, B-I-N-G-O, and Bingo was their name-o.*

This simple textual change reinforces an idea of gender diversity and honors young people who identify as TGE.

Teachers can consider gender diversity when selecting posters displayed in classroom spaces as well as any multimedia materials, like YouTube videos, that are integrated with learning activities. Sharing a broader variety of gender diversity helps students envision a broader spectrum of gender possibilities. As students progress through school music programs, music teachers have opportunities to incorporate more music-specific, thoughtful language in rehearsal and classroom settings, which can also reinforce gender diversity. For example, you can say "parent or guardian" as opposed to "mom or dad," as the former is more inclusive of all family structures. Thoughtful language use for TGE students is no different and is one part of communicating openly and vulnerably with TGE students.

Maintaining Open Lines of Communication

One of the most important takeaways for music educators in working with TGE students is to maintain an open and ongoing line of communication. As referred to in Chapter 1, students' identities may be in flux and pronouns may change from week to week (or even day to day). We as caring educators must courageously engage in dialogue with our TGE students—taking their lead whenever possible (Frohard-Dourlent, 2018). Communication cannot be forced, as evidenced by Lu's (he/him; transgender man; white) experience with a voice teacher:

> And my teacher didn't really understand. Every week I'd go into a lesson and she'd be like, "Oh, have you started hormones? What's going on?" And for like weeks and weeks, I had to be like, "I will tell you when it's happening. It's fine. It'll happen eventually. But like, trust me, you will—I'll talk about it with you."

In this instance, the teacher's insistence that Lu discuss his hormone replacement therapy was interpreted as intrusive. A more inclusive path would have been for the teacher to maintain a supportive role and to allow Lu to approach this sensitive topic, if he chose to do so. These conversations may be ongoing. The most important thing is that we as educators are open to *listening* to our TGE students and letting them chart their course.

Interactions in Rehearsal Settings

Music teachers can avoid gendered terminology altogether. Instrumental educators rehearsing in ensemble settings can refer to sections within an organization. Teachers can avoid *dead-naming* TGE students (using the name that they were given at birth) by focusing on musical language, as Mari (she/her; transgender woman; Latina) illustrates in describing her college choral teacher:

> And he was so good! He basically gave me the impression that he was going to take me in if my own parents didn't take me in, you know? And he was really concerned about my home life. He also said that he wasn't blind. And he never dead-named me or mis-gendered me, and I'm sure he was very careful at times.

Similarly, Lu (he/him; transgender man; white) describes a situation in which he had an ongoing dialogue with his collegiate choral director about voice parts after he began hormone replacement therapy with testosterone:

> It was basically like I would just go to him and be like, after that first concert or after that tour, I was like, "I need to change parts—this isn't an option anymore." And so yeah. I kind of had to just tell him what I needed and hope that he would be fine with it, which he, for the most part, was.

Choral conductor-teachers can approach rehearsals with a variety of academic language options. In Chapter 6, we will discuss ways to avoid and disrupt the habit of using gendered vernacular of choral rehearsal settings.

Considerations for Music Teacher Educators

TGE music educators must navigate their gender identity and expression in school systems, perhaps in ways similar to TGE students. A recent line of scholarship in music education research describes the unique plight of TGE music educators (Bartolome, 2016; Bartolome et al., 2017; Bartolome & Stanford, 2017; Silveira, 2019). Pre-service music teachers need support from music teacher educators to develop a positive sense of self-efficacy in who they are as people, in addition to developing skills as music teachers. In the following story, Brendan (he/him; transgender male; white) describes his experience with a mentor while student teaching in a middle school:

> I started transitioning my senior year of college, when I started student teaching. Because I knew—and I was like, "well, I cannot be in the classroom as anything other than Mr. M. That would be awful." So, I went and that's where I started truly identifying as a male. And prior to student teaching, that whole first semester I started doing the legwork for it. I started seeing a therapist and I'd told each of my friends, "Hey, so this is something I'm dealing with. Just stay tuned." And they're all supportive. And then I reached out to one of my cooperating teachers and I student taught in [a Northeastern US state]—small, kind of rural and suburban communities—I wasn't sure how my identity was going to go down, but the schools were wonderful. And part of the reason the one school in particular was pretty great was because of my middle-school band cooperating teacher. He is actually a gay man and he has a partner. And he was just so with it. And I think honestly, his experiences as a gay man made it so much easier for me to connect with him and him with me. We still keep in touch and he's one of the best mentors that I've had. So, following that experience student teaching, I moved placements to another district. It was difficult when I moved to a school district with a larger minority population and less resources. It was challenging to work with the middle-school age group, but especially because the things that I was hearing the students say about me. I was like, "Whoa, okay." I know nobody else is dealing with this when they're student teaching. But, anyway, that wasn't something that I would bring up when I went back for the monthly seminar meetings with the rest of my peers.

Brendan describes some unique interactions with students in which he struggled with advocating for himself and "taking away from the lesson":

> Some of [the students] were wonderful and really with it, and would correct their friends, be like "He and Mr." And other ones were like, "What? Mr.? Are you kidding?" And it was difficult to sometimes address [it] because I didn't want to take away from the lesson and away from the classroom time, but clearly, I had to redirect some things and just normalize it.

Music teachers working in school classrooms also explore ways to negotiate their personal and professional identities. Max (he/him; trans man; white), a middle-school instrumental teacher, describes the quandary of how "out" to be at school. Here the small semantic distinction between "on" the desk and "in the desk" may symbolize a larger struggle around identity negotiation at school:

> I have a pride flag on my desk. And I have a trans pride flag inside my desk and I just, I don't feel comfortable putting it out for just me, you know? I feel like I'm kind of

> waiting for one of my kids to, one of my current students at least, to come out to me as trans so that I can put the flag on the desk for them. Cause I don't want to hide, but I don't want to make the room all about me. So, I don't know. I should just put the flag on my desk. I know it's not a big deal. It's just, it's inside my desk right now. But I bet if I put the flag out, someone will come to me, you know. I bet there's a kid waiting for me to put the flag on my desk and then they'll come to me.

In following up with Max between the interview and final publication, he writes:

> Shortly after our interview I did put the trans pride flag out on my desk! And it was great because a few weeks later, one of my students came to me after class and talked to me about my trans pride flag, and then asked me my pronouns. A few weeks after that, a student I didn't know was with some of their friends (who are my band students) in my classroom and saw the flag. The student was like, "I have that same flag!" and proceeded to pull it out of their backpack. Since then I've had several other students give me art they created involving the rainbow and trans pride flags, which I've also displayed proudly.

Teaching people appropriate ways to communicate does not stop with the conclusion of public school. As music teacher educators uncover the talents and skills of pre-service teachers, they must also consider how they are teaching our future colleagues to teach people through music. How do we put the "people" first? This question and the ramifications of not broadening conversations in music learning spaces are certainly topics for further exploration through dialogue and research. Just as TGE youth deserve safety and empathy at school, so do music teachers who identify as TGE.

Recap

KAIZEN (they/them; gender creative; Han Chinese): My first semester I took up as little space as possible. And right before our final meeting after the performance, I emailed [the conductor] to say, to come out really, and to say this is a space that I could see being really supportive for trans guys and could we—I don't remember how I worded it—would it be okay if I invite more guys into this space and are we open to anyone who self-identifies as male? And I actually also added "and can read music and wants to sing." And he immediately was supportive and even announced, you know, replied to me in a really like kind and thoughtful email. [. . .] And he explicitly said to the group that the requirements were just that you self-identify as male and you want to sing.

Kaizen describes how their professor made a deliberate choice to honor Kaizen's gender identity. This professor could have ignored or dismissed their request. Instead, the professor chose to validate Keizen's identity and, in so doing, to expand the definition of what "men's chorus" means at that particular institution. This is a beautiful example of what we as music educators can do—*listen with empathy and act with compassion*. In this book we highlight the voices of TGE individuals so that we all can learn from their experiences. What we do with this information is up to us. Debra G. Gordon, retired professor of music education at the University of Northern Iowa, writes "teaching students to respect each other and the teacher is an integral part of the curriculum—it's a learned behavior" (2001, p. 23). Just as safe spaces do not manifest by happenstance, neither do respectful classroom behaviors. Furthermore, making initial decisions about the physical classroom or curricular materials or repertoire selection need not be made solely by an autocratic instructor. Rather, students can and should be part of ensuring a safe, productive, and gender-expansive learning environment. We advocate that respect is a commonly held value among educators. Developing respect between and among teachers and students is essential for impactful learning. Maintaining respect earned by students is a goal to which we as educators should aspire. Our students notice not only our content expertise—they notice the kind of people we are and the kind of climate we foster in our classrooms.

In this chapter we have discussed practical steps that music educators can take to become "safe people" who create safe spaces within their classrooms, schools/districts, professional organizations, and communities. We as music educators have a special role to play in the lives of TGE youth if we choose to take certain thoughtful steps. We're going to make mistakes. We are going to misstep. We may not always be perfect, and we all have things to learn, but if we place student well-being at the heart of every decision we make, we are on the right path.

Reflect/Remember

1. Are there any steps not mentioned in this chapter that could help TGE youth feel more comfortable within music classrooms?
2. Think about classrooms/spaces in your own schooling experiences in which you felt safe and supported. Perhaps you always ate lunch in the middle-school orchestra room. What steps did the teacher(s) take to

create that sense of support? How many were explicit (verbal) vs. subtle (nonverbal)? Which of these might you "steal" for your current or future classroom?

3. Remember, *always* center the experiences and wishes of TGE youth: honor their name and pronouns, but *always* ask privately and respect their choices regarding to whom they are "out." *Never* disclose a student's gender identity to anyone else without permission.

5
Empowering TGE Students with Inclusive Policies

Chapter Guide

TAVIA (she/her; Cis-het female; white): But after [my child, who is trans] did come out in eighth grade we ended up going ourselves—my husband and I and another set of parents ended up going to the district to get the [two trans] boys allowed to use the correct bathroom. So that was—I don't know that I'd say a battle necessarily. . . . It took some convincing. They were already kind of heading that way. They had already planned to eventually put up the tall bathroom stalls around all the toilets and urinals in the secondary school bathrooms, but that was for a future date. So, it did, well, I'd say not really a battle, although we did kind of threaten to bring the ACLU lawyer in. That's always a good feeling going into your boss with an ACLU lawyer's letter. Going, "am I going to have a job tomorrow? I hope so!" But for the most part people are very supportive.

The Big Picture

Policies are ubiquitous and influence many areas of our lives. Policies determine, for example, how we get a driver's license, how we apply for teaching licensure, and how we adopt a pet. Many policies exist that we may not even

Honoring Trans and Gender-Expansive Students in Music Education. Matthew L. Garrett and Joshua Palkki, Oxford University Press. © Oxford University Press 2021. DOI: 10.1093/oso/9780197506592.003.0006

think about beyond an initial reading. When is the last time you thought deeply about your school district or company policies? Music education professor Patrick Schmidt (2019) argues that (a) music educators can, and should, be a part of policy creation and enforcement (as "policy actors"), and (b) that policy be considered more broadly than a statute or rule governing some aspect of music education. Policies can be particularly influential for persons who are TGE because policies "can affirm or disavow students' identities" (Catalano, 2015, p. 275) and because those with cisgender privilege often do not view policies through a TGE-affirmative lens. Furthermore, music educators likely have many more policies than teachers in other subject areas (teachers in science or mathematics generally do not need policies about performance attire, gendered ensemble names, or overnight accommodations).

In this chapter we reveal only the "tip of the iceberg" when discussing the complex, context-dependent nature of policies that influence the lives of TGE persons in music programs:

> Policy processes and questions are deeply human. Just like pedagogy, policy is practiced by individuals, at times strategically or thoughtfully, at times haphazardly or deceivingly. Policy might be a thing, a text, but that is the tip of the iceberg. Policy process is a big colossus under the surface, and it is populated by people, that is, by us. (P. Schmidt, 2019, p. 81)

Safe people can engage in the questioning, expansion, and creation of TGE-inclusive policies within and beyond classroom spaces. This means that through policy, teachers and administrators can transform multiple learning spaces for students, including auditoriums, concert venues, or musical field trip locations. Our hope as authors is that this chapter encourages you to examine and reflect on policies in your school, community, state, and professional organization(s) and how they might be revised, or perhaps new policies created, to be as inclusive as possible for TGE students, both now and in the future.

A Reminder about Intersectionality

As we work toward equity for TGE students, we might remember that, as music education professor and scholar Bruce Carter notes, "life is too messy and complicated to simply state that being a member of one group denotes a single type of representation" (2014, p. 550). Too often, policies about

LGBTQA issues are constructed and viewed through a narrow, white lens and do not attend to elements of policy that can be, as education researchers Elizabeth Meyer and Harper Keenan (2018) note, "highly racialized." This is not unlike the struggle for Black women's concerns to be heard in mainstream feminism (e.g., hooks, 2000). In examining uniform policies as they apply to TGE persons, Harper and Keenan note that dress codes in the United States often create "gendered conditions of administrative control and regulation" (2018, p. 744). We must constantly keep multilayered identities in mind as we consider policy decisions and implementation. For example, does a policy about dress code assume that students will have the financial resources to purchase or rent attire (e.g., Bates, 2012, Shaw, 2017)? Would a dress code be inclusive of a student wearing a hijab? As music teachers, we do not always know who may enroll in our classes; for example, a new student may arrive from another district. If we nurture policies that include a broad spectrum of potential students, we as educators can be better prepared for a greater number of possibilities (e.g., Blaisdell, 2018). Remember, policies can dramatically influence the life of our current and future students, and we as teachers can be an important part of the process.

Proactive Policy Work

Advance policy planning to honor TGE persons can eliminate the need to *react* to a situation that has already occurred. When a school or school district has never had an "out" trans student, they may assume that there are no TGE students in the school, thus (a) trans students do not exist in their community, or (b) there is no need for such a policy (Woolley, 2019). In such a school or district, policies instituted after the first trans student "comes out" may be *reactive* in nature and perhaps hastily drafted. Conversely, a school or district can take a *proactive* stance by drafting inclusive policies even if there are no "out" trans and/or gender-expansive students—yet. As high-school choir teacher Peter Mullins (pseudonym) notes:

> If it's not an issue for you yet, it will be. It's not a matter of *if*, it's a matter of *when*. So yes, we should be having these discussions and laying the groundwork now so that when you do have a trans student, you're not wondering what you're supposed to do. (Palkki, 2016, p. 168)

School music teachers might encourage administrators to proactively consider policies that honor the TGE youth who are likely already present in classrooms.

Advocacy from the Ground Up

In the absence of inclusive policies, teachers, staff, and administrators can advocate for change at various levels, as exemplified in Emily's vignette in Box 5.1. The content of these policies can play an important role in the daily

Box 5.1

EMILY
choral conductor-singer
she/her
trans woman
white

EMILY: One useful policy change happened through the work of some concert office staff [at the university where I received my master's degree]. There's a packet of materials that gets given to all visiting artists, whether they're preparing conductors, or performing conductors, or not conductors at all, and one of the people who works in the concert office managed to get some language about respecting people's gender identity added to that document, something to the effect of, "Respecting people's gender identities is a vital part of working at this university. For instance, when working with choirs, we don't use words like 'women and men.'" And that's a small piece of lasting change that couldn't have been accomplished by directly confronting the particular people who'd made mistakes, because it's different people coming in and out all the time. But now it can actually have a lasting effect—you know, it's like a remedy to problems that have come up in the last couple of years that will persist and hopefully make future problems less likely.

JOSHUA: Do you know who created that language and who made it happen that it ended up in that packet?

EMILY: A staff member who's the person in charge of the concert office . . . who is the manager of the choir in question. This was in my first year, and I happened to mention to a second year student that I'd had this issue with a visiting conductor. And his student job involved working with this particular staff member, and he asked if he could talk to her about it, and I said, "sure." So he talked to her and she talked to someone higher up and said, "Hey, I think this is language we should put in these packets," and that's how it happened. Which I guess is emblematic of the fact that, again—it's not a place full of people who bear ill will toward trans people. . . . It's sort of like people are generally on board once you can tell them what it is that needs to happen.

experiences of TGE youth in schools. Music teachers may be more powerful than they realize in influencing policy change in music education organizations. This type of advocacy from the ground up can help to create policies that honor TGE youth. As Roger (he/him; male; white) says, "I do think it's important, when we're talking to upcoming educators: 'your administrators may be naive to your needs as a [music teacher].' I think we have to tactfully educate our administrators." Music teachers might start an open conversation with a building administrator as a way to prepare for working with TGE youth before they arrive in the building. An example of teacher advocacy can be found in Box 5.2. In this situation the teacher spoke with the state music education organization on behalf of his trans student. Policies will never be changed if teachers do not take action to remedy these inequities. We as teachers can make what a prominent civil rights leader, the late Rep. John Lewis, called "good trouble." Teachers who believe in equity and justice should be unafraid to speak "truth to power" and advocate for TGE youth—a vulnerable population. As music educators/scholars Randall Allsup and Eric Shieh write:

> At the heart of teaching others is the moral imperative to care. It is the imperative to perceive and act, and not look away. . . . A starting point, then: *notice* inequity. Name the inequity. There is no teaching for social justice without an awareness of the inequities that surround us, and a sense of indignation or even outrage at the "normal" state of affairs. (2012, p. 48, emphasis in original)

Educators focused on teaching people through music likely will want to commit to equity in their teaching context. It is important to note that *equal* and *equitable* are not the same things. Policies that apply to both cisgender and trans students may not be equal (meaning that everyone gets the same treatment regardless of identity, circumstance, level of ability, etc.), because TGE students more frequently face discrimination and oppression. As music educators who value respect, our goal can and should be *equity*, in which a person's treatment is consistent with their individual needs. Box 5.2 presents an example of advocacy from the ground up. The teacher telling this story is a high-school choral teacher on the East Coast who had a trans male singer who was auditioning for all-state honor choir.

Mr. Mullins had no obligation to go "above and beyond" for his trans male student in this instance; he did not have to bring up the issue at all. The fact that he did helped to change a statewide policy and has the potential to honor TGE youth in his state for the foreseeable future. This type of activism/advocacy from the ground up (Dockendorff et al., 2019; Mundy, 2013) is becoming

Box 5.2

PETER MULLINS
high-school choral teacher
gay-cisgender, white
he, him

So last April, there was something that clearly came out in every bulletin that boys can only audition for tenor and bass parts, girls can only audition for soprano and alto parts. So, at this point, Jon was still Jane, so I went to the state and said, "Here's the thing: I have a trans student." His name is Jane (this is where pronouns got fun on the phone). He wants to audition for tenor. The legal name is Jane. What can we—[*impersonating a person on the phone*] "Well we can't do that . . ." And I'm like, "Well, that's not an acceptable answer. So I'm going to have to ask you to think about this a little bit more." [. . .] And finally someone said, "Call the lawyer. Call the [state] MEA [music educators association] lawyer." And that conversation happened and the lawyer was like, "You can't say no and while you're at it, take out the 'boys can only do this and girls can only do this' policy because if you're ever taken to court, you're going to lose, and you're going to have a lot of bad press in the process. So get rid of it right now, be done with it."

Source: Palkki, 2016, pp. 186–187

more common among music educators. As music education professor Karen Salvador (2019) writes:

> Systemic change will . . . require policy work at the macro level. Actions at macro and micro levels are not mutually exclusive, nor does one precede the other. . . . Individuals can address systemic issues within their sphere of influence, beginning with the self. (p. 60)

Teachers can play a role in policy, especially when they see a student in need without policy protections. Middle-school band teacher Tavia (she/her; Cis-het female; white) says that she is known in her building for being supportive of LGBTQA students:

It's just kind of the reputation that I have in the building that I am someone that can be talked to about that. I've been advising the GSA too.

JOSHUA: Is your support of the trans community known through a safe space sticker or things that you say in class or things in your handbook?

TAVIA: Well, probably a little of all of that, but I do have safe space stickers in my room and on my door in the hallway.

JOSHUA: Are there any other teachers that have those?

TAVIA: There are some because I made a bunch of them when I made mine and put them in the staff lounge and so there are other teachers that have them up too.

Distributing Safe Space stickers is such a simple act—but one that can have major positive ramifications. Similarly, Marshall's (he/him; trans male; Asian-American) high-school choir teacher demonstrates this idea of advocacy from the ground up:

> If you refer to someone, and you use the wrong pronoun or, my God, if they even use the wrong name, [my high school choir teacher will] correct them. And recently we had student awards and I had given her mine and I was like, "Oh, they've put the wrong name" and I put a sticky note over it and put my name and [my choir teacher] was like, "I'm going to write an email to them saying that they should respect trans students and their names."

The path may be circuitous and at times uncertain, but actively advocating for inclusive policies is an important part of equity work in schools; as Patrick Schmidt (2019) explains, "justice and equity do not take place without deliberation and active engagement" (p. 25). Now that we have considered *why* policy can be impactful to TGE students, we transition to a discussion of *how* music teachers can engage with policy in meaningful ways.

The Big Question: "Is There a Policy?"

When teachers ask either of us about a situation affecting a TGE student in their school, our first question to them typically is, "Does your school or district have a policy for working with TGE students?" Very often these colleagues will respond, "I don't know." Finding out if a policy exists is a crucial first step. Teachers might ask more senior colleagues or administrators (they may also need some time to research an answer) for policy information. These policies might also be accessed on a school or district website. Inclusive policics for honoring TGE students are important to ensure equal access:

> School or district policies detailing the rights and protections afforded to transgender and nonbinary students help to ensure these students have access to an education. These policies can also serve to send the message that transgender and

> nonbinary students are a valuable and important part of the school community. (Kosciw et al., 2020, p. 81)

The first step is determining whether or not your school and/or district has such a policy in place. Once the question has been answered, you can formulate a plan.

Is There a Policy? Yes!

What to Look for in Policy Statements

You may recall from Chapter 3 that enumerated policies—those that specifically state which groups of people are protected—are important. These types of policies are particularly important for issues of gender identity, gender expression, and sexuality. Ambiguity exists in the absence of specific language, and those "gray areas" can lead to potentially discriminatory practices against the groups not referenced in policy statements. Some questions to ask while evaluating policy include, but are not limited to, the following:

1. Does the policy define "transgender" so narrowly as to exclude those who may not identify with the term, such as gender-expansive or nonbinary people (Darwin, 2020; Harrison et al., 2012; Meyer & Keenan, 2018)?
2. Are there built-in assumptions about intersectional issues such as, but not limited to, race, socioeconomic status, sexuality, ability, or religion (Meyer & Keenan, 2018)?
3. Does this policy have direct application in music settings? For example, does an existing dress code policy apply to performing ensemble uniforms?
4. Is the policy written using inclusive language?

You may also inquire whether the families of TGE students, or national organizations such as GLSEN, TSER, or NCTE, were consulted during policy construction.

Guidance from state and federal government sources also can help teachers understand policies. Even if your school and/or district does not have any policies regarding TGE students, guidance provided by the federal government may be informative. Obama-era federal guidelines from the "Dear Colleague" letter drafted by the Civil Rights wings of the US Departments of Education and Justice (Lhamon & Gupta, 2016) said that schools:

1. [May] not discriminate against trans students and should take steps to prevent [discrimination];
2. Treat trans students in keeping with their gender identity, which includes giving access to the appropriate gendered bathroom, changing room, and overnight accommodation;
3. [Use] the name and pronouns used by the student; and [allow] them to dress in accordance with their gender identity; and
4. Keep a student's trans status, birth name, and gender assignment at birth confidential (G. Beemyn, personal communication, July 27, 2016).

Even though the 45th presidential administration rescinded federal guidance concerning protections for trans students (Becker et al., 2017), some school districts still use these federal guidelines as best practice (for example, the Long Beach, California, Unified Schools; Steinhauser, 2017). Furthermore, according to the June 2020 US Supreme Court decision, "sex discrimination" under federal law includes gender identity, and this decision likely will have implications for education. In addition to the "Dear Colleague" letter, the US Department of Education under President Obama also released a document titled *Examples of policies and emerging practices for supporting transgender students* (2016). This document and others that are similar can provide blueprints for schools and districts seeking to create policies to honor TGE youth. If there are no enumerated policies in place for TGE students, music teachers may need to explore options for constructive and positive change.

Is There a Policy? No. Now What Can I Do?

Revising and Creating Policy

Music teachers can work for change in schools, districts, and professional organizations by considering how existing policies can be revised to enumerate TGE students, or by creating and advocating for inclusive policies. Organizational change can seem intimidating. Schmidt's (2015, 2017, 2019) work aims to reframe the situation as something more manageable. One person suggests an idea, that idea is developed through conversations, and over time, new or better policy language develops for the benefit of students. In Box 5.2, onc music teacher appealed to a state music education organization to affect change for trans vocalists. Sharing an idea with colleagues to develop greater understanding, in this case on the topic of trans vocalists, can be an effective way to build consensus. This constructive approach to developing policy also demonstrates the power of being proactive, as there is no way of knowing how many students may be positively impacted. We as music educators can work for change in music organizations by finding out what policies exist and then examine if they are equitable and inclusive of TGE students. If policies are discriminatory, advocate for change. Colleagues working together can ensure that professional music organizations consistently endeavor to serve all music students and teachers. Following is a description of how one school district undertook a collaborative process of policy-making:

> One Pennsylvania district made it a goal to create the best gender policy in the country. First, on the assumption that employees lacked information, not compassion, they provided training about transgender and gender-expansive children to all district employees, including administrators, teachers, support staff, bus drivers, custodians, and cafeteria workers. Second, the district invited all its employees to participate in the policy-making process, increasing transparency. The resulting team of 15 people collaboratively analyzed policies from six other districts and wrote their own supportive gender policy. The district's success grew out of a willingness to embrace the topic of transgender youth as a learning opportunity. (Mangin, 2018, p. 19)

Education and participation by multiple stakeholders created successful policy in this instance. Collaborative efforts, like the example from Pennsylvania, have the potential to unite community members toward a goal of honoring TGE students.

Music organizations such as state music education associations, state band/orchestra organizations, National Association for Music Education (NAfME) state chapters, and state chapters/affiliates of the American Choral Directors Association (ACDA) can play a large role in the experiences of TGE students. These organizations often sponsor statewide music activities like large group festival/contest, solo and ensemble festival, and honor ensembles. An organization's policies can directly influence the lives of school music students. For example, Mari (she/her; transgender woman; Latina) describes how her "best friend in high school was a countertenor, and he wanted to audition for the All-State Choir as an alto, but they wouldn't let him. He had to do bass one instead. People did not take his side." Honor choir audition policies should never state that females cannot audition as tenors. Music education researchers Matthew Fiorentino, Matthew Garrett, Nicholas McBride, Joshua Palkki, Nicholas Roseth, and Donald Taylor (2018) explored honor choir audition policies in all 50 states. Following are examples of existing policies uncovered during data collection that are supportive and less supportive of trans students.

- NOT SUPPORTIVE: It is required that the tenor and bass categories be reserved for males only and the soprano and alto categories be reserved for females only. No females may audition on the tenor or bass parts, and no males may audition on the soprano or alto parts.
- SUPPORTIVE: The Florida Vocal Association strives to be inclusive for students who identify as transgender. Transgender students may audition for the gender-specific All-State ensemble for which they identify. However, it would be expected that the student meets all of the expectations for that ensemble, including demonstrating the necessary vocal range for the voice part for which they are auditioning as part of their Vocal Quality audition. The FVA encourages its members to work with their school and county administration to ensure a positive and inclusive environment for transgender students. This may include placing transgender students in gender-specific ensembles for which they identify, modifying uniform expectations for all students, and increased awareness of transgender students' hormone therapies which would affect the singing voice.

A guiding principle is that organizations should not ask for more information than they need and should actively avoid asking for information that may force a trans or gender-expansive student into an awkward position or force them to disclose their gender identity when it is not necessary. In most cases, forms (e.g., honor ensemble audition forms) do not need to ask about sex assigned at birth or gender. Organizations may need this information later when considering hotel rooming plans, but at the audition phase generally it is unnecessary to ask.

Similarly, health forms required of students for co-curricular travel may ask for gender, but simply listing "male" and "female" as the only options is no longer adequate. Gender scholar Genny Beemyn writes, "the de facto policy is silence or omission often" (personal communication, July 28, 2020). Matt Netto, choir teacher at Patriot High School in Riverside, California, illustrates this concept in the following message from September 2018:

> Today one of my students had to fill out a form for something for choir and [the student] said to me "Mr. Netto the only choices for gender are 'male and female.' What am I supposed to do?" And I thought, "wow, how far have we come . . . this was really cool." And so, we were able to talk about how you deal with a situation like that.

In many cases, students, who often are more educated on gender issues, may be ready to make these adjustments. We as music educators, who sometimes

How do you describe your gender? Please select any/all that apply.

- ○ Cisgender female
- ○ Cisgender male
- ○ Trans male/Trans man
- ○ Trans female/Trans woman
- ○ Genderqueer/Gender-expansive
- ○ Prefer not to say
- ○ Different identity (please describe):________________________

Figure 5.1. Inclusive collection of gender data.

act as gatekeepers, can facilitate such form changes at the school, district, and state levels. An example of a more inclusive way to collect these data is illustrated in Figure 5.1.

Honor ensemble forms and policies can and should be inclusive of TGE students. Music organizations have great power in influencing the experiences of music students at state and national events that can be incredibly influential for young musicians.

Adapting Ideas from Existing Inclusive Policies

Creating better school experiences for TGE students takes time, thought, and the support of school community members. Teachers can save some time and effort by adapting ideas and language from existing inclusive policy resources. National organizations offer suggestions of, and templates for, LGBTQA-inclusive policies at district, school, and classroom levels. For example, Gender Spectrum's mission "is to create gender sensitive and inclusive environments for all children and teens" (Gender Spectrum, 2019a). In addition to providing resources for families and educational professionals, Gender Spectrum has joined a number of other national organizations, including the American Civil Liberties Union, Human Rights Campaign, National Center for Lesbian Rights, and the National Education Association, to create *Schools in Transition: A Guide for Supporting Transgender Students in K-12 Schools* (Orr & Baum, 2015). This comprehensive resource includes chapters on gender basics, considerations for school community members when designing and implementing policy, key policy elements, and appendices with additional specific examples of TGE-inclusive practices. Similar to this document, GLSEN and the National Center for Transgender Equality (NCTE) worked together to develop a *Model School District Policy on Transgender and Gender Nonconforming Students* (2018). These organizations developed this document to suggest language that can be copied into individual school district policy (for example, see *Gender-Inclusive School Communities: A Policy and Procedure Guide to Ensure the Success of Transgender Students within Pittsburgh Public Schools* in Appendix C). Model language is accompanied by commentary that further explains reasoning and background information associated with policy suggestions.

While some school districts may choose to begin with templates and models from some of these leading LGBTQA organizations, others may wish to consider specific examples of established policy. The Pennsylvania district described in the previous section of this chapter might serve as a model. Another district-level model can be found in the Los Angeles Unified School District policy. In 2014, the district implemented a policy bulletin that provides schools and teachers with general guidelines in the areas of: (a) privacy and confidentiality; (b) official records; (c) unofficial records; (d) names/pronouns; (e) restroom accessibility; (f) locker room accessibility; (g) sports, athletics, and physical education; (h) school activities and programs; (i) course accessibility and instruction; (j) dress codes/school uniform policies; and (k) student safety (Sadowski, 2016). The opening statement of the bulletin succinctly describes the purpose of the policy:

> This policy reflects the reality that transgender and gender nonconforming students are enrolled in the District. Its purpose is to advise District staff regarding issues relating to transgender students in order to create and maintain a safe learning environment for all students. The guidelines provided in this Bulletin do not anticipate every situation that might occur with respect to transgender students. The needs of each transgender student are unique. This policy should be interpreted consistent with the goals of reducing stigmatization and ensuring the integration of transgender students in educational programs and activities. (Sadowski, 2016, p. 167)

Policy statements that include the reasons *why* they were created can assist others in creating successful documents in different community contexts.

On a scale beyond that of educational policy, trans advocate Heath Fogg Davis wrote *Building Gender-Inclusive Organizations: The Workbook*

(Davis, 2018)—a companion to the 2017 book *Beyond Trans: Does Gender Matter?* (Davis, 2017). This helpful workbook includes several exercises, writing assignments, and even "scripts to convince your colleagues to implement gender-inclusive practices" (p. 12). Davis's materials can provide assistance for teachers who might need to build bridges of support among faculty colleagues or within a community prior to drafting policy language. Music teachers may find easily transferable materials from these broader resource documents that will work in the classroom and associated music-learning environments and organizations. For information on other helpful resources, see Appendix B. When referencing national policy models and resource tools, teachers will need time to reflect on their communities to find meaningful applications of TGE-related policy language.

Importance of Community Context

Music teacher educators stress to pre-service teachers the importance of knowing who lives and works in the communities around local schools (Heath, 1983). Understanding the values of a community can better inform conversations around equitable policies for TGE youth. What is considered routine in Los Angeles or New York City may be considered radical in other geographical regions of the United States. District policies about trans issues can be quite divisive in some areas. Victoria (she/her; female; white) is a high-school choral teacher and mother of a trans daughter in elementary school who describes such a controversial moment in her Michigan school district:

> Our principal has been really good about not sharing too much, but she has shared that she's gotten some phone calls. I think the one that she's talked about the most is, she got a phone call that said, "I hear you're teaching transgenderism at your elementary school." And her response was something like, "well, what we're teaching here is respect, and love for all, and compassion. And if you need to have a conversation about other things at your house you can, but it's, it's ridiculous to think that we're promoting a certain way of life." [. . .] I sometimes giggle to myself like—if we were really trying to make people be other than who they are, then we're not doing a very good job because, like Gabriella said, she's still the only transgender kid there after two years! [*chuckles*] It's not working [. . .]. You know, I think you look at all these kids, especially this young, she's so . . . she's just so . . . *who she is*, and she doesn't have any other motivation behind it.

Victoria and her family have worked with their school district to ensure that policies are inclusive for their daughter and future TGE students and their parents–policies that have student well-being at the heart of every decision.

Placing Students First

We as music educators should work to implement plans and policies that place students first. Once teachers understand legal protections for TGE students, and a plan is in place to create space for a positive school experience, implementation of that plan can be seen as a continuation of a journey—one that involves frequent reflection and adjustment. In a best-case scenario, family members and school employees will support TGE students. State or local laws might be in place affording specific protections, or district policies may emphasize inclusion of LGBTQA students. As Genny Beemyn notes, "if a city or state has a nondiscrimination policy inclusive of gender identity, a public institution has to follow that policy, which can be important leverage in advocating for the need for a school or district policy" (personal communication, July 28, 2020). If one or more parties involved do not know about a student's gender identity or plans to transition (if applicable), additional steps are necessary to ensure the safety of the student. To help illustrate the types of situations that might arise in which students and their rights need to be placed first, we offer two scenarios taken from different school districts in the same state. Both situations incorporate context about students, family members, teachers, and school administrators.

> *SCENARIO 1: Marcus teaches middle-school chorus in a suburban school district. He advocated for LGBTQA student protections in the district before he ever had a student disclose their sexual orientation or gender identity to him. Marcus's efforts were successful, and the district has explicit policies in place that prohibit discrimination based on gender. This fall, Marcus met with Jodi, a new student who identifies as trans, her supportive parents, and school administrators. The parents noted that they were aware of the district policies and had chosen to move into the area because they felt that their daughter would be safe and have greater opportunities for success than in their former school district. With policies in place, Jodi and her family found it easy to navigate the school system. Marcus felt comfortable empowering Jodi to succeed in her new music environment.*

Families supportive of their TGE children will likely research districts and schools, looking for inclusive policies that will support their loved ones (e.g., Slesaransky-Poe et al., 2013). In Scenario 1, the inclusive policies were important enough for the family to seek housing in that particular school district.

> *SCENARIO 2: Ellen teaches elementary general music and middle-school band in a rural school district. At the end of the last school year, Ellen was called to a meeting*

> *with school administrators in which she learned that one of her elementary students was planning to transition over the summer and Greg would begin his first year in middle school living full-time as male. With no formal district policy in place, school administrators worked quickly with the parents and the regional ACLU chapter to develop guidelines for the fall. Ellen was also supportive of Greg and his family as she had known them for a number of years and was fond of the young student. Greg's gender identity was revealed initially only to teachers with whom he would have direct contact. School administrators arranged for district-wide in-service training to educate faculty members about TGE students and the issues that can arise in school settings. Greg continued to thrive at school and the community celebrated him by acknowledging who he was and by getting on with the daily routines of rural community life.*

Greg's family was also supportive of him, and they were willing to take a chance by attempting to work with district and school administrators. This scenario illustrates what can happen when a group of adults is willing to listen and learn in an effort to support and honor a student. Perhaps equally important, the district chose to embrace the situation and learn as a collective unit, creating a larger opportunity for equity within the school system.

Placing students first in conversations about equitable treatment is essential to protecting the well-being of young people. *Teachers should ask to whom a TGE student is "out" at home and at school so as to not inadvertently disclose their gender identity to the wrong person(s)—especially parents.* Music teachers may need to have discussions with parents about rooming assignments, names in concert programs, etc., and a conflict may arise if a parent is not supportive. Open and supportive communication with students can be beneficial to maintaining trust and finding a plan that will work in a specific context.

Improving School Climate

American psychologist Abraham Maslow is perhaps best known for his Hierarchy of Needs, in which the idea of "safety" is foundational to students' ability to process academic content (Maslow, 1943). Music teachers typically know students from a variety of grade levels, and many students are able to identify the school music faculty. With this level of visibility, music teachers have an important role to intervene when they hear transphobic or homophobic comments in school. For example, Camden (he/him; trans man; Latinx/white) describes instances in which harassment never occurred in the presence of his teacher:

> [Bullying never happened] in class, but after we were dismissed, and we were waiting for the bell to ring. I heard a lot of people say stuff like that. And I also talked to my choir director about it and he had a talk with everyone about it, which was nice, but I don't think it really helped at all. Ever since I heard them using words in a derogatory way, I was honestly afraid of what they would say about me being trans.

Students will likely avoid inappropriate behavior in front of teachers they consider safe and protective of marginalized populations, like TGE students. For this reason, music teachers may want to work with other teacher colleagues and potentially the entire school staff to help educate other adults about what to listen for and when they might expect to hear inappropriate language.

Mystic Rose (she/her or they/them; gender nonconforming; Latinx) reminds teachers that when harassment is reported by a student,

> listen to the concerns of the student. Take them very seriously, because it could cost them a life if the schools are not careful. Because it's not just suicide without cause, there is bullying and harassment which weighs down the heart and soul.

Recall that the 2013 School Climate Survey published by GLSEN reported that about half of respondents "[participated] in band, orchestra, chorus, or choir (47.9%)" (Kosciw et al., 2014, p. 58) and that up to 41% of TGE persons attempt suicide (e.g., Maguen & Shipherd, 2010; Terada et al., 2011).

One of the reasons that these problematic discourses persist in schools is that peers, staff, and faculty do nothing to stop harassing or bullying behavior. In a survey of self-identified LGBT teachers regarding workplace climate, researchers Tiffany E. Wright and Nancy Smith discovered that "LGBT students in schools in which principals do not intervene when homophobic and transphobic language are used, frequently and consistently hear disrespect for them condoned" (2013, p. 9). Sometimes teachers are the culprits of bullying-type behavior, as described in Chapter 2—and sometimes they are the victims of bullying, as Sage (he/him; Trans Masculine non-binary; Latinx/white) says about his time teaching high school:

> I had a kid who was super homophobic and ended up harassing and assaulting me over a period of nine months. The school didn't do anything. [. . .] My principal actually said to me "this is Trump's America. You should probably just get used [to the discrimination]." I ended up acquiring Complex PTSD because of this incident and having to file with worker's compensation. I was off work afterwards for over a year, and I could no longer work with children and teens because of the damage

> done to my brain from the lack of administrative intervention that could have stopped the harassment. [. . .] People don't realize that queer, trans and gender non-conforming teachers are at risk too.

Joshua experienced much more bullying as a teacher than he did as a student, which made it difficult for him to connect with students. Matthew, however, recalls a greater amount of harassment during his student years in secondary schools than in his time as a secondary-school teacher. As authors, we hope that these differing experiences help readers to understand how much personal stories and contexts can vary.

Music educators have a responsibility to protect students in their schools by clearly signaling that any form of bullying or harassment is unacceptable (Carter, 2011; Taylor, 2011). Any form of harassment that is witnessed by a teacher, *whether or not those students are enrolled in the teacher's class*, needs to be dealt with swiftly and firmly. Bullying or taunting that is witnessed by a teacher and not followed up on can be taken as a tacit endorsement of that behavior. Zooming out, we as authors ask: if not us, who? If not now, when? We all have choices to make about inclusivity, and today is a great day to make the choice to be inclusive.

Flexible Policies to Broaden the Scope of Inclusion

Policy impacts students whom we know—those who are in our classes now—as well as students we may have in the future. If the intention of policy is to create a more inclusive environment for TGE students, then the enumerated language should include "trans" and "gender-expansive" to incorporate a broad spectrum of students. Teachers engaging in policy revision and creation should negotiate an appropriate balance between specificity and generality. Educators and scholars Meyer and Keenan (2018) warn against policies that are too specific or centered around an individual because: "there is simply no singular definition of 'transgender.' When institutions develop policy in the name of trans inclusion, they run the risk of simultaneously codifying what it means to be trans and limiting whose gender expression may be protected by such policies" (p. 737). If a policy is created with one specific person in mind, or because of the needs or desires of one particular TGE student, it may not serve other students in the future. This does not mean, however, that policies inspired by individual situations are entirely inappropriate. Policies should be clearly written and with enough flexibility to be applicable to a diverse set of students/families across time. Just as with musical performance, perfection is not achievable. We do the best we can with the knowledge that we have, and then we edit and adapt as necessary.

Music Education–Specific Policy

Engaging with policy for the first time or in contexts larger than music classrooms may seem intimidating or overwhelming. Again, working with colleagues can provide a sense of teamwork and unity when working to honor TGE students. Starting small may be more appealing for some readers. In the closing section of this chapter, we suggest some practical applications of policy that have a direct impact on the daily school experiences of TGE students.

Names and Pronouns in School Documents

Plans to ensure a safe and healthy environment for TGE students include steps to safeguard student privacy around their name and their pronouns. School officials are ultimately responsible for finding ways to honor students' wishes while also meeting recordkeeping and reporting requirements. As an example, student identity documents that reveal information about their name and sex assigned at birth might be kept in an administrator's secure files. The school's record systems could then use the name and gender marker that match the student's gender identity (Orr & Baum, 2015). If school record systems have the capability of indicating students' proper name and pronouns, then teachers and other employees are less likely to make errors in addressing students and honoring their wishes. If not, school officials should look for a system with this type of capability.

Music educators often interact with students' names publicly in the form of concert program personnel lists. Music teacher Patrick Aguayo in the Campbell Union School District in California suggests a creative way to honor TGE student names in concert programs, even in instances in which parents are not supportive. Mr. Aguayo gives every student the opportunity to list a nickname in concert programs, thus normalizing the use of an alternate name for all students. Marshall's (he/him; trans male; Asian-American) experience is similar:

> [At my school] in concert programs and anything performance-wise they ask students if they go by a different name, cause I have a lot of friends that go by other names, especially my non-binary friends. They always ask first. They're like, "what name do you want to have on the program?" And so obviously I always choose my preferred name.

Lived experiences of TGE persons can help music teachers understand the importance of using appropriate names and pronouns. Elliott (he/him; trans gay male; white) and his mother and middle-school band teacher Tavia (she/her; Cis-het female; white) relay their experience with a legal name change and the impact on school records:

ELLIOTT: By the time that I'd actually come out at school, my name had been legally changed and stuff.

TAVIA: No.

ELLIOTT: Oh—well then, they were all very good about it. [*both chuckle*] They were very good about it, especially after I got my name changed and stuff, cause it's easier to just have it on the roster and then just go off that if they didn't really know me all that well before. A lot of the teachers did know me before, but a lot of them didn't as well. If they did just like very briefly though, so they didn't really know me.

TAVIA: Well that actually is something that's changed since we started all this. Essentially at the time we couldn't change his name in the rosters in PowerSchool until it was legally changed and now, they will allow parents to request name changes even if it's not. So, there's progress.

JOSHUA: That is big progress.

TAVIA: Yes. Yeah. It's nice to not have a substitute teacher outing kids, you know.

Music teachers can make small changes in classroom guidelines and policies to honor TGE students' chosen names and pronouns. Still, other changes may extend beyond the scope of music classrooms, into facilities like auditoriums or school performing arts centers. TGE music students may require affirming policies to access facilities, such as restrooms and changing facilities.

Restroom Access

Access to public facilities in US schools remains a challenge for TGE youth. Policies regulating restroom access, in particular, can vary from one school facility to another. Music teachers should ensure that they understand the implications of laws and policies surrounding restroom use, because they directly impact the daily activities of TGE student musicians. In recent years, various states enacted laws to restrict the rights of TGE persons' use of public restrooms (e.g., Davis, 2017; Rogers, 2016; Schilt & Westbrook, 2015). These broad policies directed toward public facilities also influence public-school restrooms (Beese & Martin, 2018; Berglin, 2017). The thrust of many of these policies mandate that students use the restroom associated with their assigned birth sex (Steinmetz, 2015). In addition to legal barriers, TGE students also face stigmatizing and discriminatory district and school policies that force them to use a "single-stall washroom [which] also risks isolation and targeting as the Other" (Ingrey, 2018, p. 781). With the recent Supreme Court ruling (*Bostock v. Clayton County*, 2020), protecting LGBTQA persons from workplace discrimination, restroom restrictions for trans persons are beginning to change. In August 2020, two US appellate court decisions referenced *Bostock v. Clayton County* (2020) in affirming that public schools should allow trans students to use the restroom facilities congruent with their gender identity (*Adams ex rel. Kasper v. School Board of St. Johns Co.*, 2020; *Grimm v. Gloucester Co. School Board*, 2020). It is likely that these decisions will continue to impact school policies, and music teachers will want to remain informed about any changes in order to support the well-being of TGE students.

You may be asking yourself, "Why does a music teacher need to be so involved with students' access to restrooms?" With TGE students, the effect of not being able to use the appropriate restroom can have damaging physical and psychological effects (e.g., Beese & Martin, 2018; Davis, 2017; Ingrey, 2018; Schilt & Westbrook, 2015). Kristie Seelman, a researcher from Georgia State University, analyzed a subset of data from the National Transgender Discrimination Survey to explore the experiences of 2,772 trans college students in accessing housing options and bathroom facilities that matched their gender identity. Keeping in mind the importance of intersectionality, Seelman discovered that:

> transgender people of color, those who are younger, those with a disability (physical, learning, or mental), and those more frequently perceived as transgender are more likely to be denied access to appropriate bathrooms or other facilities due to being transgender or gender nonconforming. (2014, p. 199)

Considering the fear and misunderstanding around trans issues in schools, it is perhaps unsurprising that some of these so-called bathroom bills in the United States have been purported to "protect normal people" from "men in the women's room" (Grinberg & Stewart, 2017). As we have learned in recent court cases, these tropes are unfounded and discriminatory toward TGE students.

Music teachers actively participating in music professional organizations can also impact positive change for TGE persons. As members of music professional organizations, we can work with leadership bodies to develop affirming policies that may impact access to appropriate facilities. Michael (she/her; trans female; white) describes the quandary of bathroom use at professional events:

> As I continued to attend conferences, I would always make arrangements for restrooms at the conference site before the event. Several conference sites accommodated me by setting up an "all gender" bathroom. At some point, ACDA [American Choral Directors Association] started getting really, very supportive of the trans community by putting pronouns on the name tag. But with my particular situation, this presented a challenge. I am attending this conference presenting as female. I haven't used a male restroom in 10 years. I have had some bad experiences in male restrooms and I've never had a bad experience in a female restroom, so I use a female restroom. But if a female-presenting trans woman walks into the restroom with a name tag with the pronouns "he/him," it is uncomfortable. I have since changed my pronouns professionally and socially to align with my presentation as a trans female.

Policies that support TGE persons can make a difference in daily experiences. Those of us who are not members of the TGE community should speak with TGE persons or individuals who serve as informed resources to help develop supportive policies. In the absence of clear policy, however, the potential for confusion and continued discrimination persists.

According to Temple University professor and trans scholar Heath Fogg Davis (2017), schools who had trans students who desired to use the bathroom that aligned with their gender identity often created "makeshift policy" (p. 59). As Andy (he/him; FTM transgender; white) says:

> Our bathroom situation here is not great. Luckily, I'm only here for a couple of hours a day, so it's not that bad. But yeah, I think we only have one gender-neutral restroom and it's like all the way away from all the academic classes. So, you know, it's an extra time away from class.

Similarly, Gabriella's (she/her; female; white) elementary school agreed to let her use a staff bathroom in second grade, as noted by her mother Victoria (she/her; cis female; white):

> She was kind of okay with that because in first grade things got really confusing in the boy's bathroom with all these little tiny kids going, "Hey, you're in the wrong bathroom." And she'd be like, "no I'm not." And it was just confusing.

This connects to our earlier discussion of *proactive* vs. *reactive* policy-making. If a policy is hastily created to meet the needs of one particular student, it may not receive the time, attention, and nuance required. Such a policy also runs the risk of establishing a "victim/savior relationship" in which TGE persons are victims in need of cisgender saviors. Recall from Chapter 2 that we aim to highlight the resilience of TGE youth, rather than relying on a deficit model that frames these students only as victims.

Access to Changing and Dressing Rooms

Music classes and activities often include components that are co-curricular and/or extracurricular in nature. Producing a school musical or variety show is one example of an extracurricular activity that requires thoughtful planning for TGE students. Access to school changing or dressing room spaces should also be inclusive, in line with the argument for equal access to school restrooms discussed previously. Music educator Elizabeth (she/her; cis female; white) describes her district's gym policy as it applied to one of her trans students: "There were accommodations for changing in gym class. She had a, basically a private room if she chose and it was very much left up to the student." It is important to note that discrimination and fear often surround "masculine-appearing and androgynous women, as well as to transgender women who are readable as transgender" (Davis, 2017, p. 57). Trans women (and especially trans women of color) remain vulnerable due to a lack of education and understanding around facility access and TGE persons, in general. Teachers should remember that not all TGE students *want* a separate, single dressing room facility. It is important that you consult with the student first, if appropriate. If the student is "out," additional conversations with their parent(s)/guardian(s) and building administrators may be necessary to ensure the health and safety of the student.

Planning for School-Related Travel

As with dressing room accommodations, we as music teachers can have an open dialogue with our TGE students to see how *they* feel about their rooming assignment for school-related travel. The "Dear Colleague Letter" suggested that TGE persons be allowed to choose housing "consistent with their gender identity" (Lhamon & Gupta, 2016, p. 4) and be protected from being relegated to single rooms. However, "nothing in Title IX prohibits a school from honoring a student's voluntary request for single-occupancy accommodations if it so chooses" (Lhamon & Gupta, 2016, p. 4). Additionally, recent court decisions affirm the rights of TGE persons to use facilities congruent with their gender identity (*Adams ex rel. Kasper v. School Board of St. Johns Co.*, 2020; *Bostock v. Clayton County*, 2020; *Grimm v. Gloucester Co. School Board*, 2020). Teachers will want to review school and local policies to learn whether or not TGE supportive guidelines are in place.

Conversations with supervising adults may be required, especially if a TGE student is not widely "out." Teachers should consult with their administration, school-, district-, and state-wide policies. Here, mother of a trans son and middle-school instrumental teacher Tavia (she/her; Cis-het female; white) describes navigating her son's experience in band camp.

TAVIA: When Eli went into high school, it was the first time for band camp that they were dealing with that. [He and another] student . . . were both transitioning at the same time. And they were like, "okay, what do we do?" And you know, we're trying to figure out ways around it. We're like, okay, maybe we put out a survey about which kids wouldn't care if they stayed with a trans kid and would their parents mind and this and that. And we put together an idea, the high-school director and I, and then we went to the principal at the high school and she said, "no, that would put too much pressure on these two boys, and it might out them. You may not do that." We're like, [*surprised sounding*] "Alright!" And so, what we, what we ended up doing is, we went with some kids that they knew they were comfortable with and contacted the kids and the parents and said, "Hey, would you be okay being in the same cabin . . . ?"

JOSHUA: Because you wanted to or because the school said that you had to?

TAVIA: [*pause*] I don't know if the school said we had to because we had kind of come to it with that already. They might've said we had to if we hadn't proposed it. And it made it especially tricky because these two boys were definitely not stealth. They had both transitioned at the beginning of eighth grade and everyone knew them before. So that would be something that if they just fell in with the extremely Catholic family that was not supportive, then there would've been issues.

Eli's experience is encouraging and provides a model of an administrator who was sensitive to the needs of TGE students. Situations like this can provide a blueprint for teachers and administrators wondering how to navigate these tricky waters. While not every music educator will face situations involving overnight accommodations, many will face the question of what their students will wear for performances.

Inclusive Performance Attire

Music ensemble uniforms have been a topic of great interest in recent years. As TGE students become more visible (and numerous) in school music programs, teachers face difficult and context-dependent decisions about performance attire (see Box 5.3). It is time to begin questioning the tradition of

Box 5.3

SUSAN
Choral teacher
cis, white
she/her

SUSAN: [My trans student] first came to me before they outed themselves to me, they said, "I am not interested in auditioning next year for our choir." And I said, "well, why not?" And they said, "well, I really don't feel comfortable wearing a dress" and that is how they approached it. And I said, "That's no problem. You don't have to wear a dress." They replied, "well, that's a big problem." And I said, "Is that something that we should look at? Do you want me to look into that further? Because I have no problem with that." And they were being very iffy about it. So I approached the advisor of the GSA, saying, "Let's look at some costuming options where we can still have sort of a uniform look, but not be obvious about it, so we can be accommodating to some of our students who are not comfortable wearing dresses or tuxedos." He suggested that I contact the student leadership of the GSA. The leadership and I spent the entire summer looking at all kinds of concert clothes and came up with what we felt was a neutral and stylish way of presenting ourselves, which was essentially a tux kind of jacket and then skirts or slacks. But when I took it to the next administrative step, that person was adamant that "no, that looked too regimented and girls wanted to feel pretty, and this didn't make them feel pretty." My response was, "It's concert wear. No big deal." However, they were concerned about the show choir and the girls having to give up their sparkly dresses. My response was, "Well, we're not asking them, this is for my choirs." And they replied, "concert wear is just a costume and people just need to get over it." My response was, "no, that's not the issue. I think we've got something going on here that people cannot necessarily think about putting on a costume and feel comfortable singing with their voice." So it's not only a vocal image, it's a physical image and a vocal image combined. They would not budge. So as a result, this student said, "no, there's no way I'm going to ever sing in a dress. I will not."

JOSHUA: So did that student leave choir at that point?

SUSAN: They did.

requiring our students—especially in public institutions—to choose between two traditional clothing options that reify the gender binary. We as authors wonder: Why have tuxedos and dresses become the standard for so many schools? If we pause to consider this tradition, we may realize that visual conformity has become an unquestioned norm that can change (Blaisdell, 2018; Palkki, 2020b). We as teachers must ask ourselves: Is an ensemble looking cohesive more important than ensemble member comfort? Because gender is a spectrum, we should find ways to get away from binary choices. Abby (they/them; Gender Non-Binary; Black) describes the unique quandary of finding attire for the Trans Chorus of Los Angeles:

> We are still in the process of finding what our real look is because so far that's been one of the craziest discussions among this chorus. Because trans men are built a different way than trans women. So, you can't really find a uniform look for everybody. [. . .] That has been one of the hardest things this chorus has had to deal with. A uniform look. Something that makes everybody feel good and is cohesive—that appeals to trans men and trans women. We're experiencing this now [. . .] vocal breathing while wearing binding because that constricts a lot of your breathing. And most of the guys are going to be bound until their affirmation surgeries.

Abby highlights the important fact that TGE musicians who are binding their chest may experience difficulty breathing, which obviously can affect one's ability to sing or play a wind instrument (more on this in Chapter 6).

Music educators wishing to get away from binary performance attire have an increasing number of gender-neutral options. Some school choral programs select choir robes as their performance attire. Some band programs choose to perform in their marching band uniforms throughout the year. Additionally, ensembles may select a uniform top and require that performers obtain a black dress, skirt, slacks, or pants to complete the look. In the changing gender landscape of the twenty-first century, music teachers may need to decide whether or not some of the traditional music ensemble uniforms (e.g., dresses and tuxedos) best honor the gender identities of all students. As Avery (he/him or they/them; agender; white) describes:

> In my high school wind ensemble, we had to wear gendered uniforms for concerts, which was a little uncomfortable. It would have been better if they had just made a blanket "everyone wear all black" policy to be more inclusive of non-binary genders. Marching band was fine because all the uniforms were the same for everyone, but I still had to change clothes in the women's room. I didn't particularly

> enjoy that, but I never said anything because I didn't yet have the knowledge nor language to describe why. It wasn't until college that I gained that insight.

Similarly, Mystic Rose's (she/her or they/them; gender nonconforming; Latinx) professor used humor in discussing uniforms: "whatever you want to wear you can wear." And she made that note to everybody. "Whatever you want to wear, you can wear, just make sure it's black, no strong scents, but deodorant is not optional."

At minimum, we as a music education community can move away from a two-options-only paradigm that reinforces the gender binary. Having a third option (for schools that may have just purchased new tuxedos and dresses, for example) is a place to start. Music educators may explore a "concert black" approach in which every student dresses in all black within specified guidelines to ensure that all outfits are school-appropriate. For example, singers in the Michigan State University Women's Chamber Ensemble wear a personalized version of concert black (within guidelines) with a "pop of color":

- Dress: Solid black top, dressy black slacks or long skirt, solid black dress shoes.
- Concept: ONE jewel-tone colored accessory of your choice: scarf/pin/tie/hair accessory/dress shoes (substitutes for black)/etc.
- Personalize to suit YOU. (S. Snow, personal communication, August 12, 2020)

Conductor-teachers may consider working with local retailers to provide all-black "separates" options (e.g., two cuts of pants and a skirt matched with three different tops). Examples of inclusive uniform policies are provided in Appendix C. Perhaps in the future, music teachers could employ fashion designers to create gender-neutral uniform options.

Recap

The reality of honoring TGE students' wishes can be challenging, and teachers may be called upon to make difficult decisions. As an important first step, teachers should acknowledge a student's gender identity. This action plays an important role in a young person's academic and personal development. Next, teachers and school district personnel can educate themselves by locating resources to help bring about policy change and alter previously held biases through appropriate dialogue.

Reflect/Remember

1. Reflect on your own memories of participating in school music programs. Make a list of ways that classroom language or school policies reinforced the gender binary. Next, create a list of ideas you might use to disrupt classroom language that embodies the gender binary. What ideas do you have to help ensure equal access to school music programs for TGE students?
2. Create a list with two columns, as illustrated in Table 5.1. On the left, write down commonly used phrases, both in society and in classrooms, that are "gendered." For example, do you refer to a co-ed class as "you guys"? Do you use the word "gals" or "ladies" to refer to female students? On the right, create a parallel list of more inclusive terms that could be used. For example, "you guys" can easily become "y'all" or "friends."

Table 5.1 Inclusive Conversation Tools

From:	To:
Hey guys!	*Hey y'all!*
Ladies and Gentlemen . . .	*Folks . . .*

3. Navigating the legal landscape for LGBTQA individuals can be tricky, as laws and policies continue to change. What generalizations can you remember from this chapter about existing local and state laws designed to prohibit discrimination against TGE persons? What legal protections protections exist in your state or school district that help protect TGE students?

6

Celebrating TGE Singers in Choral Classrooms

Chapter Guide

JOSHUA (he/him; cis male; white): As secondary choral people, what advice would you have for your colleagues about honoring trans youth?

QUINCY (he/him; male; white): Educate yourself. I think that's the biggest thing. And I mean, obviously the people who are reading your book already have got that message. But then to just start, you know, start by asking pronouns in your audition forms or whatever step you can take, renaming your ensembles, whatever step you can take to start going down the road and don't feel like you have to be perfect and have it all solved on day one. But just start.

+++

DANA (she/her; female; white): When I sing in a choral environment, whether it's rehearsing or performing, my mind seems to float up out of my body. I soar to a place where my center is no longer inside my physical boundaries. Rather, it's in free space along with the centroids of the other singers as we chorally merge our spirits together. It's the summation of all of us in that choral space, where I am pulled to and where I love being. To me, being unified while making something beautiful is the closest one can get to heaven.

Honoring Trans and Gender-Expansive Students in Music Education. Matthew L. Garrett and Joshua Palkki, Oxford University Press. © Oxford University Press 2021. DOI: 10.1093/oso/9780197506592.003.0007

Choral Music as a Gendered Enterprise

Choral conductor-teachers empower singers to make music together. Music professionals also have a history of approaching choral music in gendered ways, and we as authors posit that these gendered traditions may be unnecessary. As the people in choral ensembles change from one year or performance season to the next, the needs and goals of the organization may change as well. The gender spectrum is expanding, and an increasing number of trans and gender-expansive (TGE) singers are members of our ensembles. These singers may identify themselves to teachers or they may choose to observe if and when it will be safe to do so. Subtle corrections to unnecessary gender references, like the one illustrated in Box 6.1, signal to TGE students that chorus ensembles are safe spaces. Choral conductor-teachers can be a force for good in the lives of LGBTQA persons (Garrett & Spano, 2017; Palkki & Caldwell, 2018; Womack, 2017). Jaqui (she/her; cis female; white), a private vocal instructor working with TGE singers, describes how she develops constructive student–teacher relationships by placing her students, in this instance Ty, first:

Box 6.1 Singing Inclusively

Dr. Vaughn stepped on the podium and began choral rehearsal silently. Students moved together, mostly in unison, through a series of stretching and relaxation exercises. Dr. Vaughn said, as he slowly brought his motions to a stop, "Please join me in welcoming Laura to the podium this evening as she leads us in breathing activities." Dr. Vaughn moved away from the podium as the eager undergraduate music education major started a sequence of echo consonants. Laura stepped back into her section and Dr. Vaughn led the group in a round of friendly applause, and then he began his next set of instructions, "Please take out your singing straws and find an 'A' together, on an [u] vowel." As the students gathered their straws and began to gently sing, Dr. Vaughn noticed that the sopranos and altos engaged far faster than the tenors and basses. "Gentlemen," Dr. Vaughn began, "my apologies . . . tenors and basses, could you please join us a little more efficiently?" Dr. Vaughn felt the embarrassed rush of a red face as he realized that he had slipped into an old habit of addressing his chorus, but he recognized that the need for change outweighed the discomfort of a simple mistake—and the choir kept singing.

> Prioritize the relationship first; build a relationship with them and listen to their input about things. I know a lot of people in my situation would frown at the way that I'm handling Ty, but I'm not going to steamroll over Ty's preferences because mental health and dysphoria are a really big deal—and triggering mental health issues or dysphoria could be the end of that relationship, could be the end of them loving music. And in my opinion, that is so much more important. And then as the relationship is built, then you slowly pepper in ways to get them to enjoy the parts of their voice that could have made them dysphoric in the past.

Similar to Jaqui's experience and the vignette in Box 6.1, we might ask ourselves how *our* gendered traditions can be modified so that singing occurs in a more inclusive community.

Context matters, particularly when values and goals play an important role in that context. Performing in an ensemble requires individuals to agree to create music together. How can we, as choral conductor-teachers, demonstrate through words and actions that we truly value the idea of being together in community? Choral music education professor Dustin Cates notes in a study exploring trans-inclusive practices among choral educators, "participant comments describing challenges addressed barriers to gender inclusivity with students, faculty, administration, parents, and the community. Others conveyed a lack of knowledge or appropriate training to make informed teaching decisions in support of students identifying as transgender" (2019, p. 72). Ideas and exercises discussed in this chapter may function as part of that training to disengage from learned gender practices. Choral conductor-teachers can thoughtfully consider and adapt materials most appropriate for individual classrooms. In addition, we encourage you to connect with colleagues (including us!) as you navigate how these ideas and activities might work within the context of your school, district, community, or organization.

A Reminder about Intersectionality

Choral music and gender intersect in complex ways. Western European choral music has a long history as a gendered art form. Music from this tradition is rooted largely in white, Eurocentric tradition and practice (e.g., Edidi et al., 2020). Along those lines, a majority of published choral music composers are cisgender white males. As a result, choral conductor-teachers can still struggle to diversify composer representation, beyond the cis/white/male paradigm. There is still ample room for teachers to select music that reflects the diversity represented by the people in the communities we serve—a tenet of Culturally

Responsive Pedagogy (e.g., Bond, 2017a)—especially as female, TGE, marginalized, and minoritized composers increasingly publish more music. Choral conductor-teachers may wish to consult resources listed in Appendix B to help ensembles to be more inclusive of intersectional gender diversity.

Considerations for Single-Gender Choirs

The Myth of the Gendered Voice

Many of us grew up in choirs in which there were tacit assumptions about the gendered nature of the human voice. Just as gender is a social construct—as are culture- and context-dependent norms around masculinity and femininity (Palkki, 2015a)—so too are stereotypes about the gendered nature of human voices. One of our collaborators, Riley (they/them or he/his; non-binary man or trans masculine; white) describes their voice classification journey:

> I'm non-binary, but I lean a little more towards male in general. Now that I'm in college for vocal performance, I've been using the term Countertenor or male Mezzo, since I plan to keep my voice as it is. [. . .] I'm lucky to have supportive people including voice teachers, since I'm trying to figure out how to enter the professional opera world as a trans singer.

Riley's supported choice of voice labels exemplifies a type of empowerment by their teachers. In other words, their teachers are honoring who Riley is as an individual.

Voices are not inherently gendered. How a listener—a telemarketer, for example—determines whether to address you as "ma'am" or "sir" depends upon a perception about the range of your voice. There is no such thing as a "male" or "female" voice, but there is a difference in how voices are perceived in our society (and these perceptions can be questioned). Some men have high voices and some women have low voices. Consider assumed cisgender female singers like Karen Carpenter, Tracy Chapman, and Etta James, who sang in a rich contralto range, and assumed cisgender male singers like Justin Timberlake, Pharrell Williams, and Adam Levine, who regularly use their high range throughout a song. Aaliyah (she/her; trans woman; Black) says:

> I've always had a high voice. It's natural for me, you know? [. . .] All the singers that I listened to, they also sung alto. So, it was like Patti LaBelle and Diana Ross and Brandy and—you know—I wasn't really listening to Mariah. [. . .] I guess I mean Patti sings high but she's always at that . . . [*trailing off*] Maybe that's where I get my

> range from is Patti. The choir would trip out cause I'll be singing with the baritones [and then change to the treble range]. It's like, "okay! She got range!" So, I just—I'll go back and forth.

Aaliyah's story illuminates an idea that voice labels can be flexible, and those labels can defy the notion of a "single story" (Adichie, 2009). Voices are what they are—it is we as listeners who impose gendered connotations onto the sounds that we hear.

To better understand how gender is reinforced in vocal music, we can explore singing and vocal pedagogy research. Researchers have coded the act of singing as feminine in many studies (Elorriaga, 2011; Green, 1997; Hall, 2005; Harrison, 2007; Heywood & Beynon, 2007; Koza, 1993b; Legg, 2013)—a manifestation of the construct that one's vocal range can be perceived as "feminine" or "masculine." These studies seem to suggest that in Western societies, high pitch is coded feminine and low pitch is coded masculine. This type of gendered music perception can be explained more specifically through voice science.

The fundamental frequency of an individual's voice is an acoustical property related to formants, or concentrations of vocal energy. These perceived fundamental frequencies persuade us to distinguish voices as masculine/lower or feminine/higher. Put simply, the higher the fundamental frequency, the higher the voice; the lower the fundamental frequency, the lower the voice (Azul, 2013). Voice scientist and educator Ingo Titze (1994) notes that the fundamental frequency of a voice perceived as male is 85 to 180 Hz. On the contrary, the fundamental frequency of a voice perceived as female ranges from 165 to 255 Hz. The higher the frequency, the higher pitches sound to the listener. JB (they/them; Non-binary; white) describes how they learned about fundamental frequencies of the speaking voice:

> The person who got me interested in measuring my own voice [frequencies] was also talking about how men's and women's voices, in terms of their resting fundamental frequencies, are a lot closer than people often think they are. Or, at least, a woman's speaking voice, on average, sits a lot lower than people think it does.

We, as listeners, reinforce these gendered stereotypes when we hear a person's speaking range and make a decision about what the speaker's gender is (or may be): "Listeners may have different ideas of what constitutes a masculine/feminine voice, further complicating the process of gendering a voice" (Azul, 2013, pp. 82–83). In other words, gender is in the ear of the beholder. These gendered connotations, however, can unduly influence how we label choral ensembles.

Ensemble Names, Goals, and Structure

As the gender landscape in the United States continues to expand, the associated gender spectrum becomes more complex. Choral conductor-teachers may find it necessary to re-examine the structure, goals, or names of their ensembles, particularly if a gendered context warrants further discussion. For example, if college women wish to sing tenor or baritone in a traditionally single-gender college men's ensemble, what types of conversations might take place to ensure that stakeholders are comfortable and feel included? Music education professor Stuart Chapman Hill (2021) writes, "An ensemble's name, as discourse, can communicate much about that ensemble's function, values, repertoire, membership, leadership and so forth" (p. 62). Will a "women's choir" at the high-school level serve the needs of all women, including trans women who sing in the lower octave? Will a "men's choir" be inclusive of trans men who formerly sang soprano, or still wish to? There are no easy answers, and reflective conversations likely will be necessary. Choral conductor-teachers should learn as much as they can about gender and how it influences their choral philosophy and pedagogy. If they discover incongruence, perhaps changes are necessary to appropriately address the situation.

The presence of gendered choirs in the United States is a mainstay in communities. Some common examples of these organizations include collegiate glee clubs, treble choirs with feminist roots, boy choirs, and "single-gender" collegiate a cappella groups. Many of these ensembles have proven vital to identity development for males (Elorriaga, 2011; Ramsey, 2013) and females (Bartolome, 2013; Sweet & Parker, 2019), and thus personally important for many individual singers. Women may feel empowered through membership in an ensemble with feminist roots. Likewise, male singers may feel more comfortable singing in lower voice choirs or college glee clubs. These choral traditions hold great value to the musicians who sing in school and community ensembles. Conductors and ensemble members wishing to continue with a gendered ensemble paradigm, however, should consider ways to be inclusive of TGE singers, as Camden's (he/him; trans man; Latinx/white) experience illustrates:

> It was very fascinating because I hadn't really sung that much that summer and coming back and seeing what notes I could hit—what notes I couldn't hit anymore—was super interesting. And then, [my high school choir teacher] just came to the consensus that I'd fit into the beginning tenor/bass choir. And I was ultimately, as my voice kept changing, placed as a baritone/bass—very affirming to me.

Camden felt more comfortable singing in a lower-voiced choir, and that decision was supported by his director.

The names of single-gender choirs can also impact how students engage with these choral ensembles. Matthew served as faculty advisor to a men's glee club at his university for a number of years. Students approached him wanting to open participation to anyone wanting to sing music written for tenors, baritones, and basses—regardless of gender—and, at the same time, maintain the name of the group. The group has existed since the mid-1800s, and some of the university alumni sing in the organization as community members. These topics were important components in conversations with current and former members of the organization, as they determined how best to proceed. In other words, the current students acknowledged the significance of the ensemble's past while wanting to move forward with a more inclusive ensemble in a contemporary context. The organization is now thriving with participants and officers of diverse gender identities. Keizen (they/them; gender creative; Han Chinese) shared their experience singing in a men's chorus as someone who identifies as gender creative,

> I just walked in and they—you know, they aren't auditioned and just welcome everyone and there's plenty of room because who wants to sing in a men's chorus? [*laughs*] And it was just such a wonderful experience. I just struck gold right away. I didn't have really high expectations. I thought this was just something to do with people together and I might not get along with them and that would be fine. But it turned out to be just the most magical, transformative ensemble experience and spiritual experience for me. And I just completely fell in love with it. I didn't really love choir before coming into that. And obviously I've just been completely converted.

The positive experiences illustrate how choral conductor-teachers can create more open spaces within the paradigm of a gendered ensemble. Remember that these two organizations chose to maintain a traditional name out of a deeply rooted sense of history. In other situations, additional changes may be warranted.

Have You Spoken to (a) TGE Individual(s) in the Process?

Ensemble name changes may be necessary to embody an inclusive space for music making. Choral conductor-teachers seeking to rename an ensemble to better serve student needs may choose to engage student members in open dialogue about the reasons for a potential change. Victoria (she/her; female; white) describes her experience working with a trans student:

> I had Jack who was transitioning female to male and Jack was new to choir, so wasn't quite ready to sing in the advanced SATB group but was ready for the advanced treble group. Which at that point was still called "Advanced Women's Ensemble." And Jack is the kind of person who I could sit down with and go, "okay, I'm not sure how to, to proceed. So, here's what I'm thinking and can we, can we just talk this out a little bit? This is where you belong vocally, I think and I'd like to rename the group, if you're comfortable with that." [. . .] I was so worried about not doing any vocal damage in the process of supporting him emotionally. But he has a strong desire to sing tenor and I just wasn't sure what to do with that. [. . .] I just was wrestling with how to go forward. [. . .] I can see that the social aspect of [ensemble singing] is just as important in retrospect. So, we changed the names of those groups.

After a compassionate student-teacher discussion, Victoria chose to change the name of her choral ensembles. She honored her student in making that change, in light of what was a complex decision for her as she considered the vocal and social aspects of ensemble singing. There are many options when renaming a choral ensemble. Music education professor Dustin Cates writes, "Many of these gender-neutral ensemble names utilized musical terminology in foreign languages, the school's mascot, references to voice parts, or other variations" (2019, p. 67). Choral conductor-teachers could benefit from their singers' creativity in determining a new ensemble name.

One of the prevailing mantras of the ongoing movement for social justice and human rights is "no talking about us without us" (e.g., Wolff & Hums, 2017). In creating policies about ensemble names, it is vital that we, as choral conductor-teachers, speak with any "out" TGE singers in the ensemble or at your institution. Remember that some TGE persons identify within the gender binary and are comfortable with gender labels, while others may feel uncomfortable enrolling in a group called a "women's choir" or a "men's choir." After discussing the journey taken by the ensemble that he leads in becoming "Aurelia" rather than "Women's Chorus," Hill (2021) encourages us to consider the following three questions:

1. *Who are we?* Who are the current and prospective members of this ensemble, and does our name signal to them that they belong? Who is our intended audience, and do they sense from our name that we have something to offer them? Despite all good intentions, is there anything about our name that fails to welcome singers, prospective singers, or audience members fully? For example, is this a gendered chorus or a voice-type chorus? [. . .]

2. *What are we about?* Even if you have never discussed them explicitly, your ensemble almost certainly has a definable set of values. Does the choir's name reflect what it does especially well, what its function is in the broader choral ecosystem? For example, does "madrigals" accurately describe your musical prowess? Does "chamber" reflect the nature of your musical activity?
3. *Where are we going?* I mean this both locally and universally. Where is your ensemble going, and where is choral music going? Choral music rests on rich tradition, but ACDA's mission explicitly embraces contemporary practice. How do ensembles balance tradition and evolution? [. . .] (pp. 68–69)

Conductor-teachers working *with* students—specifically TGE students—can and should engage in open dialogue to determine how ensemble goals and policies align with regard to gendered ensemble names. Remember that our singers are unique people with many identities, thoughts, and feelings. The possibilities are limitless and the positive impact on TGE singers will be immeasurable.

Inclusive Vocal Pedagogy

Teaching *People* to Sing

Choral conductor-teachers can constructively contribute to healthy singing for TGE singers by focusing on healthy singing for all singers. We, as authors, advocate the idea that we teach *people* through the art of music. The singers, as the individuals who possess the vocal instruments necessary to form choral ensembles, come first. TGE students bring their own skills and lived experiences to our classrooms. Some TGE singers strive for their vocal identity to match or align with their gender identity, while others are comfortable without this type of alignment. JB (they/them; Nonbinary; white) shares advice to choral educators about placing trans singers in ensembles:

> You put them in the choir that validates who they are and that they're going to want to show up to everyday. In the culture where our school choir program is a family, students only choose to be a part of families where they feel seen and where their identity isn't up for debate.

Similarly, Abby (they/them; Gender non-binary; Black) speaks about focusing on an individual's vocal abilities within the context of an all-trans chorus, rather than trying to label the voice with a specific gender category:

> There are some people that want their voices to align with what society has said a woman should sound like or a man should sound like, but I like to encourage them to work with the voice that you have, not the voice that you wish you had. Yeah, I wish I could get up and hit notes that Sam Smith opens up his mouth and just throws out. I can't do that anymore—it just doesn't happen. But you can learn to use your instrument to the best of your abilities. So, for me, this journey of what is a voice, especially in the trans identified spectrum, I've had to suspend everything I've learned about voices and really only focus on the human instrument that is creating that voice.

Abby suggests that vocal teachers help singers work with the voice that they have now, in an effort to guide them to the voice to which they may aspire. How do we, as choral conductor-teachers, balance the needs of TGE singers with the overall vocal needs of an ensemble?

Singers likely will engage in music making more deeply if they feel respected and comfortable in the choral classroom. Developing an atmosphere of trust with TGE individuals is an important part of honoring their choral/vocal experience (Kozan & Hammond, 2019). Choral conductor-teachers, then, will want to consider how to use a *both/and* approach when negotiating decisions about vocal and emotional health of TGE youth. In other words, teachers will want to consider both the emotional and the vocal health of the singer when determining how to improve group vocal technique. Louisiana State University voice professor Loraine Sims notes, "the most important thing for you as a teacher is to be open-minded enough to treat [TGE students] with respect and try to support them however possible" (2017, p. 281). One of our collaborators, Jaqui (she/her; cis female; white) describes how she works to establish trust with one of her trans high-school students:

> Ty has a treble clef voice and I had a conversation with Ty. I said, "what is more important to you? Your voice affirming your gender identity or doing what is 100% healthy and pedagogically sound for your voice?" And he said, "gender identity," so we went that route. So, he will be singing tenor again next year. And I get it. I like it. I think he understands that it's not 100% perfect training for his voice to always be singing low, but sometimes there are things more important and there are ways to support his upper register that don't involve dysphoria in public.

Once an atmosphere of trust and respect has been established, students will likely be able to focus more intentionally on improving vocal skills and technique.

When teachers are aware that a person who identifies as TGE will be singing in a choral ensemble, a one-to-one conversation will be helpful in learning about specific vocal goals or challenges for that individual. Jaqui's conversations with Ty illustrate the type of casual conversation that puts students at ease when speaking with an adult. Discussions with TGE youth should incorporate learning about the *person*, in addition to learning about their goals and developing a plan for vocal success. Brainstorming ideas with students or guiding them in constructive ways can empower their learning and set them on a trajectory for musical success (e.g., Bond, 2017b). If, as teachers, we are uncertain whether we may be teaching a TGE student, there are fairly simple ways that we can establish an inclusive environment for all singers.

De-Gendering Voice Part Labels

Choral conductor-teachers may choose to reframe the language used in choral classrooms as they acknowledge that choral ensembles can be gendered spaces. Matthew recalls conversations with many of his middle-school singers in which he would ask, "What voice part(s) have you sung before?" as he was getting to know new students. Often, his students would enthusiastically blurt, "*I'm* a soprano!" or "*I'm* a tenor!" Trying to convince young people that they are, in fact, *themselves* first and that they might *sing* one or more vocal parts is fascinating, to say the least. Using accurate musical terminology, like traditional SATB voice part labels, can certainly help teachers avoid directly gendering singers with "girls/ladies" or "boys/men." Choral conductor-teachers can signal their openness to gender diversity by avoiding gender-binary terms in school music settings. Rex (they/them; non-binary; white) describes the gendered language often heard in choral music settings:

> Because it's like, "okay, the women are going to sing now, the men are going to sing now," right? Women over here to do this, men over here to do this. And so, there is just like the general gendered aspects of choral culture.

Soprano, alto, tenor, bass (SATB) labels also can carry gendered implications. If you were to close your eyes and think of a well-known soprano, whose personage do you envision? More specifically, what is the gender identity of that well-known soprano you pictured? You likely recalled a cisgender female singer from the classification of soprano. Recognizing that SATB labels may be problematic for some TGE singers, choral conductor-teachers may want to apply some creativity when referring to voice part assignments. Director of Choral Studies at Purdue University–Fort Wayne, William Sauerland (2018) synthesized research and offered practical suggestions to consider more gender neutral labels of Voice/Part I, II, III, etc. These labels can already be found in published music written for three-part mixed voicing and some treble- and lower-voiced ensemble works. Michelle (she/her; transgender female; white) describes her ideas about voice parts in her role as conductor of an all-trans chorus:

> We don't identify voice parts. What we do is, if we do two parts songs, she just says, "Michelle, you can sing the low part" or whatever. She doesn't say "you're a bass, you're alto, you're soprano" or whatever. She just kind of fits us in wherever we can feel comfortable because I asked her, "what would you classify me?" As she said, "I don't do that." She just uses us as we can fit into the music.

Choral conductor-teachers working with children's and youth choirs could create section labels with input from young singers. One way that we, as music teachers, can approach group singing more inclusively is by focusing on student-centered learning and leadership activities.

Applying a "Plus One" Approach in Choral Classrooms

Choral conductor-teachers can broaden the scope of instruction to include healthy singing techniques for TGE students by adopting tenets of Universal Design for Learning (CAST, 2020). Universal Design for Learning (UDL) is a framework to help teachers optimize learning using multiple means of student engagement, information representation, and demonstration of acquired skills. In other words, if you think about one way you might teach sight-reading skills (e.g., developing solfege skills) to students and you add one additional way to do that (e.g., allowing more advanced students to sight read using a neutral syllable like [du]), your learning activity would incorporate UDL with a "plus one" approach. Choral conductor-teachers already teach using UDL tenets when giving verbal instructions and then reinforcing those with physical gestures or conducting. Applying healthy vocal techniques that can assist TGE students in their singing, like those mentioned later in this chapter, can allow teachers to differentiate instruction without singling out any one student or group of students. A team of applied voice instructors writing for the National Association of Teachers of Singing Journal (Manternach et al., 2017) wrote about the need to avoid a one-size-fits-all approach when working with singers: "we should not expect that teaching singers who openly identify as transgender should somehow follow a formula any more than the other singers who walk into our studios" (p. 84). Choral conductor-teachers can easily begin to meet the individual vocal needs of TGE singers by employing a UDL-inspired "plus one" approach to healthy group-singing techniques. Teachers applying these techniques help to ensure that they are balancing the emotional and vocal health needs of the student. Sauerland (2018) summarized the importance of focusing on TGE *persons* who are also singers: "A teacher's awareness of how gender impacts music spaces coupled with physiological knowledge of transitioning voices is important to effectively teach this population" (p. 226). Choral conductor-teachers might equate "transitioning voices" with adolescent singers. An adult's vocal instrument, however, can also be affected by physiological changes.

Understanding Voice Masculinization and Voice Feminization

Gender identity and voice identity intersect in ways unique to us as individuals. TGE persons wishing to align their gender identity with their vocal identity may do so through a process of voice masculinization, a lowering of the speaking and singing voice, or voice feminization, a raising of the speaking and singing voice. Sage (he/him; Trans Masculine Non-binary; Latinx/white) shares:

> I started testosterone in January 2018. My endocrinologist started me on an incredibly low dose. [. . .] When I was placed on a higher dose, then all of a sudden, I was hoarse, and my voice was cracking, sounding like a teenage boy. By this time, I'm teaching college. It wasn't something I could hide, nor did I want to, so I'd tell my classes, "you can laugh. It's okay, because *I'm* going to. I think this is hilarious." But it gave me a way to talk about being trans because it was so there. And for me the cracking was a source of happiness because I was getting somewhere.

It is extremely important to note that this type of alignment between gender and voice identity is not a part of every TGE person's journey (Palkki, 2016, 2017). Michael (she/her; trans female; white) describes the intersection between her vocal identity and gender identity,

> I think it's in flux. I wish that when people heard my voice, they would think female. But I also feel very self-conscious about changing my voice at home. If I was living alone and not married and didn't have kids, I might actually practice with a

> higher pitch, softer and more colorful inflection, and work to develop a more feminine voice. I did recently buy an app which has voice lessons for trans females. And I did actually try the app out, but only when everybody was at school and work. [. . .] I know that these lessons are something I'd have to practice more than just once a day to hear results. Maybe I will slowly adjust my voice, but the truth is that I identify strongly with my natural voice, and if I ever adjust my voice to match my gender identity, I want to transition slowly while retaining the best parts of my voice.

As TGE students choose to engage choral conductor-teachers in conversations about their gender and vocal identities, teachers should remember to listen carefully to students, offer guidance from the perspective of a vocal teacher (not a health specialist), and seek additional resources as needed. Once again, the people that we are teaching come before the subject and art of music.

Choral conductor-teachers speaking specifically with trans singers should consider appropriate language. This discourse can be tricky, as terms change from acceptable to problematic over time. Voice instructor Liz Jackson Hearns and college voice professor Brian Kremer describe the difference between problematic language of "female to male (FtM)" or "male to female (MtF)" and the more widely accepted "trans male/trans masculine" and "trans female/trans feminine,"

> [FtM and MtF] imply that the individual was once one gender and then changed or switched to the other. Although the individual's birth-assigned sex is listed first, that person likely never identified as that gender. The notion that a trans person changed *from* female *to* male or *from* male *to* female is not correct as this is confusing birth-assigned sex with a person's self-identified gender. (2018, p. 21)

Speech pathologists concur with the use of the more appropriate "trans male" and "trans female" terminology (Södersten et al., 2019) for TGE persons who identify with the gender binary. Keep in mind, however, that there are trans persons who still use the terms FtM and MtF, which reinforces the idea that there is no monolithic TGE experience. Choral conductor-teachers now have a growing number of print, online, and professional development opportunities from which to choose when seeking pedagogical guidance for working with TGE singers. Prior to 2017, much of the research and pedagogy was focused within the field of speech-language pathology. In recent years, a number of texts have been published that apply science from speech and language specialists to singing contexts. See Appendix B for a listing of publications that create connections between research and praxis.

Voice Masculinization

A trans adult male seeking a lower pitched speaking and singing voice may take testosterone to begin voice masculinization. Hormone replacement therapy (HRT) involving testosterone will cause a drop in the fundamental frequency of the voice by thickening the vocal folds and effectively lowering the perceived sound of the voice. These changes in the physiology of the vocal folds are permanent and the decision to engage in voice masculinization is deeply individual. Likewise, the rate, duration, and overall quantity of voice change will be unique to each trans person undertaking HRT. Initial changes in the vocal folds may result in a period of vocal instability, during which parts of the range may be inaccessible, and this likely will stabilize over time. Further changes will include a loss of accessible pitches in the higher vocal range and an increase in accessibility to pitches in the lower vocal range. The quality and clarity of timbre may also change over time, and these aspects of the voice may be improved with careful training. Avery (he/him or they/them; Agender; white) described their vocal changes,

> The voice is such a personal, vulnerable instrument, and it can often be tangled up with dysphoria and shame. During my first two years on testosterone, I had a large "hole" in my range—from the B-flat below middle C to the E above middle C—where no noise would come out or my voice would crack if I tried to sing. This was exceedingly frustrating, and I admit to pushing much harder than I needed to in order to get the notes out. Intentional vocal rest and passaggio-bridging exercises helped a lot: quietly humming slides up and down, getting used to where my voice was sitting that particular day. My range was continually changing, and every day I would have to re-learn that muscle memory. Having the critical ear of a musician, but little vocal control, it felt like a true curse. I knew the notes I wanted to sing, but actually hitting them was like throwing a dart at a dartboard from across a freeway.

While adult voice changes may appear to have similarities to those that occur during adolescence, in the body of a person assigned male at birth, choral conductor-teachers should carefully consider context when making that type of analogy. The physiological changes in an adult and an adolescent are different (Hearns & Kremer, 2018; Sweet, 2020), and the perception of change by a teacher may not mirror the perceptions of the individual experiencing these changes (Meizel, 2020). High-school student Elliott (he/him; trans gay male; white) says:

> I want my voice to be deeper just because I feel like it would help me pass better. So, I do have this sort of connect with like, "Oh yeah, in order for me to sound more

> masculine, even though that's, you know, just kind of whatever, *[chuckles]* I want my voice to be deeper." Even though I know a lot of cis guys who have voices who are a lot higher pitched than mine, but I still feel like I want my voice to be deeper as like—it would feel better.

Choral conductor-teachers aware that a trans student is engaging in voice masculinization should check in often with the singer to listen and provide appropriate guidance through a period that may be marked by diminished range and increased rate of vocal fatigue. Teachers may need to help TGE persons navigate choral part-singing to accommodate the individual's changing vocal range with the range and tessitura of a corresponding musical line. We discuss this in more detail a little later in this chapter.

Voice Feminization

A trans adult seeking to raise the fundamental frequency and alter the timbre of their voice will most likely explore options outside of hormone therapy. Unlike the physiological changes caused by the introduction of testosterone to the body, an adult trans person taking estrogen, a female hormone, will not experience any noticeable change in their speaking or singing voice because once the vocal folds have lengthened due to puberty involving testosterone, they will never shorten without surgery. Instead, trans persons may choose to feminize the voice by working with a speech therapist or with assistance from voice feminization applications (see Appendix D for specific references). Gradual work to increase the fundamental speaking pitch takes time, patience, and practice, as Dana (she/her; female; white) describes:

> A convincing female voice becomes kind of an obsession for most TGs [transgender persons] during transition. It started that way for me but became much less afterwards. There's a terror of being busted, "clocked" in TG lingo. In a way, women seem to sing when they speak. In other words, singing naturally puts you (or at least me) into a female voice mode. The trick is to think of singing when you're talking. Listen to women sing and speak. It's not just higher and softer. Their vocalizations are filled with subtle variations impossible for me to describe, but filled with emotion, passion, love, sweetness, and female power, just like singing.

Choral conductor-teachers should know that the process of attempting to raise fundamental pitch can be vocally fatiguing, due to potential increases in tension within the structures of the vocal instrument. Careful warm-up and laryngeal relaxation exercises may be beneficial in reducing this type of vocal fatigue (Lessley, 2017). Again, the decision to achieve a different quality of speaking and singing voice is personal, and some trans persons are perfectly comfortable singing in a tenor or bass range, including trans women (Palkki, 2020a).

In addition to voice therapy, a number of surgical methods are available to raise the fundamental frequency. Sauerland discusses some of these procedures in greater detail, noting that the surgeries have focused on three strategies: "increasing vocal fold tension, decreasing vocal fold length, or decreasing vocal fold mass" (2018, p. 39). Vocal music professionals express caution to singers pursuing these types of phonosurgeries, since "results for singers are not well documented, however, and a trans singer considering voice feminization surgery would benefit from the support of a complete voice care team, including the singing teacher" (Hearns & Kremer, 2018, p. 133). College voice professionals have also expressed concern as to the lack of documented long-term results of these types of surgeries on individuals who wish to pursue singing (Sauerland, 2018; Sims, 2017). Choral conductor-teachers can remain focused on developing healthy vocal techniques with singers seeking to feminize their voice. It is important to recognize that the processes for voice feminization may be fatiguing. Teachers will want to maintain open and frequent communication with their singers and consider appropriate pacing of singing, including brief opportunities for intermittent vocal rest, to negotiate vocal and personal goals.

Our voices are inimitable parts of who we are in the world, and the sounds that we produce through speaking and singing identify our presence to those around us. Trans individuals may pursue voice masculinization or feminization as part of the gender-expression journey. Similarly, gender-expansive individuals may also express gender identity and expression needs related to the pitch or timbre of their voices. For example, a gender nonbinary person may wish to lower a higher speaking and singing voice, so their vocal identity aligns with their gender identity. Choral conductor-teachers wishing to attune themselves to the vocal needs of TGE students will want to create safe learning spaces that allow room for student-centered interactions (Sauerland, 2018). It also may be helpful to remember that vocal development is a journey that lasts a lifetime for singers. The guidance that we, as voice professionals, offer in the present may have long-lasting ramifications for an individual's ability to enjoy singing throughout their lifetime. For this very important reason, choral conductor-teachers must understand the physiology of the vocal instrument and the pedagogy behind healthy singing techniques. In other words, the science behind the art of singing impacts the joy we experience through the act of singing. Ethnomusicologist Katherine Meizel speaks eloquently about the intersecting complexities of meaning associated with our voices:

> The voice, as both biology and culture, reflects and contributes to the diversity of gender variance in human life. And on the journey, transvocality, instead of providing a map between one place and another, inscribes a network of paths to navigate the borderscape of voice. It does not necessarily represent a vocal liminality between two states but, rather, an instrument through which an individual may embody and identify with more than one sonic expression of self. (2020, p. 157)

We return, then, to the concept of intersectionality as a way to acknowledge the complex associations between gender identity, expression, and voice identity.

Healthy Group Vocal Technique in Choral Classrooms

Goals for Healthy Singing

Voice professionals teach healthy singing techniques to their individual students, which then transfer easily for use in choral ensemble settings. Voice professor Loraine Sims (2017), who has taught and interviewed TGE singers, suggests the following overarching goals for working with vocalists: (a) establish goals for singing, (b) develop solutions for anticipated or observed vocal challenges, (c) build solid foundations for healthy vocal technique, and (d) choose repertoire that will help students achieve singing goals successfully. Choral conductor-teachers hopefully will notice similarities between Dr. Sims's voice studio goals and benchmarks that might serve to focus group vocal techniques in ensemble classrooms. We, as authors, also advocate for a process of establishing age-appropriate and achievable vocal goals with choral ensembles. Specific vocal practices and exercises that directly benefit TGE singers and, simultaneously, aid in the development of healthy singing habits for all can be grouped into five areas:

1. Rehearsal pacing;
2. Breath activation and awareness;
3. Phonation and resonance building;
4. Developing flexibility throughout vocal registers;
5. Improving freedom of articulation.

Choral conductor-teachers may consider moving from one area to the next sequentially as a way to activate the body, mind, spirit, and voice. The accompanying exercises could also be incorporated at any point into a choral rehearsal, as a means to reinforce healthy singing technique.

Vocal Rehearsal Pacing

Vocal rehearsals equate to physical workouts, especially considering how much energy is expended by two small folds of vocal tissue and the associated muscular systems of the body that coordinate for singing. TGE singers, particularly those engaged in voice changes, may experience vocal fatigue more quickly when speaking or singing for extended periods. Honor choir conductors often will carefully pace singing in rehearsal blocks with less vocally intense activities because younger singers' voices also tend to tire quickly. One way to ensure a well-paced vocal rehearsal is through the use of semi-occluded vocal tract exercises (SOVTEs). A team of vocal experts led by University of Iowa choral music education professor Jeremy Manternach (2019) suggests that choral directors likely have used SOVTEs without necessarily knowing they were doing so. Lip trills, tongue trills, and sustained singing on voiced consonants (e.g., [m], [n], [v], [z]) are examples of SOVTEs. These exercises create back pressure on the vocal folds (see Figure 6.1), which essentially allows for "gentler vibration and more overall sound" (Manternach et al., 2019, p. 48).

Another effective set of SOVTEs involves speaking or singing through a narrow straw (Titze, 2006). A leader in voice science, Ingo Titze models straw singing techniques through a video link on the Voice Science Works website (Irene & Harris, n.d.). Considering that TGE singers may be working with limited ranges, choral conductor-teachers may find it useful to limit the range of vocal glides or slides with straw singing to intervals of a major third or a perfect fifth to start, and then move to wider intervals or voice range extremes as students develop additional skill with straw singing. Similarly, teachers should instruct students to sing within a range that is most comfortable for them during vocal glide activities. Straw singing can easily be used at any

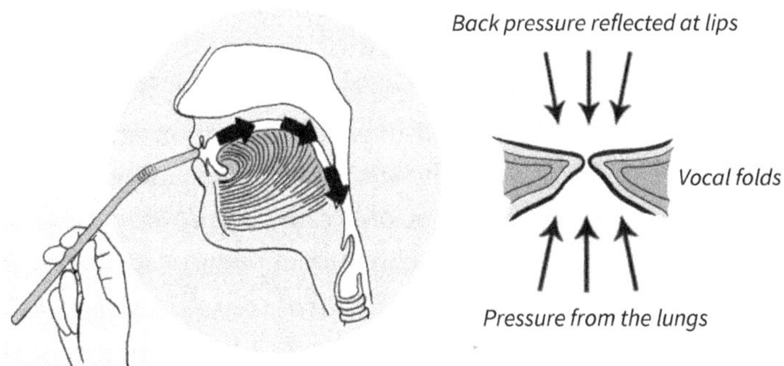

Figure 6.1. Back pressure achieved through straw singing (www.voicescienceworks.org).

point during a rehearsal, with any piece of vocal music, to help singers produce a fuller, more consistent tone with less physical effort.

Breath Awareness

Breath functions as the power source for singing, and taking time to physically prepare the body for deep breathing builds a foundation for an effective choral rehearsal. Choral conductor-teachers should be aware that some TGE students may choose to wear body-altering garments as a way to express their gender identity, including chest binders which can restrict upper chest motion or corsets which may restrict both abdominal and chest motion (Peitzmier et al., 2016). If a student chooses to share information about wearing these types of garments, remember that the disclosure was likely made in confidence. Any suggestions you may offer about the potential impact of the garments on the student's singing goals should be made with care or perhaps withheld altogether.

Body mapping allows singers to reconnect with their body and raise awareness of breath expansion and postural alignment. One effective method of developing breath awareness involves having singers lie on their back, feet flat on the floor, with knees bent at an approximately 45-degree angle to encourage a natural curvature in the spine, and then proceed to engage in slow, deep breathing. Guide students to be aware of their breath in, and out, concentrating on how their deep breaths feel and where they sense expansion and contraction. Encourage students to release tension in their lower back, allowing the spine to sink into the floor. Continue this guided sense of relaxation through the chest, upper body, shoulders, and neck while constantly encouraging awareness of each breath in, and out. While completing additional cycles of deep breaths, teachers can direct students to release jaw or tongue tension by allowing those structures to remain in a comfortable position. Choral conductor-teachers can remind singers how breathing helps to connect with body awareness through focused breathing activities. These types of activities may be particularly helpful with students who feel uncomfortable with their body image. Once positive connections have been made between body and breath, singers may engage in breath-activation exercises.

Through pulsing breaths with alternating unvoiced and voiced consonant pairs, singers move closer to the type of breath compression used in singing. Choral conductor-teachers can initially model patterns of three alternating consonant pairs and ask students to repeat: [f]/[v], [f]/[v], [f]/[v]. Other echo combinations may include [s]/[z], [p]/[b], and [θ]/[ð]. This activity can be slightly modified to transition from breath activation to phonation. Simply direct students to start exhalation/phonation on a voiced consonant, like [z], for four beats at a comfortable pitch, and then to switch seamlessly to a vowel, like [u], for an additional four beats at the same pitch. This transitional exercise leads naturally into more extended phonation activities.

Phonation and Resonance

Choral conductor-teachers can provide an effective foundation for choral rehearsals by gradually warming up the vocal folds and encouraging space for resonant singing. The use of semi-occluded vocal tract exercises (SOVTEs) encourages a gradual warm-up pace and reduces tension in the vocal mechanism and surrounding body tissues. Straw singing, as previously described, helps to lengthen the vocal tract and build resonant space. Singers may be able to focus more specifically on individual technique by striving to create a relaxed space in the neck and around the jaw while singing through a paper, plastic, or OOVO straw (Lundquist, 2020). Start SOVTEs in the mid-to-low register, moving first by intervals of a third, fifth, and gradually up to and beyond an octave for a gently paced warm up. Trained musical theatre performer MJ (she/her or they/them; trans woman; Black) speaks of her experience with lip trills as a phonation exercise as suggested by her voice teacher:

> Lip trills. It's funny. We start up with lip trills and then from lip trills, we go through different passaggi with the lip trills. Because mostly with people, when they think of lip trills, they think of the siren. We don't want to do the siren because we don't want to negate our middle and head because everybody just goes all the way up. Like [*performs siren*] just go up to the siren and they forget everything in between. And that's what we need to work on is everything in between. So that was new information to me. And while we were doing it, the first few times were a little hard and then once I started doing it every day, it became a lot easier for me. So now there isn't much of a break from my head voice to my falsetto. There really isn't a break. It's just a placement thing. It's just a little flip, and even though everyone says it, they don't tell you how to navigate that flip. So yeah, [my voice teacher has] been helping me navigate through that.

A list of suggested phonation exercises to help build warm, consistent resonance can be found in Appendix D.

Developing Vocal Flexibility

Once singers have had an opportunity to gradually warm up their instrument and build resonant space, choral conductor-teachers may begin the process of guiding students through the *passaggi*, or transition points between voice registers. Trans students engaging in voice feminization or masculinization may experience fatigue with too much repetition of these vocal exercises. Teachers may offer that all ensemble students return to straw singing, singing on a voiced consonant, or simply taking a moment to rest and relax the neck and jaw muscles, as well as the larynx, if they are experiencing tension or strain while singing. The exercises in Appendix D include suggestions for specific vowels and consonants to aid in coordinating resonance and appropriate placement of the lips, tongue, and jaw—all components associated with our vocal articulation system.

Improving Articulation

Choral conductor-teachers can constantly monitor singing tension by listening for strained production, or hyper phonation, and by visually observing signs of tension in the neck, jaw, lips, and tongue. When singers attempt to access lower pitches, they may press or constrict muscles in the neck to "reach" notes that are still in development. On the contrary, when a singer seeks higher pitches, they may push their vocal mechanism upward in the neck to "hit" notes in the upper extremes of their vocal register. Lu (he/him; transgender man; white) describes a voice jury, or exam, during which his upper register was uneasy:

> The best example of this was on my jury. I had all this music learned super well. I had to switch one out three weeks before my jury cause it was just not an option, but the day of my jury, I sang my first song and the high notes were very scary, but I sang it and it was fine. I didn't crack too much, but then for the second song the jury panel said, "okay, what is the best song that you can sing that is going to feel good today?" And like none of the other ones were, they all had a note or two that was no longer an option.

By putting too much pressure on their vocal folds, a singer may experience an abrupt break in phonation, which can be physically uncomfortable and lead to vocal damage if attempted repeatedly over time. By incorporating a [ja] syllable and legato-style singing, specific exercises encourage a gentle stretch and relaxation of the tongue muscle (see Appendix D). Some students may sing with too much breath in the tone, known as hypo phonation, which can be the result of the vocal folds not closing properly. Singers who undergo hormone replacement therapy (HRT) involving testosterone may experience a tonal gap between accessible pitches. These students can benefit from exercises designed to find glottal closure, like a comfortably pitched "uh-oh." Suggested articulation exercises in Appendix D are intended to aid singers in reducing vocal fatigue by releasing tongue and jaw tension.

Inclusive Choral Techniques

Vocal Identity and Gender Identity

Joshua's dissertation research highlighted the unique quandary of the connection (or lack thereof) between a TGE person's vocal identity and gender identity. A 2017 *Choral Journal* article based on the last chapter of the dissertation chronicles the idea of a disconnect between gender identity and vocal identity, using the label "gender trouble":

> Some choral conductor-teachers may already have experience with a similar construct: it is not only trans singers who face "gender trouble" in the choral context—countertenors or cisgender females who sing tenor can be considered "voice variant"—where there is some disconnect between one's perceived gender and one's voice (Bond, 2017b). [. . .] Some trans singers may revel in the fact that their voice does not match society's notions of how their voice should sound (Zimman, 2014). Other trans persons consider the voice a vital way that they "do" their gender in society. Choral music educators can determine through conversation the level of connection, if any, between a trans student's voice and gender identity. Based on this conversation, a personalized voice part plan can be devised. Conceptually, this is similar to middle-level choral educators who modify, adapt, or compose voice parts to fit the vocal range of singers in the midst of the voice change (Ramsey, 2008). Vocal health should always be taken into consideration, of course, but the connection between the choral experience and gender identity may determine whether or not a student continues to sing in choir. [. . .] One necessary caveat here is that if a choral music educator determines that a student is not able to sing healthily in their preferred voice range, a rapport should be developed between student and educator in which the teacher is comfortable recommending that the student stay on the same voice part that they had previously been singing—at least temporarily. (Palkki, 2017, p. 25)

In light of this variability, it is important that choral conductor-teachers are sensitive when helping TGE singers find the appropriate voice part in a choral setting. Dane (she/her; trans woman; Black [African, Cuban, Indigenous]) recalls a sense of loss during adolescent voice change:

> Puberty was—the voice change . . . was very traumatic for me. I can definitely tell you that much. Because I loved being a soprano. I loved it. And it wasn't—it really wasn't—it didn't have anything to do with my gender expression, and I know what you mean by, like, some people are like "oh my god my voice." I totally get that. For

> me it was more like, it was just like beautiful. Soprano, to my ear, I could listen to a soprano, whether she's a gospel soprano, an opera soprano (a good one), I could listen to them all day.

Again, for some individuals, vocal identity is central to who they are in a given context. A disconnect between vocal identity and gender identity can be troublesome for some and traumatic for others. On the contrary, TGE persons can also feel no sense of disconnect between their vocal and gender identities, as evidenced by Sara (she/her; woman; white), a participant in Joshua's dissertation: "I'm a girl and I'm bass and I own that" (Palkki, 2016, p. 137). Vocal development, like identity development, is unique to each individual, which is why we, as authors, continue to emphasize that we teach *people.*

Voice Part Assignments

Some TGE singers will be very easy to place within the typical SATB (soprano, alto, tenor, bass) framework of a choir. As Emily (she/her; trans woman; white) says: "The fact that I'm a tenor—the relationship between me and my voice doesn't feel dysphoric in itself, without the intrusion of a conductor mis-gendering me." In other words, Emily would only find rehearsal troubling if a director referred to the tenors by gender (e.g., "Let me hear all the men sing their tenor and bass parts"). Consider another possible scenario: if a trans woman arrives at an audition singing a bass aria and is comfortable singing bass in choir, then a simple solution has presented itself. However, the conductor-teacher should remain cognizant of gendered language despite this. *Remember that we as educators likely will have TGE students who are not yet "out."* Other TGE singers' placements will take more time and care because they may wish to sing a voice part that helps them affirm their gender identity.

Flexible Voice Leading

Teachers of TGE students wishing to make a significant voice part shift (e.g., from soprano to tenor) will need to develop a personalized approach for those students, not altogether different from that of middle-school choral educators who create edited or "hybrid" voice parts for students with changing voices (e.g., Bowers, 2008; Ramsey, 2008; Palkki, 2017). Consider a situation in which a trans male who previously sang soprano and now prefers to sing tenor joins your choir. The student has a developing lower vocal range, and he can sing the tenor line consistently in several pieces of music you have programmed.

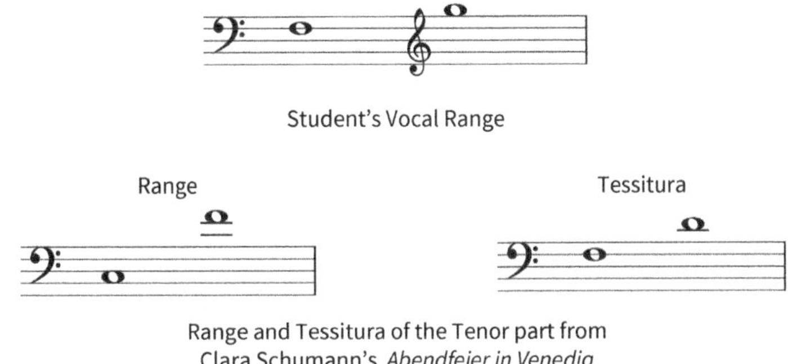

Figure 6.2. Vocal range and tessitura illustration.

Still, there are other selections in which the tenor line dips below this singer's accessible range. What do you do? Figure 6.2 illustrates the student's vocal range and the range and tessitura of the tenor part for one of your selections, Clara Schumann's *Abendfeier in Venedig*. With careful score study and conversation with the student, you both identify places in which they can move from the tenor line to the alto line, and vice versa, to continue to sing without interruption. Figure 6.3 illustrates an excerpt from Schumann's score, indicating the opportunities for flexible voice leading.

Seating and Standing Arrangements

Choral conductor-teachers create seating and standing arrangements to improve the overall sound of vocal ensembles. Balance and blend of an ensemble can be impacted by the location of individual singers within a vocal ensemble. Choral conductor-teachers wishing to learn more about choral configuration may be interested in Kari Adams's overview of the topic (2019). Whether or not an "out" trans student is involved in a choir, teachers should carefully consider seating and standing arrangements. With thought and careful planning, choral conductor-teachers can design arrangements in which TGE singers can be successful and comfortable vocally and socially. For example, a transmasculine singer in the alto section may wish to wear a tuxedo, as opposed to a concert dress. As a way to honor this TGE singer, the teacher may have them stand at the edge of the alto section, next to the tenors. Vocally, the singer will remain within their voice part block, and they will likely feel more comfortable standing next to similarly dressed performers. Camden (he/him; trans man; Latinx/white) reinforces this idea to aid conductor-teachers with seating and standing arrangements:

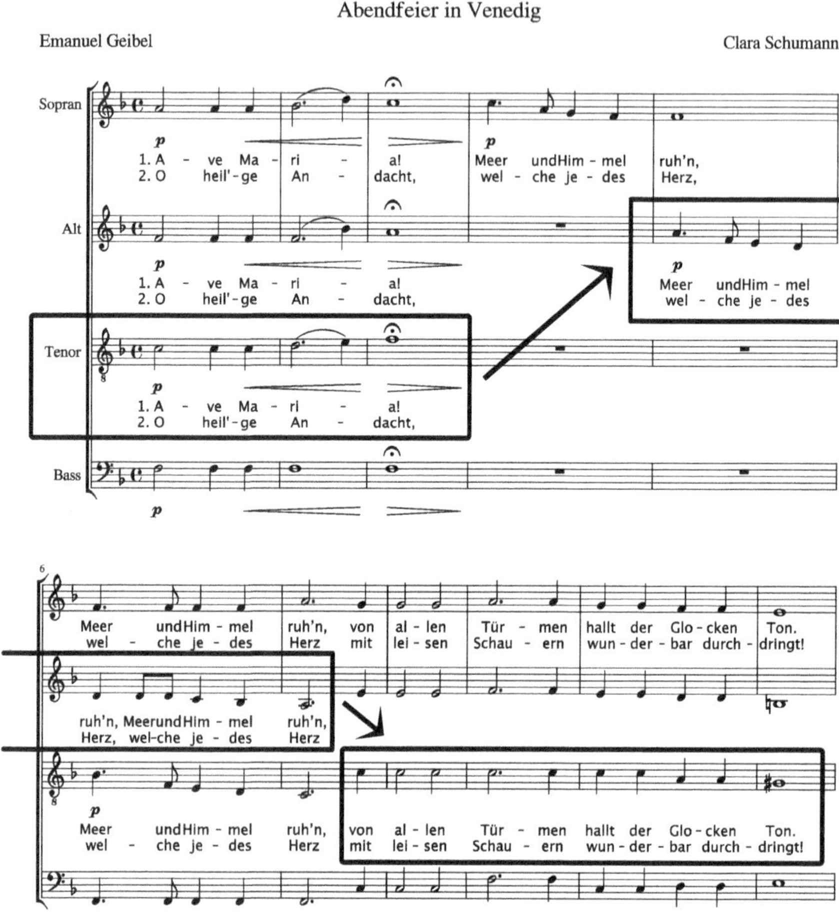

Figure 6.3. Flexible voice leading in Clara Schumann's *Abendfeier in Venedig.*

> Remember that in a choral setting there are many ways to allow your students to feel more comfortable regarding the pitch and resonance of their singing voice. You can place trans/gender-expansive students in a SATB choir (if applicable) and allow them to sing with a voice part that matches their gender identity. For example, a transgender man singing with the tenors or a transgender woman singing with the altos (if they are not on hormone replacement therapy). You can also place trans individuals next to those wearing the same concert attire as them if it is not gender neutral. For example, placing a trans woman next to everyone else wearing dresses instead of making them stand out in the middle of all the tuxedos.

Such careful standing arrangements may be less crucial visually if all students wear more gender-neutral uniforms, as discussed in Chapter 5. Likewise, ensembles singing in mixed formations (e.g., vocal quartets distributed equally on choral risers) offer greater options for TGE persons. Flexible singer placement can help alleviate student discomfort, particularly in honor choir settings where other options may not be readily available.

Rehearsal Vernacular

Choral conductor-teachers often refer to tenors and basses as "men" and sopranos and altos as "women." While this would not be a problem for anyone singing a voice part that matches their gender identity, it can serve as an obstacle for TGE singers (e.g., a trans woman who sings bass). Mari (she/her; transgender woman; Latina) discusses this "degendering" of choral rehearsal pedagogy:

> The most helpful thing would be to fundamentally take gender out of pedagogy because we overly emphasize gender. Music teachers that teach instrumental ensembles or instrumental lessons don't feel a need to impose a gender on the instrument. That's just not important. And we can do the same as vocal teachers by speaking about the voice as an instrument—contextualizing singing tenor as if a student is picking up a tenor sax or singing soprano as if a student is picking up a flute. We can psychologically rewire ourselves, for example, by addressing "sopranos and altos," rather than addressing "girls" or "ladies." It's not that it's toxic or that most people aren't cis. It's really just that cisgender-normative language is counterproductive even for cis singers.
>
> Most of the students that I've taught have been young cis women. Some of them go to college only having sung alto two for all of their high school experience because that's what they were told to do in choir. And then, they discover that they're a soprano. So, even for cis people, it's limiting specifically for teachers to pigeonhole their students or their young singers in any capacity at all. Soprano, alto, tenor, bass, they're voice parts, sure. But they're really just instruments that students are picking up. In the same capacity that some musicians play flute and trumpet and horn, some singers can sing tenor and soprano and alto, you know? Taking gender out of voice classification is so simple, and I think it's extremely helpful.

Once again, it is important to recall that some TGE persons seek alignment between their vocal identity and their gender identity, while others do not. Mari's comments also serve as a reminder that choral conductor-teachers can move students from one voice part to another while their vocal instruments are still developing, as this process aids in expanding vocal range and improving associated aural skills.

Choral conductor-teachers can label and use voice parts when referring to specific sections, as a simple way to remove gender from classroom language; similar to removing "boys and girls" from our vernacular with younger students, "ladies and gentlemen" (and other binary terms) should also be discontinued to promote a more inclusive music-making environment. Aaliyah (she/her; trans woman; Black) describes an instance in which a gender noncomforming singer in an LGBT chorus felt unwelcome when the conductor said,

> "Ladies and gentlemen," and this person just got outraged and was like, "I can't believe this." And then this person ended up leaving and Trevor [the conductor] was like, "What did I do wrong?" And I was just like . . . When it comes to non-gender conforming people, really—it's hard, you know?

Matthew grew up in the Southern United States and can relate to the challenges of changing old habits. He had to unlearn the "boys and girls"/"ladies and gentlemen" language that he had always heard used in school music settings. He changed his rehearsal vernacular with repeated *intentional* practice, over time. He still makes mistakes from time to time, acknowledges them, and moves on with rehearsal activities. Choral conductor-teachers easily can move away from gendered language by reframing a gendered mindset to one that focuses on more accurate language in rehearsal settings. For example, if you want the sopranos and altos to sing, simply say "sopranos and altos" (or "trebles"); if you want the tenors and basses to sing, ask for "tenors and basses" (or "low voices"). These distinctions may become even more prevalent when performing treble- or bass-clef only repertoire, as our collaborator Dana (she/her; female; white) discusses:

> JOSHUA: Did you ever feel uncomfortable singing tenor?
>
> DANA: Only when there's a TBB arrangement just for guys. I feel uncomfortable and prefer not to participate. My main choral group did one not too long ago: "Stand by Me." No way I was going to get up with all the guys, and that was OK. I also love to slide over to the alto section when we do an SSA piece. It would be very awkward to sit it out with the guys with all the ladies standing and singing.

As choral conductor-teachers, we can change our rehearsal vernacular with thought, intentionality, and repeated practice over time. Another way we can be more deliberate about inclusive rehearsal practices is to address the context of text in the pieces we program.

Contextualizing Heteronormative and Cisnormative Texts

The study of texts used in choral repertoire can aid teachers and students in understanding possible connections between text and music and leads to stronger expression of the composer's musical intent. We, as choral conductor-teachers must take time to research the context of the text, just as we take time to complete formal and musical analysis prior to rehearsal. Singers should also have opportunities to learn about poetic text and to identify meaningful ways to musically express that text. Composers often set poetic texts that speak to the ideas of love and relationships. Many of these texts describe heterosexual relationships between two people assumed to be cisgender. Choral conductor-teachers can engage ensemble members in dialogue that assists with contextualization of these types of texts. Avoiding these brave, vulnerable conversations may alienate queer students, who are often unable to see themselves in the context of the poetry. Choral conductor-teachers who make the effort to speak with students about heteronormative and cisnormative texts, specifically, can make an important difference in the ensemble experiences of TGE persons.

There are various options for ensemble leaders and participants to consider when programming music with text. Perhaps the least helpful option is to study and perform a piece without any discussion of the text. In doing so, students and teachers bypass any opportunity to establish connections between music and text and consequently, musical expression during performance may be limited, at best. A second option requires conductor-teachers to build in rehearsal time for discussions that contextualize text and to discuss potentially challenging or problematic aspects of the poetry. This approach takes time and planning, but conductor-teachers would also be demonstrating respect for students and for the music by facilitating thoughtful conversations. Finally, a third option is to collectively arrive at a decision not to study and perform a particular work because of a problematic text. The conductor-teacher may wish to have a "plan B" selection in anticipation of this particular outcome. Both the second and third options would open a space to consider the *context* of the text. Audience members might also be interested to learn more about a given text through an announcement from the podium or a program note in which choral conductor-teachers could provide a synopsis of in-rehearsal discourse—thus extending the learning process from the classroom to the performance space.

Musicians benefit from the ability to make connections between the music they perform and their own lived experiences. Consider two examples in which a small amount of teacher-student discussion could help students better understand the context of a choral text. In the first example, a conductor-teacher programs Brahms's "Neckereien" (1864), translated into English as "teasing." In this Romantic period part-song, the poet depicts a dialogue between a male suitor and the woman who wants little or nothing to do with the person pursuing her. A brief conversation about the back-and-forth banter of this text would place the story in an appropriate historical context. A choral conductor-teacher could simply add that while this particular text describes a heterosexual flirtation, they value and respect queer viewpoints, even though those perspectives are not represented in this text. Out of such a conversation, the ensemble may arrive at a decision to focus on the teasing aspect of the interpersonal exchanges, which Brahms highlights in his setting of the two characters. In another example, ensemble leader chooses to program "Where Your Bare Foot Walks" by David Childs (2009). The composer sets this text by Rumi, in part, as an expression of love. Close study of the actual text, however, reveals no gender distinctions in deeply felt expressions of love from one person to another. Teacher-student dialogue about this text could potentially lead into a focus on compassion and romantic love between two individuals, regardless of gender identity. TGE singers may more readily relate to this poetic expression of love, facilitated through conversation and study of the music and text. Keep in mind that these types of rehearsal conversations need not be led solely for the purposes of honoring TGE students, but rather as a way to include them in music-learning activities: contextualizing potentially heteronormative and cisnormative poetic texts enriches music-making experiences for all vocal ensemble participants.

Constructive dialogue to further musical understanding can be a valuable component of gender-complex education (Rands, 2009). Recall from Chapter 2, the four components of Rands's approach to help teachers and students explore gender diversity:

1. Reflect on ways that gender operates in classroom situations.
2. Respect the idea of gender diversity in spectrums.
3. Analyze how gender is represented in classroom situations.
4. Create gender equity for all students.

The types of rehearsal dialogues discussed in the previous examples would meet each of the components of the gender-complex approach to education. One of our collaborators, Emily (she/her; trans woman; white), speaks to the importance of creating gender equity for all students through the process of repertoire selection:

> I think one of the things that doesn't get talked about often enough is the repertoire issue. It goes beyond the question of giving varied repertoire to your treble and tenor-bass ensembles. People also need to think about the way gender gets articulated in mixed rep—you know, "here's the verse where the sopranos and altos sing the words of the pretty young maiden, and then here come the big strong men. . . ." It's a matter of extending your thoughtfulness about repertoire beyond the question of "what am I having the treble chorus sing" and asking what sexist or binary reinforcing or whatever messages might the content of even a mixed piece send.

Choral conductor-teachers have a shared responsibility to consider the texts of chosen repertoire and how those texts may affect students, especially students from marginalized populations such as TGE youth. Teachers need not address this process alone, however, as students may be empowered to assist through facilitated conversation.

Recap

The choral classroom environment involves many issues that can be perceived as highly gendered. Through small, mindful changes, choral conductor-teachers can honor TGE students and create a more welcoming space for singers who want and deserve to feel supported and safe. These mindful changes are often successful because of open, respectful conversations between teachers and students. When ensemble stakeholders understand the goals and the structure of a performing group, the focus of interpersonal interactions can be more centrally focused on people making music. Choral conductor-teachers can be a major force for good in the lives of TGE persons, particularly as educators continue to learn about vocal pedagogy that supports healthy singing. As conductor-teachers, we may never know that we *have* or *have had* TGE persons in our classrooms. We can, however, demonstrate respect for TGE singers through thoughtful application of inclusive choral techniques. If we lead with respect for the persons in our learning environments and we strive to honor TGE singers in our ensembles, choral conductor-teachers can realize opportunities to be a positive force in the vocal experiences of TGE students.

Reflect/Remember

1. Reflect on your own vocal pedagogy knowledge/training. How does the material covered in this chapter align with what you already know? How might the vocal pedagogy principles outlined here best serve singers in your ensembles?
2. Make a list of what you consider to be gendered aspects of the choral program(s) with which you are associated. How does the gender binary manifest? Are binary uniforms used? "Single-gender" choirs? Once you have completed your list, consider which of these aspects might be changed and what steps you might take in that process. Also consider what stakeholders besides yourself might assist with any changes.
3. Review the contents of your personal choral octavo library, your school/church choral library, and/or your state's required repertoire list. Identify titles that have highly "gendered" texts and devise possible inclusive teaching plans for those pieces. How will you honor TGE students in your music-making experiences?

7
From Our Collaborators

Trans and gender-expansive (TGE) persons have a great deal to share with school music teachers. Stories (especially positive stories) about TGE persons are necessary to create understanding and empathy in a society where conceptions about gender are expanding (Namaste, 2000; Wilchins, 1997). One of the purposes of this project was to help trans musicians (and teachers of trans musicians) to portray "[their] own narrative" (Wilchins, 1997). The final chapter of this book is, therefore, from our collaborators. As Lu (he/him; transgender man; white) so eloquently states:

> I should be more involved in [the trans] community, but I haven't yet had the chance to, but I think that's definitely something I can see myself doing as well. Just, you know, the reason you're doing these interviews is there's all this research coming out that the trans voices are not as centered often. We are talked about, but we are not the ones talking.

Self-ownership of trans persons' stories by those to whom they belong is a cornerstone of transgender theory. Nagoshi suggests, "in [transgender theory], embodiment is seen as an essential component of the self" (2014, p. 86). In addition, Trans-identity theory proposes an "explicitly self-constructed aspect of identity, one that derives meaning from the narrative of lived experiences" (Nagoshi et al., 2014, p. 87). Finally, "Trans studies also have the opportunity to move away from purely theoretical discourse and move toward issues of the agency of real transgender individuals" (Nagoshi et al., 2014, p. 88). Learning with and from TGE persons honors their lived experiences and creates opportunities for strong music-learning communities.

In an effort to lend credence to the voices of our collaborators, we wanted them to have the last word in this book—an attempt to mitigate the unbalanced positionality that we referred to in the Introduction. As our collaborator JB (they/them; Non-binary; white) notes:

> Every group, especially those that are not in power, not in leadership, every group represents one tile, one color on the mosaic of people in our world. Some groups

Honoring Trans and Gender-Expansive Students in Music Education. Matthew L. Garrett and Joshua Palkki, Oxford University Press. © Oxford University Press 2021. DOI: 10.1093/oso/9780197506592.003.0008

> are recognized, celebrated, but not empowered, which is to say, they are not the ones in power. Everyone deserves to be represented by a seat at the table.

To that end, we asked each person the following question: "If you had an opportunity to stand in front of a room of music educators and tell them what you think they need to know about honoring trans and gender-expansive youth, what would you say to them?" Their uninterrupted and inspiring responses follow. Listen, and hear their voices.

Aaliyah (listen to Aaliyah's advice in ▶ Audio 7.1)

(she/her; trans woman; Black)

Just to be aware cause . . . some people just don't like to be called certain things or certain names, and I think they should always be like—before they even like sign up for a class, it should be a questionnaire: This is how you identify cause you know, sometimes some applications would ask you, "well what's your government name?" "What is your preferred name?" So, under your preferred name they should be saying "what is your gender at birth and what is your preferred gender?" Or "your preferred pronouns?" [. . .]

Also, to be mindful to people bullying these people cause there's always going to be somebody in the class that doesn't care. I think it should be like, at the beginning of the class say—not really point out people that are trans or non-gender-conforming, say, "Hey, we're a school that does not discriminate on race, gender, creed. If I find out that you are making fun of or bullying somebody that you may not understand or you don't get along with, we will ask you to leave the class." You know, there should be [a] certain type of consequences because that's how these kids in high school are dying because none of the teachers are—[*trailing off*] it needs to be more education [for] teachers, parents. Maybe there should be, especially at parent-teacher meetings, they need to talk about that, you know? Or like— do they still do introductions when you go to the colleges? Maybe like at those introductions, [say] "this is a school that teaches equality, and this is what's going to be happening on this campus. If you don't feel comfortable, then maybe this is not the school for you."

Selected lyrics from Aaliyah's single "This Is Me" (Daniels, 2019):

> *This is me*
> *This is who I am*
> *Never gonna change to make you happy*
> *Cause you don't understand*

I lived a life to make everyone happy
But now I'm free
Free to be the me I want to be
No more hurt, no more pain
No more heartache
No more lies, who I am
I will not break [. . .]
I am the woman that you see today
And I'm not going away
Love and respect me
Take me for who I am
Accept me for being me
I'm still the same person inside now
Just living in my truth
Now that I've lived a life that the world wants me to be.

Abby (listen to Abby's story in ▶ Audio 7.2)

(they/them; Gender non-binary Black)

I learned something great from Joe, when [he] went back to Kansas and he was telling me about one of the students. When he was taking roll, he called them by their name, and the other student who said, "no, no, they go by Jack now." And he was so impressed that it was the student that was teaching him something. And so, if I was in front of a bunch of people K through 12, I would say really listen to the kids. Listen to how they present themselves. You might want to call him a boy soprano, but you don't call her a female soprano. So why does this kid have to be a boy soprano? Why are you giving him that little marker on there? Listen and help them develop their voices. Because if you help them develop their voices, they're going to develop their minds and it's just going to be an amazing new journey for this next generation. Really not adding your perception to it—not adding how you grew up and how you think a boy is or how a girl is or this or that. Really you have to go in there with a very gender neutral slate in order to really understand and help them along their musical journey. [. . .]

The journey that you're about to take as a teacher is such an amazing journey and they're at a point where they are now removing the gender spectrum and really accepting a new gender variance. I think that these teachers will already know this, but I want to encourage them to remember that the foundation you lay in that child today is what's going to take them all the way through their lives. [. . .] You're laying down a foundation that is so strong that you'll never know what you're doing. But just do it well and enjoy that process and enjoy these kids. Cause 20, 30, 50 years down the line, you see the fruits of that labor, you know? I think that's what's so great about what they're about to do. I love that you're doing this for educators because we are in a new realm of music—new realm of the world. When you and I were kids, if you're a boy, you were going to be T1, T2, bass, baritone. And if you sang in the soprano or alto range, they would say, boy soprano. But they never did that with the female identified. You're either soprano or alto. But now these future educators will know it's so much more than that. And they'll start helping people develop their voice in their instrument. Way beyond where we were years ago.

Andy (listen to Andy's advice in ▶ Audio 7.3)

(he/him; FTM transgender; white)

I would say make [trans and gender-expansive students] feel supported but don't make them feel ostracized, cause sometimes by being over, I don't want to say over-supportive, but like making a bigger deal about it than it needs to be kind of ostracizes a person from their peers. Something [my high-school band director] did, we've always been pretty close. So, like the end of my sophomore year he could kinda' tell that something was going on, that I was not in a great place. And so, he took me in his office and was like, you know, "What's going on?" And he was one of the first teachers I came out to. I think knowing that music attracts queer people. I don't know why, but you know, that's always been a big community. And to realize that music is an outlet for a lot of queer folk and that you should expect that you're going to have queer people in your class.

Avery (listen to Avery's suggestions in ▶ Audio 7.4)

(he/him or they/them; Agender; white)

If you're a music educator, know that one of the greatest things you can do for your trans and gender-expansive students is to put them in the driver's seat. Talk with your student ahead of time to determine what they are and aren't comfortable with. Listen to their concerns and take concrete steps to address them. Normalize gender-neutral language and pronouns and model the behavior you want to see from your class. Most importantly, create a safe space for whole-ensemble discussion around these important topics, even if you think they don't have much to do with music. They do, and it *will* have an impact.

Brendan (listen to Brendan's recommendations in ▶ Audio 7.5)

(he/him; transgender male; white)

Give students options. Be aware of different options and things that you may not expect. Even if you don't think anyone is going to take you up on it, offer . . . something that really helped for me was when people would just offer, "we can use different pronouns if you want. Just let us know." Posing that to your students makes it easier for them to talk to you later and to come to terms with it themselves. I think just saying you support people. Even if you don't know if they need the support. Saying it again and again even if you think it's redundant. To whoever is struggling, especially a high school kid, that's got to mean the world—or middle school even.

I think it's helpful to post up resources in your classroom even if you think no one is going to need them—just have them there. If no one looks at them, fine. Even if it's good for one kid, that's great. I don't know why but that sign I saw in the cafeteria of the college I went to for music camp . . . it had the male symbol, male symbol and the female symbol, female symbol together—homosexuality with the symbols or whatever—REALLY impactful. That was not even for me, but I got something out of it. You never know who's going to be affected. I would just say have the resources available and state your support even if you don't know who needs it.

Camden (listen to Camden's advice in ▶ Audio 7.6)

(he/him; trans man; Latinx/white)

Please allow your trans and gender-expansive students to correct you if you make a mistake. By encouraging your students to correct you, it puts you in a position that shows them that you don't know everything about their community and that you're passionate about being educated. Also, please ask your students what you can do for them to make them feel the most supported in your classroom, whether that's everyone sharing their pronouns, using gender neutral language, implementing gender neutral concert attire (if possible), etc. Please openly and frequently talk about your goal of making your classroom a safe space for trans and gender-expansive people. [. . .] Also, if you have a transgender student who is stealth (meaning that they are perceived as the gender they identify as to society and do not want to disclose they are trans to other people), try and think ahead in regards to situations that may "out" them as transgender. For example, talk to the student privately about where they feel comfortable changing or being fitted for concert attire. Lastly, by creating such a comfortable and safe space for these students, it will encourage others to come out and be their authentic selves as well.

Dana (listen to Dana's story in ▶ Audio 7.7)

(she/her; female; white)

When you're a transgender [TG] child, you're aware of gender differences, but not overly burdened with them. If I think back on being three or four, I remember having mostly girlfriends and not so many boyfriends. I was aware of the gender disconnect, but it didn't affect me emotionally. However, when I hit junior high, the hormones started flowing, and I became very aware of my gender identity issue. I used to kid myself that I would outgrow it. We all embrace our sexuality in different ways, but for TG people this is where the gap starts to open. The good news is that kids today have access to information that didn't exist for me, so coming to grips with the TG state of being is easier, but never easy. It's very hard to come out to yourself and almost impossible to come out to others. TG kids are desperate to find out who they are. Parents and teachers need to remember that they have instant access to both good and potentially harmful information, so caution and supervision are essential.

I believe as humans, when we feel that people have our backs and they're on our side and there's others like yourself (and you probably have this understanding too)—that's what I'm looking for. Personally, I don't want to shout it from the rooftops. If people ask, I tell them I used to be TG, now I'm just an ordinary woman, and that's what I always wanted to be. I don't want to make a big deal out of it. Sometimes it's almost intimidating because, "Oh, you're transgender, we love you." I don't want any of that. I just want to be one of the girls.

When dealing with transgender children, or adults for that matter, don't make a big deal about it. I think you need to be aware of a transgender child in a classroom or other adult supervisory situation. This is helpful because you can watch to see if there's any protecting or guidance needed or if there's any bullying or abuse taking place. It's certainly your job to be vigilant for that. But even if it happens, be discreet. If you aren't, you're just going to draw attention to the whole situation, potentially making it worse.

Dane

(she/her; trans woman; Black [African, Cuban, Indigenous])

For me personally I think schools can stop being a part of the problem. [. . .] I think that we can make an environment in school that does not need to model the pain and the trauma that we face outside of school—that we have faced growing up in school that then becomes the norm of society. I think that we can really make bullying not okay. We need to have trans people really in the schools, teaching. We need to have training—we need to have the states paying for trans people to come and train teachers how to teach trans students. We need to re-vamp the way we teach history, and in particular US history, and the United States of America, because we need to add back in that trans identities and queer identities existed in Indigenous cultures. [*long pause*] And we need to stop allowing our teachers to bring their own prejudices to school. [. . .]

And we also need more queer teachers who are willing to actually stand up for queer students. 'Cause oftentimes I find that people in positions of power are afraid of losing their power and their privilege, RIGHT?! . . . they'll let other people just kind of flounder and drown, and then we have this same structural oppression being perpetuated. And it's 20 years later, and someone like you is sitting with someone like me once again saying, "what can we do to make things better?"

Elliott (listen to Elliott's recommendations in ▶ Audio 7.8)

(he/him; trans gay male; white)

I would say just one: don't make a huge deal about them being trans and, you know, things like that. 'Cause a lot of people, they want to pass—like stealth. They [trans guys] just want to be seen as a guy. So just refer to them as a guy and their name and stuff like that. And then just be accepting of them. Just be there for them if they need some extra support, whether they don't have supportive parents or they don't have other supportive teachers or kids are bullying them or whatever, just try to be there for them.

Emily (listen to Emily's advice in ▶ Audio 7.9)

(she/her; trans woman; white)

There are some very concrete things that I wish music educators and choral directors knew. One is not using gendered words to refer to voice parts. And then there's the whole concert attire question, the importance of not just letting people switch to the other binary option, but instead coming up with a policy that isn't "here are two choices, pick one." [. . .] You know, come up with something, whether it's all black, or black pants or skirt and a solid-colored shirt, or whatever, something that's not gendered, and that, even if your words for it aren't gendered, isn't effectively reinscribing a binary model of the world in its particulars even if you haven't given the two options gendered names.

Granger Family (listen to the Granger Family's conversation in ⊙ Audio 7.10)

Gabriella (she/her; female; white)
Quincy (he/him; male; white)
Victoria (she/her; female; white)

GABRIELLA: It is hard. [My teachers] Sort of like, didn't really just announce to the whole class, "this girl is transgender." "Okay, okay. . . . I can tell the people that on my own," so . . . yeah.

VICTORIA (MOM): And they use your right name, your right pronouns probably?

GABRIELLA: Mhmm [*affirmative sound*]

JOSHUA: What does it feel like to be out as trans in elementary school?

GABRIELLA: Oh, it feels good to be different. [. . .]

QUINCY (DAD): If you could tell music teachers how to best honor and celebrate transgender students, what would you tell them?

GABRIELLA: Probably hang trans flags possibly, would be a good idea. And like . . . [*pause*] I don't know. Maybe I like hanging trans flags.

QUINCY: Okay, so, showing their support in their classroom?

GABRIELLA: Yeah.

JB (listen to JB's suggestions in ⊙ Audio 7.11)

(they/them; Non-binary; white)

Don't gender your [choral] ensembles, period. I know that it's easy to do and it avoids a lot of concerns. It does bring up the question of, "do students just kind of choose what ensemble they want to be in?" And the answer is, "put students in the ensemble to which they are going to want to show up every day." If you put a student in an ensemble where they're not comfortable or don't want to come to the ensemble every day, you are not serving that student. Period—as the kids say, Period!

Jessica (listen to Jessica's recommendations in ▶ Audio 7.12)

(she/her or they/them; transfeminine non-binary; white)

What I would say to those teachers who are making first steps to welcome and accommodate their trans students is to rely on the thing which connects all musicians and that's to listen . . . listen. Find as many people who are willing to talk to you about their gender and about their transition and about their journey. Find as many people who are willing to talk to you about it and just listen. . . . All too often, [cis] people are ready to give advice. "Are you sure this is what you want?" "Are you sure you're ready for this?" "Are you sure you won't go back?" I think what's really, really, really important, especially when it comes to kids, is to listen. I've met so many wonderful young trans folk from ages four all the way to adulthood. Gender isn't one of those things that people are typically—[*changing course, pause*] They know who they are. They know the things they need and the things that they want. If you try and control that in a way, if you try and give advice, even if it's coming from the best place, I don't think that's nearly as good as using your musical talent to listen.

Keizen (listen to Keizen's story in ▶ Audio 7.13)

(they/them; gender creative; Han Chinese)

Maintaining a feeling of comradery and positivity, that was something that I also really appreciated about that space [the university TTBB choir]. It's really easy in masculine spaces for the insults and the one-upmanship to come out, and that very rarely came out. I've noticed over the couple of years that some of the senior members will say something if someone says something disparaging or even disparaging self-talk or—you know, just that softness and that kindness just takes a second. And it really, I think sets a tone for the group. [. . .]

Most teachers, because we have to assert authority, we may make the mistake of making authority a habit. And sometimes we don't have authority in an area and it's so important to be ready to recognize and communicate that. So, like, one area where we need to use authority appropriately is in the example I just gave where, you know, we have to assert a norm of inclusion in our classroom best we can and maintain an atmosphere of positivity and supporting each other. And you know, in other areas, this is something that I also noticed about [my choral professor], that I might ask him a question where he doesn't know the answer and he'll immediately say that he doesn't know. And that takes discernment, which takes time and effort to cultivate. And it requires us to be humble—to have to practice humility where we don't know something. And just because the student in front of us has lived experience that we don't, doesn't mean that we demand that they teach us either. So that's something cool that I noticed when [my choral professor] says he doesn't know about something, he also doesn't require me to be the one to educate him. [. . .]

And so I think a good teacher cultivates kindness and sensitivity and resourcefulness and acceptance in a way that supports students with all kinds of, rainbows of problems. Humans, right? And that was something that I kept emphasizing—I had a presentation Q & A with some music ed majors at Benedict University and that was something that I really made the core of the presentation: that we're human beings—like there's not an "us" and "them" and like, how do I learn more about them so I can support them better? That's already—that's where the obstacle is. A good teacher is a good human being and a good teaching relationship is a good relationship—a supportive relationship between human beings. And cultivating sensitivity in general is going to make it possible for us to support everyone. Because someone who is struggling with gender identity needs the same kind of support and kindness and openness that anybody else that is struggling with sexuality or body image issues or, you know, anything. And, music and choral arts I think are especially a wonderful kind of space to work on that stuff and make those connections because it is so physical and it's so emotional. And that's really why I'm in love with it.

Kim (listen to Kim's advice in ▶ Audio 7.14)

(they/them; genderqueer woman; white/Latinx)

Listen to your children. They know themselves. People develop a sense of self much younger than typically thought. The best way to support your child/friend/sibling/etc. is to listen to them and believe what they are saying about themselves. They know themselves better than you do. It can be very difficult for them to even say something. So, if they mustered up the courage to tell you, it's important to them and what they're saying has merit. If you have a notion that your child wants to tell you something, and that you may have a feeling that it is about something as important as gender identity, then find a way to support them until they are ready to say it out loud. Create an open and honest dialogue that gives them the space to feel safe to tell you who they really are. If your child can do that, then you are doing something right.

Using the correct name and pronouns for these kids is a lifesaving act. Lifesaving! 47% of trans youth will attempt suicide if their pronouns and chosen name are not respected. 47%! That drops to the national average of 11% if their name and pronouns are respected. It is a lifesaving act. I cannot stress this enough. [. . .] Especially in the arts, this is supposed to be the safe haven for people like us, you know.

Lu (listen to Lu's story in ▶ Audio 7.15)

(he/him; transgender man; white)

I think the most important thing is just keeping an open dialogue. 'Cause like, for me, my voice was changing every week or something . . . you just kind of have to take the lead of the student, how much they want to share and how much—just kind of where their thinking is. Because like I said, with my old voice teacher, she was wanting to keep the conversation open, but I didn't want to engage with that. And so, it was very stressful on me to keep having to answer these questions that I just didn't—I didn't want to go there with her. But having a teacher now who is so open and, "yeah, we can talk about it, we can go through things." She's very careful about, if she's going to ask me a question about something physical or—you know, she's very careful to be like, "hey, can I ask this of you? Is it okay if we talk about this?" It's just all about keeping open ears to the student because they might not have an avenue through someone else, so they might want to really talk about it, or they might not want to talk about it at all—it's very case by case.

Mari (listen to Mari's suggestions in ▶ Audio 7.16)

(she/her; transgender woman; Latina)

[Don't] assume anything about a person's identity. It would be helpful. I understand teachers feeling pressured to make assumptions—to project a gender on someone just because they have paperwork to do, you know. Structurally that's the world we currently live in, but it's—[*long pause*] the more you take gender out of the music, the more you're left with just the music. And that's where we want to be.

Marshall (listen to Marshall's recommendations in ▶ Audio 7.17)

(he/him; trans male; Asian-American)

I think getting to know their students and actually recognizing names and how they identify, and kind of just letting other people know how you should approach people who are trans. The staff should also take the precautions to educate themselves as well as their students on trans-related issues.

I think that one thing that all teachers should know is that you just have to be respectful toward students of all types of identity. Honestly, everyone is just trying to find who they are, and at this age, it's something really crucial yet confusing. The best thing for teachers and adults to do, is to just respect people's decisions. We should also normalize asking for people's name and pronouns, never assume them, as a lot of trans students are unable to transition, or even appear as their true self. Affirming their identity, using the correct name and pronouns, and correcting other students and teachers should be the very bare minimum. Even if you don't necessarily agree with the LGBT community, the least you can do is respect them as a person, it isn't really that hard to do so. If someone were purposefully calling you by the wrong name and pronouns, you'd be irritated and offended as well, so why do that to someone else because they're different from you? Honestly, you should just practice listening to other people and actively using correct names and pronouns toward trans students. Try putting yourself in their perspective.

Mason (Pseudonym) (listen to Mason's story in ▶ Audio 7.18)

(he/him; Trans Man; white)

I'm trying to learn that for myself so I can give what was given to me. I don't know why I felt so connected. I mean the one teacher I connected to pretty heavily was gay, but I didn't know that for a long time. So, I know there's something he must have done that made it feel like I could go to him, but I can't pinpoint it. I think just being open all of the time—it's just the way he was. A lot of teachers are . . . you know, putting up a teacher front, which is good, but when you have teachers that are very clearly, you know, this is how they react and they act and you can just vibe with them for the lack of a better term, it makes it easier to talk to them 'cause you feel like you're talking to a person and not a teacher.

Max (listen to Max's story in ▶ Audio 7.19)

(he/him; trans man; white)

It's all really subtle . . . I feel like you don't get the effect you want by just declaring "this is a safe space." In my experience that actually feels kind of dangerous, especially from cis, straight people or from privileged people in general, because often when privileged people declare something, they don't want to know that it's incorrect. So, they say, "This is a safe space and you're welcome here." And it sometimes has the opposite effect, I feel, because I think, "Okay, well I understand that you want it to be a safe space, and that your classroom being a safe space is important to you. And now I don't know if I can tell you if it's a safe space or not." So instead of declaring it, I don't mention it. If it comes up though—when things come up that are gendered or racial or touch on privilege things, that's when I make sure that my response to those things is appropriate for the space. And as much as I can, confirm to the not-so-privileged that they're safe and welcome.

So, like, for example, when my gay kid dances in class, I know that the other students are watching my response. They're also watching each other's responses. I make sure that my response to that is to be delighted with it because it's great. He's a good dancer too, you know? And for it to be genuine joy at seeing this personal expression. Or if it's not an appropriate space—this particular kid is very good at choosing appropriate times to express himself—but if it was an inappropriate time, I try to make sure that the discipline is about appropriateness of time and not appropriateness of action. And we need to make sure, especially with marginalized kids, that when they do something that isn't appropriate, that we make sure that we are clear about what exactly was inappropriate. Like, we shouldn't just say, "this bothers me." Otherwise, we risk the student thinking it's something about their core self that is inappropriate. I think that's the other thing I do—whenever I have any sort of event like that in class—I always spend time reflecting: "How did I handle this? Was this the right way to handle it? How did the kid feel afterwards?" And if the kid was upset about it, was it because they needed to be corrected? Or was I putting my own perspective and comfort over theirs? [. . .] I've practiced a lot apologizing to kids, because they deserve apologies when we mistreat them. I feel like that's something a lot of teachers really don't do. They feel like they lose power if they let kids know they've messed up. [. . .] But no—the kids will give you more power if you can make them feel like they actually have a voice. [. . .] I don't ever decide that I've succeeded at giving my students a safe place. 'Cause it's not my choice—the kids will tell me if I've succeeded or not.

And they need to . . . feel able to say that stuff to me. And so, I can't ever say I'm done because then I'm back to declaring my classroom is safe instead of actually making it safe. So, I think I'm doing okay based on what I observe from the kids. I think my space is safe based on the way that they treat me. But, you know, I'm working on it.

Melanie (listen to Melanie's advice in ▶ Audio 7.20)

(she/her; Transgender female; white)

Remember that you're teaching a human—that you're teaching somebody who—they may be different, but they have emotions, they have feelings, they have thoughts, they have hearts. And I think sometimes we get really lost on—the humanity gets lost and buried in the label. I think that's probably number one. I think number two is, it's okay to not know something, and it's okay to educate your own ignorance or to try and clear up your own ignorance. But while doing so you need to make sure that you're trying to be as respectful as possible. And if you do make a mistake—because we all make them—'fess up, apologize. Because you don't know necessarily how your words might impact somebody. But then move on. It's like when my dad would mess up—sometimes somebody would just get so hung up on a pronoun when they misgendered me and I'm like, "stop drawing attention to it." You know, an apology is okay. Move on. Don't expect trans people to educate you. For a lot of people, I've been their first trans person . . . I've kind of accepted that's my life. And, you know, that's who I am. It's not who other people are. Also, your trans student might know as much about trans things as you do, which might be nothing. They might not have—most of them probably will by this point know something, but they might not. And so, it's important for you to know—it's important for you to understand some of the intricacies of the trans experience because it is confusing. It's also important to try and keep up with everything that's changing because it's constantly changing. [. . .]

Just know that you're not perfect. And mostly just with your student, the most important thing is how comfortable they feel and that they feel loved and respected by you. Because at the end of the day, you might be the only person that shows them that love. You might be the only person that shows them that they matter—that who they are is valid and any mistakes that you make, whether it be a slip up in pronoun or a slip up in name or something, they will probably forgive as long as they know at the end of the day, you care for them and you're trying your best. And I think that's important because I think a lot of people think, "well, I'm just going to mess it up." And if your trans kid knows that you care about them and that you're supporting them in whatever way that you can, or at least trying to learn, they're going to have a lot more patience and a lot more understanding than if they think that you're not.

Michael (listen to Michael's advice in ▶ Audio 7.21)

(she/her; trans female; white)

One of the first things I wanted to share is that gender transition is one of many types of transitions which also happens to be very visible. Though, in important ways, it is not much different than the transitions experienced by their classmates. It's simply more visible. So, whereas Sally, who is experiencing a horrible divorce between her parents, this is an emotionally destructive transition. Another kid may be dealing with an abusive parent, a hidden and traumatic transition. And these are all transitions. Middle school kids are going through puberty, and this can be a very difficult transition even for the cisgender student. So, it just happens to be that you have a classroom of kids who are going through a myriad of transitions. This one transition, the gender transition, happens to be very visible. Gender transitions do not make them so incredibly different from everyone else in the classroom. I think it is important for the educator to see them in that context, not only with the age they are teaching, and the group of kids that they are teaching.

Every gender transition is different, and there are a myriad of gender identities—a beautiful, gorgeous rainbow. It is fascinating to see how each trans kid develops—what their colors are in the rainbow. Each trans identity is unique and each identity is valid. We are our best selves when we are open to their identity and however they express themselves. Of course, gender transition is a very tough transition, especially if there's difficulty at home. Acting out might not necessarily be something that is intentional misbehavior, if such a thing even exists. There is a reason behind it. I think that they need somebody to listen to them. The teacher has a golden opportunity to be that active listener.

I feel it is important to understand that it is very hard for the parents, even the parents with the best intentions. I am not speaking of the parents that will start quoting Bible verses and everything like that. I think that there is a—I really have very little patience for people who do not accept trans people because of the Bible—whether that's based in fear or whether that's based in laziness. The Bible—as well as other books of faith—have been interpreted time and again to suppress others and to maintain power. However, there are parents that just care so deeply about their child, and gender transition is something new to them. It is possible they have never, up to this point, experienced being emotionally connected to anyone in the trans community. (Thank goodness the media is beginning to change it in that way.) But it is a scary time and it's a huge transition for these parents. In a perfect world, the child is listened to and supported unconditionally by the parents and the teacher. As a teacher, you can usually tell when a parent cares deeply about their child and they're struggling with something, and they should be listened to. The more they are able to be supported as parents, the better it is for the child.

Michelle (listen to Michelle's suggestion in ▶ Audio 7.22)

(she/her; Transgender female; white)

If I had to tell them one thing, I would maybe just say, allow your students to find their own voice. Don't force them into something that they can't do or don't want to do and just accept them for where they're at in their vocal performance and just blend that in with the other voices.

MJ (listen to MJ's recommendations in ▶ Audio 7.23)

(she/her or they/them; Trans woman; Black)

First of all . . . I feel that you should let the child come to you and express who they are. Don't try to force it out of them, because a lot of these kids live in traumatic environments where they don't have freedom to be who they are. They're just so closeted and they're closed in by their parents, by their siblings. So, yeah, when they come to school, it's like their chance of a little bit of freedom. So, let them enjoy that freedom. Don't take it away from them and let them be who they are and let them come to you and say, "this is how I identify, these are my pronouns." [. . .] Let them come out to you. Don't force it out of them, let them be who they are. And also, if another child is picking on them, because they wear makeup to school, or they're wearing dresses, or, you know, feminine clothing, you should stick up for them.

Because that makes us trust you even more. When you don't stick up for us, when you just let things happen [*changing course*] . . . and I know it's like, it's kind of hard to navigate student and student harassment and bullying and situations like that, because you don't want to put your job at risk as well. . . . But if you can fight in a logical way, and that would consist of . . . okay, if there's a situation where someone is being bullied or harassed because of the clothing that they choose to wear, then you should sit down with the student who was bullying and say, "okay, cool. . . [that's not okay]." And with the student that decides to cross dress or wear feminine clothing and try to be more comfortable with their identity, we should have a conversation and sit down and say, "okay, cool . . . that's not okay. Especially in my classroom." You don't want to create a hostile environment for anyone because: (a) that prohibits learning, and (b) people feel that they can't express themselves. So, you should say, "in my classroom, people can express how they want to express." And try to word that in a way so people who are very religious or have, you know, other ideas, they won't bring that to the classroom. But as far as expressing themselves creatively, which they are, then that is encouraged in your classroom, and you should say, "bullying of any kind . . . will not be tolerated in my classroom at all." And that will open up a child more—just hearing those words, "bullying will not be tolerated." . . . that they can express themselves creatively. When you say those words to a child, it is just opening them up and they can actually say, "okay, cool, I can trust this teacher. I can trust this class. I can actually come here and express myself. I can be who I want in this classroom." Because they don't get to do that at home. So, having that opportunity will mean the world to them.

Mystic Rose (Pseudonym) (listen to Mystic Rose's advice in ▶ Audio 7.24)

(she/her or they/them; gender nonconforming; Latinx)

I would say, listen to your students. Listen to what they have to say. Just know that they're speaking from the heart and that they're speaking to you in confidence. So, take a listen to what they have to say. Be ready to have your arms open because it's really scary to come forward with your trans identity. It is also very important to just be open to wanting to learn with them and get educated about them when they are wanting you to understand something. When we're teaching, we make relationships with our students? We become a family with our students and sometimes members of a family need more attention than others. We need to be mindful of what we say. Be mindful of the jokes that go around in the classroom. You are the first line of defense when it comes to that. You have to make [people] stop [telling] trans and gay jokes. You are there as a guardian to this person in a way where you're guarding their self-esteem. You're guarding their identity. You're guarding their personality and soul. So, it's very important that you're cognizant of what's being said in your classroom. Being cognizant of what's going on and be vigilant in case they're being bullied. Even outside the classroom too, you need to make sure that they're safe because being trans openly is opening yourself up to a whole bunch of unnecessary BS. [. . .]

Be kind and love. Being a trans youth in particular is really hard on the individual because it's already really hard because you're young and people are going to say, "You don't know any better. You're too young to know what you want," which is not the case. You know, I feel like everybody knows who they are when they realize who they are and no one just does it for attention, as society likes to think most trans people do it for. Just be kind to people. You don't have to accept it, but you could just not say anything if you don't agree with it. Don't say anything. There's so much hate in this world that I feel like if we were all just a little bit kinder, I feel like there would be less of a suicide rate in the trans community and the gay community too. There would be less hate for people who are attracted to people within the trans community. There would be less de-stigmatization with all of it. Just be kind.

Percy (listen to Percy's suggestions in ▶ Audio 7.25)

(they/them; Nonbinary; Asian-American)

I think the first thing that I would say is understand why they're there. Understand why they want to go into that program and want to express themselves as they do through that program. They may not necessarily have the chances to express themselves at home, but while they're at school at a sort of safe place, you have to honor why they're there. You have to honor everything that they want, everything that they have in mind. So, make sure to have that in your mind as you're looking at them and teaching them.

While you're performing, you sort of feel more like yourself because you feel sort of separated from everything else. You're controlling everything that you do. You're controlling how you move, how you speak, how you sing. That's something that you can control. And, when students go into the vocal music program, they have an audible control over what they do and how they express themselves. So, if they use different pronouns than what you see online, like in a roster, honor that because that's what they want. That's what they want people to see. That's how they want people to see themselves. They don't want to see them as anybody else, but themselves and going into our programs, vocal music programs, so on and so forth, they have that opportunity.

Phoebe

(she/her or they/them; non-binary; white)

If standing in front of a room of educators and asked what they need to know about honoring trans and gender-expansive youth, my priority would be to remind this room that there is no one rule when it comes to the trans and gender-expansive population. All of us are different, individual people with our own needs, and while there are certainly practices that can help us, we are all going to have different experiences and different types of support we're looking for. The best way to support and honor trans and gender-expansive people is to treat us as people, not a monolith—all different persons with different stories to tell and different ways of being best supported. Just as with all other people, learn about who we are and what we need as individuals. Your understanding will develop from knowing us for who we are.

Rex (listen to Rex's advice in ▶ Audio 7.26)

(they/them; non-binary; white)

I mean, I think part of my advice would just be, believe them. Believe what they tell you. Believe, who they tell you they are, even if you don't know what it means, even if you don't understand it, even if there's a part of you that doesn't want to believe them, believe them, you know? Let them define who they are. Let them define who they are and let them figure those things out for themselves. [. . .]

[My friend who is a high school choir teacher] is someone who saw children coming into her classroom and seeing a lot of LGBT youth and trans and gender-expansive youth coming into her classroom. And she asked the question, "what do I do to make sure they feel like they belong here?" And then she figured it out and she listened to them. . . . So many of them don't have places—they cannot go home and be who they are, right? There are kids that she has, who their parents want to kick their children out of their homes for being who they are. And so, she has been able to do things, like she doesn't say "men and women," she doesn't use those terms. She uses different section terms for everything now. And she has also figured out different music to use [. . .] when she auditions folks, right? Everyone is placed in a safe section just based on what their vocal range is. Their actual vocal range—not what it's expected to be—not what people will assume it is, but by what it actually is and then that's how sections are created. And so, she has done such incredible work at making sure that anyone that walks into that room, regardless of gender and gender experience, is going to feel like they belong there, you know?

And the other thing too, we need to give folks an opportunity to actually explore their gender, because the reality is that we are all living in this world that is highly gendered. And in the society that, you know, even if you are able to find gender affirming, trans affirming spaces, that's probably like one place of a million that you're able to go to, right? Because the rest of the world is not accepting in that way. And so being able to work with kids as they are figuring out what is authentic to them. And so, if their expression is one way one day and different a different day, great—affirm that, you know? It doesn't need to be made a big deal.

And let people wear what they want to wear, we don't need to have "tenors and basses are in suits and ties" and "sopranos and alto are in dresses and pearls." You don't have to have that, you know? You can look uniform without having to have gendered clothing expectations. And so that's another thing people need to take into consideration is, if you want uniformity that's okay. And how can we make sure that uniformity is also still being affirming to anyone that's in that room regardless of gender? So, I feel like there's just so many small things—small changes that can happen. And that's the other thing too: it's not a lot of change that needs to happen. Actually, the smallest changes are what's going to make the biggest impact. And so, if you are able to just allow for that, that is going to make a world of a difference, and quite honestly is going to end up saving a life at some point or another. Because that is one of the things that people aren't realizing is the prevalence of suicidality among the trans community and especially the younger trans community. That literally having one supportive person in someone's life completely can change things, you know? That can be the difference between them living and dying.

Ryder (listen to Ryder's recommendations in ▶ Audio 7.27)

(he/him; TransMan; not specified)

Number one, stop saying "guys and gals, boys and girls." Get it out. The gender terms have to go. That's number one. The wardrobe costuming: either make it gender neutral or let people pick. [. . .] Try not to separate via traditional gender: do it by vocal range. [. . .] In terms of what those generations are feeling and what those generations are expressing and experiencing, stay connected. Stay connected to your kids. Stay connected to what your kids are connected to.

Sage (listen to Sage's story in ▶ Audio 7.28)

(he/him; Trans Masculine Non-binary; Latinx/white)

First things first, using correct names and pronouns is not optional. It's not optional because 50% of trans kids will try and commit suicide due to lack of familial and societal support. That percentage drops to a typical cis teenage range if people just use trans kiddos' name and pronouns—that's it. And it doesn't have to be everybody. It has to be at least one person. I typically tell the student teachers I supervise, "your belief system or religion may not include trans people, but it certainly includes children and saving children's lives. Your belief system would work to keep a child alive or save their life, so use names and pronouns as a lifesaving act for a child, as your motivation if you have to. Because even if your belief system doesn't include trans people, it does include keeping children safe and healthy. So, this instead is not a political act, it's a lifesaving act.

Teachers have a lot to work to do to be aware and start to shift their biases. That is super important to me. But what is more important is that they take their responsibility seriously as a supportive person to a trans child. So, I also have a pretty serious conversation about what we mean by "it only takes one person" to be supportive to save the life of a trans child. The thing is, you cannot guarantee somebody else will do it. I tell them, I have now given you this responsibility. It is yours . . . if you feel like that you shouldn't take this mantle, sorry, your awareness makes it your responsibility. You have to find a way to be supportive. This responsibility is even greater for teachers in the arts. Most of the time, kids feel safe in the arts, but they may not know that their specific teacher may not be a safe person, so there's an assumption there. I've seen teachers who are not supportive of trans kiddos do some major damage.

Often, kids will come out to a music or a theater arts teacher much sooner than they would come out to, say, a chemistry teacher. And the hardest part is, that even though it's an old teaching adage, we can't actually leave our bias at the door. We carry those with us. That said, as a teacher we have to step back, admit we have biases, and that we need to do the work to break down the biases that put our children at risk. The willingness to be aware is the most important piece. We all have bias, period. I believe humans have to have bias because we have to categorize. For example, a couch and a tiger are relatively the same size. One we can relax into, one we should probably run away from. Our brains need to categorize quickly so that we can move on to other things. The trouble is that our categorizing has socially constructed meaning superimposed on it. Teachers come to the profession with deeply ingrained biases towards certain students, and to be a good teacher, they need to know that we all have bias, that we all categorize, but that we can't stay there. It is not an excuse. If something makes me wildly uncomfortable as a teacher, I have to look at it and ask, where did this come from? But also, is my acting on my discomfort worth the life of a child? With trans children, that is a real choice teachers have to make. That's huge. It's a huge responsibility.

The other piece of advice is to watch the minutiae. It's the small things that make the biggest difference. How do you take attendance the first day? Do you call out first names? Uh . . . don't do that. [*chuckles*]. It's so ingrained in us to take attendance this way, that a small change is often mind blowing for educators. Instead, take the roll by last name and first initial. Or send a sign-up sheet around instead. If you're worried about names being different enough that you won't be able to take attendance, ask a student to include a birthday or a student ID. You could also send around little index cards and ask students to write how they want to be addressed. Or ask, is there something I need to know to help you learn? When describing it, I always add gender identity. Some students want me to know that they're trans, but they don't want me to out them, so I typically ask how students want to be addressed in class? How do you want me to address you with your parents? How do you want me to address you outside of this classroom? You have to ask all these questions because kids have different levels of safety in different places. And that is something cis people don't think about that at all. They think, "Oh, well, they ask me to call them this pronoun here so that goes for everywhere."

Also, you have to be aware of and know your state's policies and Education Code and it's different everywhere. I would look for if there are safeguards so that you have a leg to stand on, when a parent comes in and says, "why didn't you tell me my kiddo is queer/trans?" Though, I want to say, "because I don't out people," it's a much better idea to work emotionally connected with parents, but also have the ed codes ready to cite, and explain why the codes are in place, which is typically about children's physical and emotional safety. Another piece of advice—and this is a big one— is the thing that I come back to over and over: rapport, rapport, rapport, rapport, rapport, rapport! If you don't have rapport as a teacher, you're going to lose everybody. They have to trust you before they can learn.

APPENDIX A

Glossary

Before jumping into definitions, it is important to acknowledge the evolving and living nature of these words and their meanings. Some terms are commonly understood, while others are considered controversial. LGBTQA vocabulary will continue to change—as it should—as people and contexts change. We endeavor to define key terms, nevertheless, with the hope that the curious reader might take to the internet (e.g., Gender Minorities Aotearoa, n.d.) to monitor the transformation and evolution of these ideas over time.

AFAB Assigned female at birth.

Agender An umbrella term that a person uses who does not have a gender or who describes themself as being gender neutral. *It is best to ask someone how they use this term.*

Ally A term used to describe someone who is supportive of LGBTQA individuals and the community, either personally or as an advocate (Parents and Friends of Lesbians and Gays [PFLAG]).

AMAB Assigned male at birth (see *assigned birth sex*).

Androgynous Having elements of both femininity and masculinity.

Assigned birth sex The assignment and classification of people as male, female, intersex, or another sex, assigned at birth often based on physical anatomy at birth and/or karyotyping (Trans Student Educational Resources [TSER]).

Cisgender/cis A term for someone who exclusively identifies as their assigned birth sex. The term *cisgender* is not indicative of gender expression, sexual orientation, hormonal makeup, physical anatomy, or how one is perceived in daily life (TSER).

Cisgender privilege Rights or advantages given to persons whose assigned birth sex aligns with socially sanctioned gender categories. Some forms of cisgender privilege include: having a government-issued identification that accurately represents one's identity; not being forced "to adopt a different gender presentation" (Johnson, 2013, para. 18); not being denied medical care; not being refused "access to, and fair treatment within, sex segregated facilities" such as bathrooms, homeless shelters, prisons, and domestic violence shelters (Johnson, 2013, para. 17).

Cisnormativity A term describing the assumption that all people are cisgender.

Clocking "The term 'clocked' is used to reflect that someone transgender has been recognized as trans, usually when that person is trying to blend in with cisgender people, and not intending to be seen as anything other than the gender they present. Another word is 'read,' as in 'She read me,' or 'I got read as trans'" (Ennis, 2016, paras. 20–21).

Closeted Describes a person who has not disclosed their sexual orientation or gender identity.

Coming out For most people who are lesbian, gay, bisexual, transgender, and queer, the process of self-acceptance that continues throughout one's life, and the sharing of the information with others; sometimes referred to as *disclosing* by the transgender community. There are many different degrees of being out: some may be out to friends only, some may be out publicly, and some may be out only to themselves. It's important to remember that coming out is an incredibly personal and transformative experience. Not everyone is in the same place when it comes to being out, and it is critical to respect where each person is in that process of self-identification. It is up to each person, individually, to decide if and when to come out or disclose (PFLAG).

Deadname The birth name of someone who no longer uses that name. TGE persons may select to use a chosen or claimed name, rather than their birth name. *It is inappropriate to refer to a TGE person by their deadname.*

Equality The state of being equal, especially in status, rights, or opportunities.

Equity The quality of being fair and impartial.

FTM or F2M A trans male/masculine person who was assigned female at birth (PFLAG). *Some trans persons find these terms offensive.*

Gay The adjective used to describe people who are emotionally, romantically, and/or physically attracted to people of the same gender (e.g., gay man, gay people). In contemporary contexts, *lesbian* is often a preferred term for women, though many women use the term *gay* to describe themselves (PFLAG).

Gender A set of socially constructed and context/culture-dependent ideas and behaviors.

Gender-affirming surgery, gender-actualization surgery, gender-reassignment surgery, sex-reassignment surgery Surgical procedures that can help people adjust their bodies to more closely match their innate or internal gender identity. Not every transgender person will desire or have resources for surgery. This term should be used in place of the older and often offensive term *sex change*. Also sometimes referred to as *sexual-reassignment surgery* (or SRS), *genital reconstruction surgery*, or *medical transition* (PFLAG). *It is inappropriate to ask about gender-affirming surgery. These highly personal questions can be triggering.*

Gender binary The concept that there are only two genders, man and woman, and that everyone must be one or the other. Also implies the assumption that gender is biologically determined (PFLAG).

Gender dysphoria In 2013, the American Psychiatric Association released the fifth edition of the *Diagnostic and Statistical Manual of Mental Disorders* (DSM-V) which replaced the outdated entry "Gender Identity Disorder" with "Gender Dysphoria" and changed the criteria for diagnosis. The necessity of a psychiatric diagnosis remains controversial, as both psychiatric and medical authorities recommend individualized medical treatment through hormones and/or surgeries to treat gender dysphoria. Some transgender advocates believe the inclusion of gender dysphoria in the DSM is necessary in order to advocate for health insurance that covers the medically necessary treatment recommended for transgender people (Gay & Lesbian Alliance Against Defamation [GLAAD]).

Gender-expansive An umbrella term that acknowledges the variety of gender identities and expressions in children, youth, and adults.

Gender expression The outward presentation of a person's femininity, masculinity, or other socially gendered traits, including choices of clothing, hairstyle, voice, and body language.

Gender fluid A term used to describe someone who moves between or among two or more gender identities or expressions. *It is best to ask someone how they use this term.*

Gender identity A deeply held internal sense or feeling of being a particular gender or genders. For trans persons, their assigned birth sex and their gender identity are not necessarily the same.

Gender nonbinary A term used to describe people who experience their gender identity and/or gender expression as falling beyond the categories of man and woman. They may define their gender as falling somewhere in between man and woman, or they may define it as wholly different from these terms (GLAAD).

Gender nonconforming A term used to describe people whose gender expression is different from conventional expectations of masculinity and femininity. Please note that not all gender nonconforming people identify as transgender; nor are all transgender people gender nonconforming. Many people have gender expressions that are not entirely conventional; that fact alone does not make them transgender. Many transgender men and women have gender expressions that are conventionally masculine or feminine. Simply being transgender does not make someone gender nonconforming. The term is not a synonym for transgender or transsexual and should only be used if someone self-identifies as gender nonconforming (GLAAD).

Gender policing An experience that occurs for individuals who are perceived as not adequately or accurately performing their gender (Ivey, 2016).

Genderqueer An umbrella term, similar to *gender nonbinary*, that refers to a person whose gender identity and gender expression fall beyond the categories of male and female.

Gender roles Gender roles in society means how we're expected to act, speak, dress, groom, and conduct ourselves based upon our assigned sex. For example, girls and women are generally expected to dress in typically feminine ways and be polite, accommodating, and nurturing. Men are generally expected to be strong, aggressive, and bold. Every society, ethnic group, and culture has gender role expectations, but they can be very different from group to group. They can also change in the same society over time. For example, pink used to be considered a masculine color in the United States, while blue was considered feminine (Planned Parenthood).

Gender socialization The process by which an individual is taught how they should behave as a boy or as a girl. Parents, teachers, peers, media, and books are some of the many agents of gender socialization (PFLAG).

Gender spectrum The concept that gender exists among fixed points without needing to be confined to a binary.

Gender variant A term, often used by the medical community, to describe children, youth, and some individuals who dress, behave, or express themselves in a way that does not conform to dominant gender norms (see *gender nonconforming*). People outside the medical community tend to avoid this term because they feel it suggests these identities are abnormal, preferring terms such as *gender expansive* and *gender creative* (PFLAG).

Heteronormative Of, designating, or based on a worldview which regards gender roles as fixed to biological sex and heterosexuality as the normal and preferred sexual orientation (*Oxford English Dictionary*, n.d.).

Heterosexism Prejudice or discrimination against people who are not heterosexual. Also: the belief that heterosexuality is the only normal or natural sexual orientation or identity (*Oxford English Dictionary*, n.d.).

Heterosexual Sexually or romantically attracted to, or engaging in sexual activity with, people of the opposite sex (*Oxford English Dictionary*, n.d.).

Homophobia An aversion to lesbian or gay people that often manifests itself in the form of prejudice and bias. Similarly, *biphobia* is an aversion people who are bisexual, and *transphobia* is an aversion to people who are transgender. *Homophobic*, *biphobic*, and *transphobic* are the related adjectives. Collectively, these attitudes are referred to as anti-LGBTQ bias (PFLAG).

Intersectionality "People's lives and the organization of power in a given society are better understood as being shaped not by a single axis of social division, be it race or gender or class, but by many axes that work together and influence each other" (Collins & Bilge, 2016, p. 12).

Intersex/differences of sexual development (DSD) Refers to individuals born with ambiguous genitalia or bodies that appear neither typically male nor female, often arising from chromosomal anomalies or ambiguous genitalia. Medical professionals often assign a gender to the individual and proceed to perform surgeries to "align" their physical appearance with typical male or female sex characteristics beginning in infancy and often continuing into adolescence, before a child is able to give informed consent. interACT: Advocates for Intersex Youth opposes this practice of genital mutilation on infants and children (PFLAG).

Latinx A person of Latin American origin or descent (used as a gender-neutral or nonbinary alternative to Latino or Latina) (*Oxford English Dictionary*, n.d.).

Misgender To refer to someone, especially a transgender or gender-expansive person, using a word, especially a pronoun or form of address, which does not correctly reflect the gender with which they identify (PFLAG).

MTF or M2F A trans female/feminine person who was assigned male at birth (PFLAG). *Some trans persons find these terms offensive.*

Mx A gender-neutral honorific salutation used instead of Mr., Mrs., or Ms.

Out Generally describes people who openly self-identify as LGBTQ in their private, public, and/or professional lives. Sometimes, individuals are outed by others who they may have already come out to. Outing an LGBTQ person without their consent is disrespectful and potentially dangerous for the LGBTQ individual. Some people who are transgender prefer to use the term *disclose* (PFLAG).

Passing/blending/assimilating Being perceived by others as a particular identity/gender or cisgender regardless of how the individual in question identifies, e.g., passing as straight, passing as a cis woman, passing as a youth. This term has become controversial, as *passing* can imply that one is not genuinely what they are passing as (TSER).

Pronoun A word used in place of a noun to refer to an individual (e.g., he, her, their, etc.). Also known as a *preferred pronoun, preferred gender pronoun*, or *proper gender pronoun*, although these terms are falling out of use because they imply something other than a "real" pronoun (and all of our pronouns are "real" pronouns). *It is best to share your pronouns and allow another person the opportunity to do the same, or not.*

Queer A term for people of marginalized gender identities and sexual orientations who are not cisgender and/or heterosexual. This term has a complicated history as a reclaimed slur (TSER).

Questioning A term used to describe those who are in a process of discovery and exploration about their sexual orientation, gender identity, gender expression, or a combination thereof (PFLAG).

Sex (sex assigned at birth) Assigned sex is a label that you're given at birth based on medical factors, including your hormones, chromosomes, and genitals. Most people are assigned male or female, and this is what's put on their birth certificate. When someone's sexual and reproductive anatomy doesn't seem to fit the typical definitions of female or male, they may be described as intersex. Some people call the sex we're assigned at birth *biological sex*. But this term doesn't fully capture the complex biological, anatomical, and chromosomal variations that can occur. Having only two options (biological male or biological female) might not describe what's going on inside a person's body. Instead of saying "biological sex," some people use the phrase "assigned male at birth" or "assigned female at birth." This acknowledges that someone (often a doctor) is making a decision for someone else. The assignment of a biological sex may or may not align with what's going on with a person's body, how they feel, or how they identify (Planned Parenthood).

Sexual orientation Emotional, romantic, or physical attraction toward other people. While sexual behavior involves the choices one makes in acting on one's sexual orientation, sexual orientation is part of the human condition, and one's sexual activity does not define one's sexual orientation; typically, it is the attraction that helps determine orientation (PFLAG).

SFAB Socialized female at birth (see also *gender socialization*). A broader, emerging term in the TGE community.

SMAB Socialized male at birth.

Social transition An expression of one's authentic gender now shared with others in the social environment. Social transition is one aspect of transitioning and often, although not always, the first action a transgender person takes to align with their internal sense of themselves as a gendered person, with the other aspects being medical, surgical, and legal (Ehrensaft et al., 2018, p. 252) (see also *transition*).

Stealth A term used to describe transgender or gender-expansive individuals who do not disclose their transgender or gender-expansive status in their public or private lives (or certain aspects of their public and private lives). The term is increasingly considered offensive by some, as it implies an element of deception. The phrase *maintaining privacy* is often used instead, though some individuals use both terms interchangeably (PFLAG). *Some people also use* passing *to describe the same phenomenon, though some trans people find the latter term offensive.*

Transition A term sometimes used to refer to the process—social, legal, and/or medical—one goes through to discover and/or affirm one's gender identity. This may, but does not always, include taking hormones; having surgeries; and changing names, pronouns, identification documents, and more. Many individuals choose not to or are unable to transition for a wide range of reasons both within and beyond their control. The validity of an individual's gender identity does not depend on any social, legal, and/or medical transition; the self-identification itself is what validates the gender identity (PFLAG) (see also *social transition*).

Trans, transgender An umbrella, or broadly encompassing term of many gender identities of those who do not identify or exclusively identify with their sex assigned at birth. The term *transgender* is not indicative of gender expression, sexual orientation, hormonal makeup, physical anatomy, or how one is perceived in daily life (TSER).

Trans* An outdated term popularized in the early 2010's that was used to signify an array of identities under the trans umbrella. However, it became problematized online due to improper usage. (TSER)

Trans woman/trans man *Trans woman* generally describes someone assigned male at birth who identifies as a woman. This individual may or may not actively identify as trans. It is grammatically and definitionally correct to include a space between trans and woman. The same concept applies to *trans men*. Please ask before identifying someone. Use the term and pronouns preferred by the individual (TSER).

APPENDIX B

Suggested Resources

TELEPHONE HOTLINES

Trans Lifeline (Trans Suicide Hotline)
877-565-8860
Trevor Project (LGBTQ Counseling/Crisis/Suicide Hotline)
866-488-7386

SELECTED PRINT RESOURCES

Learning More about Transgender and Gender-Expansive Communities

Barker, M., & Iantaffi, A. (2019). *Life isn't binary: On being both, beyond, and in-between*. Jessica Kingsley.

Beam, C. (2008). *Transparent: Love, family, and living the T with transgender teenagers*. Harcourt.

Bornstein, K. (1994). *Gender outlaw: On men, women, and the rest of us*. Routledge.

Cook, M. (2019). *Gender identity: Beyond pronouns and bathrooms*. Nomad Press.

Cronn-Mills, K. (2014). *Transgender lives: Complex stories, complex voices*. Lerner.

Erickson-Schroth, L. (Ed.). (2014). *Trans bodies, trans selves: A resource for the transgender community*. Oxford University Press.

Erickson-Schroth, L., & Davis, B. (2021). *Gender: What everyone needs to know*. Oxford University Press

Erickson-Schroth, L., & Jacobs, L. A. (2017). *"You're in the wrong bathroom!" And 20 other myths and misconceptions about transgender and gender-nonconforming people*. Beacon Press.

Feinberg, L. (1996). *Transgender warriors: Making history from Joan of Arc to Dennis Rodman*. Beacon Press.

Girshick, L. B. (2008). *Transgender voices: Beyond women and men*. University Press of New England.

Gottlieb, I. (2019). *Seeing gender: An illustrated guide to identity and expression*. Chronicle Books.

Halberstam, J. (2018). *Trans*: A quick and quirky account of gender variability*. University of California Press.

Johnson, G. M. (2020). *All boys aren't blue: A memoir-manifesto*. Farrar, Straus and Giroux.

Kuklin, S. (2014). *Beyond magenta: Transgender teens speak out*. Candlewick.

Mardell, A. (2016). *The ABC's of LGBT+*. Mango Media.

Meadow, T. (2018). *Trans kids: Being gendered in the twenty-first century*. University of California Press.

Mock, J. (2014). *Redefining realness: My path to womanhood, identity, love and so much more*. Atria Books.

Namaste, V. (2000). *Invisible lives: The erasure of transsexual and transgendered people*. University of Chicago Press.

Nestle, J., Howell, C., & Wilchins, R. A. (Eds.). (2002). *GenderQueer: Voices from beyond the sexual binary*. Alyson Books.

Pardo, T. B. (2008). *Growing up transgender: Research and theory.* Cornell University, Family Life Development Center.

Pessin-Whedbee, B. (2016). *Who are you?: The kid's guide to gender identity.* Jessica Kingsley.

Serano, J. (2007). *Whipping girl: A transsexual woman on sexism and the scapegoating of femininity.* Seal Press.

Schilt, K. (2010). *Just one of the guys?: Transgender men and the persistence of gender inequality.* University of Chicago Press.

Stryker, S. (2008). *Transgender history.* Seal Press.

Stryker, S., & Whittle, S. (Eds.). (2006). *The transgender studies reader.* Taylor & Francis.

Tannehill, B. (2019). *Everything you ever wanted to know about trans (but were afraid to ask).* Jessica Kingsley..

Tobia, J. (2019). *Sissy: A coming-of-gender story.* G. P. Putnam's Sons.

Valentine, D. (2007). *Imagining transgender: An ethnography of a category.* Duke University Press.

Selected TGE-Related Children's Books

Ewert, M. (2008). *10,000 dresses.* Penguin Random House.

Hoffman, S., & Hoffman, I. (2014). *Jacob's new dress.* Albert Whitman.

Love, J. (2018). *Julián is a mermaid.* Candlewick.

Newman, L. (2017). *Sparkle boy.* Lee & Low Books.

Patterson, J., & Barlow, C. P. (2021). *Born ready: The true story of a boy named Penelope.* Crown Books for Young Readers.

Thorn, T. (2019). *It feels good to be yourself: A book about gender identity.* Henry Holt.

Van Ness, J. (2020). *Peanut goes for the gold.* HarperCollins.

Teacher Resources

Bilodeau, B. (2009). *Genderism: Transgender students, binary systems and higher education.* VDM Verlag Dr. Müller.

Blackburn, M. V., Clark, C. T., & Schey, R. (2018). *Stepping up! Teachers advocating for sexual and gender diversity in schools.* Routledge.

Brant, C. A. R., & Willox, L. M. (2020). *Teaching the teachers: LGBTQ issues in teacher education.* Information Age.

Calcagno, J. (2017). *Rewind fast forward: A practical guide of the transgender student for teachers.* 10-10-10.

Chappell, S. V., Ketchum, K. E., & Richardson, L. (2018). *Gender diversity and LGBTQ inclusion in K-12 schools: A guide to supporting students, changing lives.* Routledge.

Ellis, S. J., Riggs, D. W., & Peel, E. (2020). *Lesbian, gay, bisexual, trans, intersex, and queer psychology: An introduction* (2nd ed.). Cambridge University Press.

Gorski, P. C., & Pothini, S. G. (2013). *Case studies on diversity and social justice education.* Routledge.

Grant, J. M., Mottet, L., Tanis, J. E., Harrison, J., Herman, J., & Keisling, M. (2011). *Injustice at every turn: A report of the national transgender discrimination survey.* National Center for Transgender Equality.

Hancock, A. B., & Siegfriedt, L. T. (2020). *Transforming voice and communication with transgender and gender-diverse people: An evidence-based process.* Plural.

Hearns, L. J. (with Maddigan, P.). (2018). *One weird trick: A user's guide to transgender voice.* CreateSpace Independent.

Martin, A. D., & Strom, K. J. (Eds.). (2019). *Exploring gender and LGBTQ issues in K-12 and teacher education: A rainbow assemblage.* Information Age.

Meyer, E. J. (2009). *Gender, bullying, and harassment: Strategies to end sexism and homophobia in schools.* Teachers College Press.

Meyer, E. J., & Sansfaçon, A. P. (Eds.). (2014). *Supporting transgender and gender creative youth: Schools, families, and communities in action*. Peter Lang.
Mills, M., & Stoneham, G. (2017). *The voice book for trans and non-binary people: A practical guide to creating and sustaining authentic voice and communication*. Jessica Kingsley.
Olszewski, A., Sullivan, S., & Cabral, A. (2019). *Here's how to teach voice and communication skills to transgender women*. Plural.
Russell, S. T., & Horn, S. S. (Eds.). (2017). *Sexual orientation, gender identity, and schooling: The nexus of research, practice, and policy*. Oxford University Press.
Sears, J. T. (Ed.). (2003). *Gay, lesbian, and transgender issues in education: Programs, policies, and practices*. Routledge.
Shane, K. (she/her). (2020). *The educator's guide to LGBT+ inclusion: A practical resource for K-12 teachers, administrators, and school support staff*. Jessica Kingsley.
Sieck, S. (2017). *Teaching with respect: Inclusive pedagogy for choral directors*. Hal Leonard.
Wells, K., Roberts, G., & Allan, C. (2012). *Supporting transgender and transsexual students in K-12 schools: A guide for educators*. Canadian Teachers' Federation.
Woolley, S. W., & Airton, L. (2020). *Teaching about gender diversity: Teacher-tested lesson plans for k–12 classrooms*. Canadian Scholar's Press, Inc.

Student Resources

Bornstein, K. (1998). *My gender workbook: How to become a real man, a real woman, the real you, or something else entirely*. Routledge.
Cook, M. (2019). *Gender identity: Beyond pronouns and bathrooms*. Nomad Press.

Family Resources

Brill, S. A., & Kenney, L. (2016). *Transgender teen: A handbook for parents and professionals supporting transgender and non-binary teens*. Cleis Press.
Ehrensaft, D. (2016). *The Gender creative child: Pathways for nurturing and supporting children who live outside gender boxes*. The Experiment.
Gratton, F. V. (2019). *Supporting transgender autistic youth and adults: A guide for professionals and families*. Jessica Kingsley.
Helsel, C. B., & Harris-Smith, Y. J. (2020). *The ABCs of diversity: Helping kids (and ourselves!) embrace our differences*. Chalice Press.
Lev, A. I. (2004). *Transgender emergence: Counseling gender-variant people and their families*. Taylor & Francis.
Meadow, T. (2018). *Trans kids: Being gendered in the twenty-first century*. University of California Press.

CURATED WEB RESOURCES

Learning More about the TGE Community

Dumlao, A. C. "100 Ways to Make the World Better for Non-Binary People" https://www.vice.com/en_us/article/evkwm4/how-to-be-an-ally-to-non-binary-gender-non-conforming-people-support?fbclid=IwAR1tCb6CEvd9ncu5M8GhX3t_8AHzbPqOAdwtDVjKbSEucTnTX8fj14eS-dA
Florin Roebig Lawfirm (Legal information on LGBTQ discrimination) https://florinroebig.com/lgbtq-discrimination/
For Families https://drive.google.com/file/d/1wJ7KxBxEd2GNL8ut7OkqXHRjop0OtJkA/view
GLSEN https://www.glsen.org/

Trans Action Kit
https://www.glsen.org/activity/trans-action-kit?emci=274c251a-6006-ea11-828b-2818784d6d68&emdi=e6a5e9e7-6e06-ea11-828b-2818784d6d68&ceid=469369
Gendered Intelligence
http://genderedintelligence.co.uk
Gender Odyssey
http://www.genderodyssey.org/
Gender Spectrum
https://genderspectrum.org/
Haimson, O. L., & Airton, L. "Making space for them, her, him, and 'prefer not to disclose' in group settings: Why pronoun-sharing is important but must remain optional"
https://medium.com/national-center-for-institutional-diversity/making-space-for-them-her-him-and-prefer-not-to-disclose-in-group-settings-why-1deb8c3d6b86
National Center for Transgender Equality
https://transequality.org/
No big deal campaign
https://www.nbdcampaign.ca/
Sexsmith, S. "Dear (cis) people who put your pronouns on your 'Hello my name is' name tag"
https://medium.com/@mrsexsmith/dear-cis-people-who-put-your-pronouns-on-your-hello-my-name-is-nametags-78c047ed7af1
Trans Equality by State
https://transgenderlawcenter.org/equalitymap
Transgender Pulse
https://www.transgenderpulse.com/
Trans Policies by State
https://transequality.org/documents/state/new-hampshire
Trevor Project
https://www.thetrevorproject.org/?
"What Does It Mean to Misgender Someone?"
https://www.healthline.com/health/transgender/misgendering
Wyss, S. E. "Thinking about a Non-Binary Gender Identity?"
https://shannonwyss.com/thinking-about-a-non-binary-gender-identity/

Education

American Library Association statement affirming the rights of transgender people
http://www.ala.org/news/press-releases/2020/06/ala-statement-affirming-rights-transgender-people
Finding a trans-inclusive college
https://www.accreditedschoolsonline.org/resources/transgender-student-support/
Gender Diversity Project (City College of San Francisco)
https://www.ccsf.edu/student-services/resource-centers/link-center/gender-diversity-project
National Association of School Psychologists Policy Statement
https://www.nasponline.org/assets/Documents/Research%20and%20Policy/Position%20Statements/Transgender_PositionStatement.pdf
Resources for Principals/Administrators
https://www.nassp.org/policy-advocacy-center/nassp-position-statements/transgender-students/
Resources for School Counselors
https://www.schoolcounselor.org/asca/media/asca/PositionStatements/PS_Transgender.pdf

Learning for Justice Website: Gender & Sexual Identity
https://www.learningforjustice.org/topics/gender-sexual-identity
Learning for Justice: Gender & Sexuality Lesson Plans
https://www.learningforjustice.org/search?f%5B0%5D=facet_content_type%3Alesson&f%5B1%5D=facet_sitewide_topic%3A
TransYouth Project & Gender Development Lab (University of Washington)
https://depts.washington.edu/scdlab/

Music and Music Education

GALA Transgender Voices. (n.d.). Gala Choruses.
http://galachoruses.org/resource-center/singers/transgender-voices
Stapleton, M. Blurring the Binary
https://blurringthebinary.com/
Trans Chorus, Los Angeles
https://transchorusla.org/
Trans Choir, Cleveland
https://www.facebook.com/Transchoircleveland/
Trans Voices Festival
https://transvoicesfest.org/

Pronouns and Gender Identity

Mary Retta. "Work sucks, especially when people get your pronouns wrong"
https://www.vice.com/en_us/article/kzmy39/pronouns-at-work-trans-nonbinary
"Bathroom Bill" Legislative Tracking
https://www.ncsl.org/research/education/-bathroom-bill-legislative-tracking635951130.aspx
International Pronouns Day
https://pronounsday.org
Los Angeles Unified School District Pronoun Brochure
https://achieve.lausd.net/cms/lib/CA01000043/Centricity/Domain/383/My%20Pronouns%20Are%20flyer%202018.pdf
"Practice with Pronouns"
http://www.practicewithpronouns.com
"Resources on Personal Pronouns"
https://www.mypronouns.org
Social Identity Worksheet
http://timeandplace.ubc.ca/files/2014/06/Appendix-2.pdf

Speech and Communication

American Speech-Language-Hearing Association
https://www.asha.org/public/speech/disorders/Voice-and-Communication-Change-for-Transgender-People/

APPENDIX C

TGE-Affirmative Policy

Policy Suggestions and Models from National and State Organizations

California School Boards Association
https://www.csba.org/~/media/E68E16A652D34EADA2BFDCD9668B1C8F.ashx
Gender Spectrum Advice on Bathrooms
https://gender-spectrum.cdn.prismic.io/gender-spectrum%2Fb631ac8b-fa0f-425f-9af1-2e3c3c745581_transgender+students+and+school+bathrooms+-+frequently+asked+questions+%281%29-min-min.pdf
GLSEN Model Policy Language
https://www.glsen.org/activity/model-district-policy-transgender-and-gender-nonconforming-students
Lambda Legal
https://www.lambdalegal.org/know-your-rights/article/youth-tgnc-friendly-schools
National Center for Transgender Equality
https://transequality.org/know-your-rights/schools
National School Public Relations Association
https://www.nspra.org/e_network/2014-02_connecting-communities
Texas Music Educators Association Code of Ethics (2.10 includes gender)
https://www.tmea.org/about/policies/code-of-ethics/

TGE Policy Resources from State and National Professional Organizations

California Choral Directors Association
http://calcda.org/repertoire-resources/lgbtq/
Chorus America
https://www.chorusamerica.org/conducting-performing/making-your-chorus-welcoming-transgender-singers
National Association for Music Education
https://nafme.org/nafme-opposes-rescinding-of-transgender-guidelines-for-schools/
National Collegiate Athletic Association
https://www.ncaa.org/sites/default/files/Transgender_Handbook_2011_Final.pdf
National Federation of State High School Associations
https://www.nfhs.org/articles/transgender-students-participation-in-school-sports-access-to-facilities/
Rhode Island Department of Education
https://www.ride.ri.gov/InsideRIDE/AdditionalInformation/News/ViewArticle/tabid/408/ArticleId/379/RI-Department-of-Education-Reaffirms-Policy-on-Protections-for-Transgender-Students.aspx
Washington Choral Directors Association
https://waacda.org/2016/03/06/safe-spaces-for-transgender-voices/

Sample School and District Policies

Arcadia (CA) School District
https://www.ausd.net/apps/pages/index.jsp?uREC_ID=976257&type=d&pREC_ID=1296129
Austin (TX) Independent School District
https://www.austinisd.org/sites/default/files/dre-surveys/17.32_transgender_students_school_perceptions_experiences.pdf
Berklee (MA) College of Music
https://www.berklee.edu/diversity/trans-resources-and-support
Bridgeport (CT) Public Schools
http://www.bridgeportedu.com/Board/Policies/2013-2014/SafeSchoolClimatePLAN12-5-11.pdf
Burlington (VT) School District
https://www.bsdvt.org/wp-content/uploads/2017/07/F-29R-Prevention-of-Harassment-Hazing-Bullying-of-Students.pdf
District of Columbia Public Schools
https://dcps.dc.gov/publication/dcps-transgender-and-gender-non-conforming-policy-guidance
Leon County (FL) Schools
https://www.leonschools.net/site/handlers/filedownload.ashx?moduleinstanceid=55747&dataid=113268&FileName=Transgender%20Transition%20Plan.pdf
Los Angeles (CA) Unified School District Policies and Resources
https://achieve.lausd.net/Page/3651
New York City (NY) Department of Education
https://www.schools.nyc.gov/school-life/school-environment/guidelines-on-gender/guidelines-to-support-transgender-and-gender-expansive-students
Pittsburgh (PA) Public Schools
https://www.pghschools.org/cms/lib/PA01000449/Centricity/Domain/1295/PPS%20Gender%20Inclusive%20Handbook.pdf
Portland (OR) Public Schools
https://www.pps.net/cms/lib/OR01913224/Centricity/Domain/4814/7.40.010-AD.pdf
San Diego (CA) Unified Schools Nondiscrimination Policy
https://www.sandiegounified.org/nondiscrimination-statement
Santa Ana (CA) Unified School Districts
https://www.sausd.us/cms/lib/CA01000471/Centricity/Domain/3975/BP%205145.3%20Nondiscrimination-Harassment.pdf
State of Colorado
https://one-colorado.org/wp-content/uploads/2017/06/TransResourceGuide_2016.pdf
Trans Inclusion Toolkit
https://mermaidsuk.org.uk/wp-content/uploads/2019/12/AllsortsYouthProject-Trans-Inclusion-Schools-Toolkit-Sept-18.pdf

Sample Uniform Policies

Possibility for High School or Collegiate Ensembles

We will be wearing separates. The uniform chairs and I have chosen three tops and three bottoms. Choose one top and one bottom in your size. See uniform chairs for help.

TOP OPTIONS
Shirt: Cut 1:
https://www.macys.com/shop/product/bcx-juniors-tab-sleeve-shirt?ID=2523427&CategoryID=17043&swatchColor=Black#fn=sp=1&spc=628&ruleId=78&kws=black%20shirts&searchPass=exactMultiMatch&slotId=53

Shirt: Cut 2:
https://www.macys.com/shop/product/van-heusen-mens-fitted-poplin-dress-shirt?ID=642851&CategoryID=20635&swatchColor=Black#fn=sp=1&spc=628&ruleId=78&kws=black%20shirts&searchPass=exactMultiMatch&slotId=45

Shirt: Cut 3:
https://www.jcpenney.com/p/worthington-essential-long-sleeve-oxford-shirt-petite/pp5007670216?COLOR=Black&%3Brrec=true&pTmplType=regular&rrplacementtype=product1_rr

BOTTOM OPTIONS:
Skirt:
https://www.macys.com/shop/product/jm-collection-diagonal-seam-midi-skirt-created-for-macys?ID=3343056&CategoryID=131&swatchColor=Deep%20Black#fn=sp%3D1%26spc%3D318%26ruleId%3D78%26kws%3Dblack%20skirt%26searchPass%3DexactMultiMatch%26slotId%3D7

Pants: Cut 1:
https://www.jcpenney.com/p/worthington-modern-fit-trouser-pants/pp5003910685?pTmplType=regular&catId=cat100250095&deptId=dept20000013&urlState=/g/trousers-womens-pants/N-bwo3xD1nopgvZ1z140ui

Pants: Cut 2: Any Stafford black dress pants that fit you
https://www.jcpenney.com/s/stafford-mens-black-dress-pants/N-7iZe3Z160Z162Zxc9?Ntt=black+dress+pants&mode=1&activeFacetId=8&view=list

From the GLSEN Model Policy Document

"Schools may enforce dress codes pursuant to District policy, but any such dress codes may not be enforced based on gender or gender stereotypes. Students shall have the right to dress in accordance with their gender identity and expression, including maintaining a gender neutral appearance within the constraints of the dress codes adopted by the school. School staff shall not enforce a school's dress code more strictly against transgender and gender nonconforming students than other students" (GLSEN, p. 7).

Sample Language from TGE-Affirming Policies

Birch Creek Music Performance Center (WI)

Birch Creek accepts and encourages the participation of students with transgender and gender nonconforming concerns. This policy is established to explain our approach to help in the assimilation of transgender or gender nonconforming students into the student population. https://birchcreek.org/wp-content/uploads/2019/11/2020-Transgender-Student-Policy.pdf

Camp Registration Form, Skyline High School (Ann Arbor, MI)

Birth date _ /___ /___

Student's gender identity is:______________________

Our standard practice is to assign cabins according to a students' consistently asserted gender identity. Please contact Mrs. Cie with questions or concerns about this.
___I prefer a gender neutral cabin
___I prefer to stay in an all biologically male cabin
___I prefer to stay in an all biologically female cabin
___No preference
What more do we need to know about you in order to make your camp experience great?
—Lyn CieChanski

Honor Choir Policy (Florida Vocal Association, All-State Omnibus)

FVA POSITION ON TRANSGENDER STUDENTS

The Florida Vocal Association strives to be inclusive for students who identify as transgender. Transgender students may audition for the gender-specific All-State ensemble for which they identify. However, it would be expected that the student meets all of the expectations for that ensemble, including demonstrating the necessary vocal range for the voice part for which they are auditioning as part of their Vocal Quality audition.

The FVA encourages its members to work with their school and county administration to ensure a positive and inclusive environment for transgender students. This may include placing transgender students in gender-specific ensembles for which they identify, modifying uniform expectations for all students, and increased awareness of transgender students' hormone therapies which would affect the singing voice.

https://fva.net/wp-content/uploads/2019/08/2019-2020-all-state-omnibus-final-2019-08-30.pdf

Name/Pronouns (California State University, Long Beach)

This course affirms people of all gender expressions and gender identities. If you prefer to be called a different name than what is on the class roster, please let me know. Feel free to correct me on your preferred gender pronouns either in person or in writing. You may also change your name for BeachBoard* and MyCSULB without a legal name change. To submit a request, go to MyCSULB/Personal Information/Names. If you have any questions or concerns, please do not hesitate to contact the instructor.

*BeachBoard is our name for D2L, a Learning Management System

Overnight Rooming (Arroyo High School and Bohannon Middle School, San Lorenzo, CA)

In the planning of sleeping arrangements during overnight activity and athletic trips, the needs of students who are transgender shall be assessed on a case-by-case basis with the goals of maximizing the student's social integration and equal opportunity to participate in overnight activity and athletic trips, ensuring the student's safety and comfort, and minimizing stigmatization of the student. In most cases, students who are transgender should be assigned to share overnight accommodations with other students that share the student's gender identity consistently asserted at school.

Any student who has a need or desire for increased privacy, regardless of the underlying reason, should be provided with a reasonable accommodation, which may include a private room.

Any alternative arrangement should be provided in a way that allows the student's transgender status to be kept confidential. In no case shall a student who is transgender be required to share a room with students whose gender identity conflicts with their own.

—Patricia E. Schultz

Sample Gender-Inclusive Choir Course Descriptions (Gilroy High School, Gilroy, CA)

CONCERT CHOIR (TREBLE): College Prep "F": This entry-level choir is open to all students wishing to learn the fundamentals of good singing technique and basic musicianship. The student will learn about proper choral tone, diction, balance, and intonation. They will also learn basic fundamentals of music reading and theory. No previous singing experience is necessary and no audition is required. Participation in regularly scheduled co-curricular performances is mandatory. Curriculum will be consistent with the Common Core State Standards for technical subjects. The GHS choirs utilize gender-inclusive language. When choosing which choir to enroll in please choose the group you feel your voice will fit best. In the past the titles were not gender-neutral, "Treble" was called "Women's Choir" and "Bass/Tenor" was called "Men's Choir." To help enroll in the correct choir, please consider Concert Choir (Treble) = HIGH voices and Concert Choir (Bass/Tenor) = Low Voices.

CONCERT CHOIR (BASS/TENOR): College Prep "F": This entry-level choir is open to all students wishing to learn the fundamentals of good singing technique and basic musicianship. The student will learn about proper choral tone, diction, balance, and intonation. They will also learn basic fundamentals of music reading and theory. No previous singing experience is necessary and no audition is required. Participation in regularly scheduled co-curricular performances is mandatory. Curriculum will be consistent with the Common Core State Standards for technical subjects. The GHS choirs utilize gender-inclusive language. When choosing which choir to enroll in please choose the group you feel your voice will fit best. In the past the titles were not gender-neutral, "Treble" was called "Women's Choir" and "Bass/Tenor" was called "Men's Choir." To help enroll in the correct choir, please consider Concert Choir (Treble) = HIGH voices and Concert Choir (Bass/Tenor) = Low Voices.

—Jonathan Souza

APPENDIX D

Vocal Exercises

Phonation and Resonance

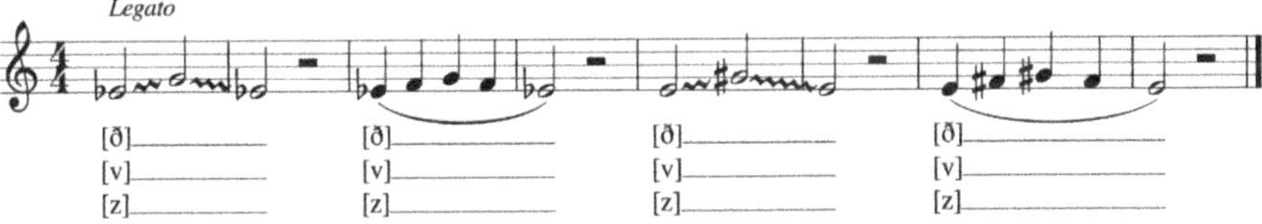

Exercise 1: Semi-occluded vocal tract glides on consonants or through a straw on [u].

Exercise 2: Semi-occluded vocal tract glides on consonants or through a straw on [u].

Exercise 3: Descending scale, close to [ŋ].

Exercise 4: Descending two-note sliding pairs.

Exercise 5: Ascending arpeggio on gradually opening vowels.

Exercise 6: Ascending alternating vowel pairs.

Developing Vocal Flexibility

Exercise 7: Descending fifth glides into lower register.

Exercise 8: Perfect fifth exercise to work through *passaggi*, or register shifts.

Exercise 9: Gradual descending octave glides into lower register.

Exercise 10: Descending melodic exercise to develop lower register.

Exercise 11: Ascending arpeggio to develop upper register.

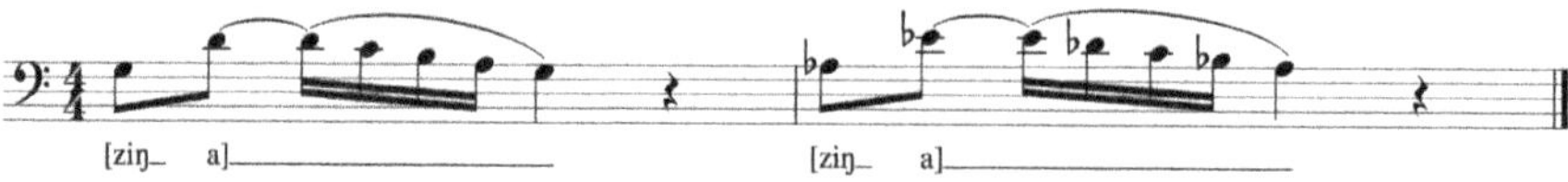

Exercise 12: Ascending melodic exercise to develop upper register.

Improving Articulation

Exercise 13: Descending melodic arpeggio to extend range and release tongue and jaw tension.

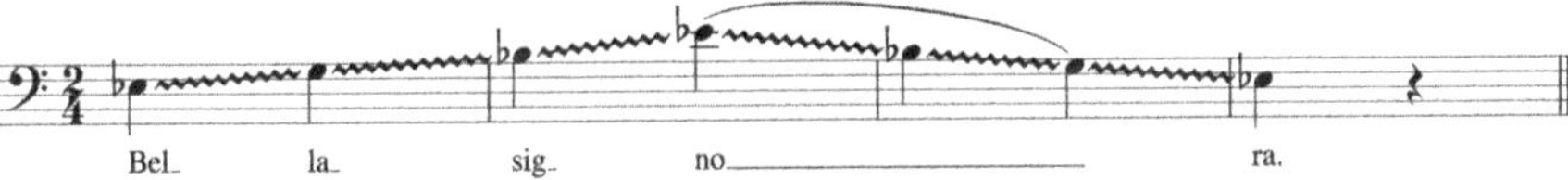

Exercise 14: Ascending melodic glide exercise to release tongue tension, sing with legato connection.

Exercise 15: Melodic exercise to lengthen vocal tract and reduce throat tension.

Exercise 16: Ascending arpeggio to release tongue and jaw tension.

References

Abeles, H. F. (2009). Are musical instrument gender associations changing? *Journal of Research in Music Education, 57*, 127–139. https://doi.org/10.1177/0022429409335878

Abeles, H. F., & Porter, S. Y. (1978). The sex-stereotyping of musical instruments. *Journal of Research in Music Education, 26*, 65–75. https://doi.org/10.2307/3344880

Adams ex rel. Kasper v. Sch. Bd. of St. Johns Co., No. 18-13592 (11th Cir., Aug. 7, 2020). https://www.lambdalegal.org/sites/default/files/legal-docs/downloads/adams_fl_20200807_opinion.pdf

Adams, K. (2019). Choral configuration: An overview of research and implications for the choral music educator. *Update: Applications of Research in Music Education, 37*(2), 24–29. https://doi.org/10.1177/8755123318783526

Adderley, C., Kennedy, M., & Berz, W. (2003). "A home away from home": The world of the high school music classroom. *Journal of Research in Music Education, 51*, 190–205. https://doi.org/10.2307/3345373

Adichie, C. N. (2009). The danger of a single story [Video file]. Retrieved from https://www.ted.com/talks/chimamanda_ngozi_adichie_the_danger_of_a_single_story

Aguirre, R. (2018). Finding the trans voice: A review of the literature on accommodating transgender singers. *Update: Applications of Research in Music Education, 37*(1), 36–41. https://doi.org/10.1177/8755123318772561

Ahmed, S. (2006). Orientations: Toward a queer phenomenology. *GLQ: A Journal of Lesbian and Gay Studies, 12*, 543–574. https://doi.org/10.1215/10642684-2006-002

Airton, L. (2018). The de/politicization of pronouns: Implications of the No Big Deal Campaign for gender-expansive educational policy and practice. *Gender and Education, 30*, 790–810. https://doi.org/10.1080/09540253.2018.1483489

Airton, L. (2019). *Gender: Your guide.* Adams Media.

Allsup, R. E., & Shieh, E. (2012). Social justice and music education: The call for a public pedagogy. *Music Educators Journal, 98*(4), 47–51. https://doi.org/10.1177/0027432112442969

Apple, M. W. (2004). *Ideology and curriculum* (3rd ed.). Routledge.

Azul, D. (2013). How do voices become gendered? A critical examination of everyday and medical constructions of the relationship between voice, sex, and gender identity. In M. Ah-King (Ed.), *Challenging popular myths of sex, gender and biology* (pp. 77–88). Springer. https://doi.org/10.1007/978-3-319-01979-6

Barker, M. J., & Iantaffi, A. (2019). *Life isn't binary.* Jessica Kingsley.

Bartolome, S. J. (2013). "It's like a whole bunch of me!": The perceived values and benefits of the Seattle girls' choir experience. *Journal of Research in Music Education, 60*, 395–418. https://doi.org/10.1177/0022429412464054

Bartolome, S. J. (2016). Melanie's story: A narrative account of a transgender music educator's journey. *Bulletin of the Council for Research in Music Education, 207–208*, 25–47. https://doi.org/10.5406/bulcouresmusedu.207-208.0025

Bartolome, S. J., Prichard, S., & Palkki, J. (2017, September). *Mx. Music teacher: A conversation about gender nonconforming preservice teachers.* Society for Music Teacher Education Symposium, Minneapolis, MN.

Bartolome, S. J., & Stanford, M. E. (2017). "Can't I sing with the girls?": A transgender music educator's journey. In B. C. Talbot (Ed.), *Marginalized voices in music education* (pp. 128–150). Routledge. https://doi.org/10.4324/9781315225401

Basow, S. (2004). The hidden curriculum: Gender in the classroom. In M. A. Paludi (Ed.), *Praeger guide to the psychology of gender* (pp. 117–131). Praeger.

Bates, V. C. (2012). Social class and school music. *Music Educators Journal, 98*(4), 33–37. https://doi.org/10.1177/0027432112442944

Becker, J. W., Peters, J., & Davis, J. H. (2017, February 22). Trump rescinds rules on bathrooms for transgender students. *New York Times*. https://www.nytimes.com/2017/02/22/us/politics/devos-sessions-transgender-students-rights.html

Beemyn, B. G. (2005). Making campuses more inclusive of transgender students. *Journal of Gay & Lesbian Issues in Education, 3*, 77–87. https://doi.org/10.1300/J367v03n01_08

Beemyn, G., & Rankin, S. R. (2011). *The lives of transgender people*. Columbia University Press.

Beese, J. A., & Martin, J. L. (2018). The bathroom case: Creating a supportive school environment for transgender and gender nonconforming students. *Journal of Cases in Educational Leadership, 21*(2), 65–76. https://doi.org/10.1177/1555458917731867

Berglin, J. (2017, February 15). Don't reduce transgender rights to bathroom access. *Education Week*. http://www.edweek.org/ew/articles/2017/02/15/dont-reduce-transgender-rights-to-bathroom-access.html

Bernstein, J. (2014, March 12). The growing transgender presence in pop culture. *New York Times*. https://www.nytimes.com/2014/03/13/fashion/the-growing-transgender-presence-in-pop-culture.html

Biegel, S. (2010). *The right to be out: Sexual orientation and gender identity in America's public schools*. University of Minnesota Press.

Bishop, R. S. (1990). Mirrors, windows, and sliding glass doors. *Perspectives, 6*(3), ix–xi.

Blair, E. E., & Deckman, S. L. (2019). "We cannot imagine": US preservice teachers' Othering of trans and gender creative student experiences. *Teaching and Teacher Education, 86*. https://doi.org/10.1016/j.tate.2019.102915

Blaisdell, G. (2018). Fostering inclusion: Unpacking choral dress codes. *Choral Journal, 59*(1), 59–64. https://doi.org/10.2307/26600192

Bond, V. L. (2017a). Culturally responsive education in music education: A literature review. *Contributions to Music Education, 42*, 153–180.

Bond, V. L. (2017b). Like putting a circle with a square: A (voice-variant) choral singer's story. In B. Talbot (Ed.), *Marginalized voices in music education* (pp. 137–152). Routledge.

Bornstein, K. (1994). *Gender outlaw: On men, women, and the rest of us*. Routledge.

Bostock v. Clayton County, 590 U.S.___ (2020). https://www.supremecourt.gov/opinions/19pdf/17-1618_hfci.pdf

Bowers, J. (2008). Building early choral experiences: Part two—The middle school choral program. In H. Michelle & J. Jordan (Eds.), *The school choral program: Philosophy, planning, organizing, and teaching* (pp. 359–374). GIA.

Brahms, J. (1864). *Neckereien* (Teasing), *Op. 31, No. 3*.

Branson-Potts, H., & Stiles, M. (2020, June 15). All Black Lives Matter march calls for LGBTQ rights and racial justice. *Los Angeles Times*. https://www.latimes.com/california/story/2020-06-15/lgbtq-pride-black-lives-controversy

Brown, B. (2019). *The Call to Courage* [Streaming]. *Netflix*. https://www.netflix.com/title/81010166

Butler, J. (1990). *Gender trouble: Feminism and the subversion of identity*. Routledge.

Campbell, P. S., Connell, C., & Beegle, A. (2007). Adolescents' expressed meanings of music in and out of school. *Journal of Research in Music Education, 55*, 220–236. https://doi.org/10.1177/002242940705500304

Carbonara, E., Parisi, F., & Von Wangenheim, G. (2008). Lawmakers as norm entrepreneurs. *Review of Law & Economics, 4*, 779–799. https://doi.org/10.2202/1555-5879.1320

Carter, B. A. (2011). A safe education for all recognizing and stemming harassment in music classes and ensembles. *Music Educators Journal, 97*(4), 29–32. https://doi.org/10.1177/0027432111405342

Carter, B. A. (2014). Intersectionalities: Exploring qualitative research, music education, and diversity. In C. Conway (Ed.), *The Oxford handbook of qualitative research in American music education* (pp. 538–552). Oxford University Press. https://doi.org/10.1093/oxfordhb/9780199844272.001.0001

Case, K. A., & Meier, S. C. (2014). Developing allies to transgender and gender-nonconforming youth: Training for counselors and educators. *Journal of LGBT Youth, 11*, 62–82. https://doi.org/10.1080/19361653.2014.840764

CASEL. (2021). *What is SEL?* https://casel.org/what-is-sel/

CAST. (2020). Universal Design for Learning Guidelines version 2.2. Retrieved from http://udlguidelines.cast.org

Catalano, D. C. J. (2015). "Trans enough?" The pressures trans men negotiate in higher education. *TSQ: Transgender Studies Quarterly, 2*, 411–430. https://doi.org/10.1215/23289252-2926399

Cates, D. S. (2019). *Choral directors' experiences with gender-inclusive teaching practices among transgender students*. Available from ProQuest Dissertations and Theses database. (UMI No. 13884557).

Cava, P. (2014). Trans etiquette. In L. Erickson-Schroth (Ed.), *Trans bodies, trans selves* (pp. 125–126). Oxford University Press.

Chappell, S. V., Ketchum, K. E., & Richardson, L. (2018). *Gender diversity and LGBTQ inclusion in K-12 schools: A guide to supporting students, changing lives*. Routledge.

Childs, D. N. (2009). *Where your bare foot walks*. Walton Music.

Coleman, N. (2020, July 5). Why we're capitalizing Black. *New York Times*. https://www.nytimes.com/2020/07/05/insider/capitalized-black.html

Collins, P. H., & Bilge, S. (2016). *Intersectionality*. John Wiley & Sons.

Comer, J. (1995). Lecture given at Education Service Center, Region IV. Houston, TX.

Conway, C. M. (2000). Gender and musical instrument choice: A phenomenological investigation. *Bulletin of the Council for Research in Music Education, 146*, 1–17.

Cooper, P. K., & Burns, C. (2019). Effects of stereotype content priming on fourth and fifth grade students' gender-instrument associations and future role choice. *Psychology of Music, 49*(2), 246–256. https://doi.org/10.1177/0305735619850624

Crenshaw, K. (1991). Mapping the margins: Intersectionality, identity politics, and violence against women of color. *Stanford Law Review, 43*, 1241–1299. https://doi/org/10.2307/1229039

Daniels, A. A. (2019). This is Me. Single. [Audio file]. Retrieved from https://music.apple.com/us/album/this-is-me-single/1447425114?i=1447425117&ign-gact=3&ls=1

Darwin, H. (2020). Challenging the cisgender/transgender binary: Nonbinary people and the transgender label. *Gender & Society, 34*, 357–380. https://doi.org/10.1177/0891243220912256

Davis, E. C. (2009). Situating "fluidity" (trans) gender identification and the regulation of gender diversity. *GLQ: A Journal of Lesbian and Gay Studies, 15*, 97–130.

Davis, H. F. (2017). *Beyond trans: Does gender matter?* New York University Press.

Davis, H. F. (2018). *Building gender-inclusive organizations: The workbook*. https://heathfoggdavis.selz.com/item/5b33dc34f6281a0430bf549d

Demby, G., & Meraji, S. M. (2020, June 27). *They don't say our names enough*. Code Switch Podcast (*NPR*). https://www.npr.org/2020/06/26/884080764/they-dont-say-our-names-enough

DePalma, R. (2013). Choosing to lose our gender expertise: Queering sex/gender in school settings. *Sex Education, 13*(1), 1–15. https://doiorg/10.1080/14681811.2011.634145

Derman-Sparks, L., & Edwards, J. O. (2019). Understanding anti-bias education: Bringing the four core goals to every facet of your curriculum. *Young Children, 74*, 6–12.

de Vries, K. M. (2012). Intersectional identities and conceptions of the self: The experience of transgender people. *Symbolic Interaction, 35*, 49–67. https://doi.org/10.1002/symb.2

DiCaro, N. (2017). *Educators' guide supporting successful gender transition: Equality, diversity and inclusion*. Middletown, DE.

District of Columbia Public Schools. (2015). *Transgender and gender-nonconforming policy guidance.* https://dcps.dc.gov/sites/default/files/dc/sites/dcps/publication/attachments/DCPS%20Transgender%20Gender%20Non%20Conforming%20Policy%20Guidance.pdf

Dockendorff, K., Nanney, M., & Nicolazzo, Z. (2019). Trickle up policy-building: Envisioning possibilities for trans*formative change in postsecondary education. In E. M. Zamani-Gallaher, D. D. Choudhuri, & J. L. Taylor (Eds.), *Rethinking LGBTQIA students and collegiate contexts: Identity, policies, and campus climate* (pp. 153–168). Routledge.

Edgar, S. N. (2017). *Music education and social emotional learning: The heart of teaching music*. GIA.

Edidi, D. F., Valverde, M. E., Rawls, M. J., & Blake, A. L. (2020, July 27). *Amplifying marginalized voices*. California Choral Directors Association Summer Summit, virtual.

Ehrensaft, D. (2016). *The gender creative child: Pathways for nurturing and supporting children who live outside gender boxes*. The Experiment.

Ehrensaft, D., Giammattei, S., Storck, K., Tishelman, A., & Keo-Meier, C. (2018). Prepubertal social gender transitions: What we know; what we can learn—A view from a gender affirmative lens. *International Journal of Transgenderism, 19*, 251–268. https://doi.org/10.1080/15532739.2017.1414649

Elias, N. M. (2019, May 23). Transgender and nonbinary gender policy in the public sector. In *Oxford Research Encyclopedia of Politics*. https://oxfordre.com/politics/view/10.1093/acrefore/9780190228637.001.0001/acrefore-9780190228637-e-1168

Elliot, P. (2010). *Debates in transgender, queer, and feminist theory: Contested sites*. Ashgate.

Elorriaga, A. (2011). The construction of male gender identity through choir singing at a Spanish secondary school. *International Journal of Music Education, 29*, 318–332. https://doi.org/10.1177/0255761411421091

Elpus, K., & Carter, B. A. (2016). Bullying victimization among music ensemble and theatre students in the United States. *Journal of Research in Music Education, 64*, 322–343. https://doi.org/10.1177/0022429416658642

Elze, D. E. (2007). Research with sexual minority youths. *Journal of Gay & Lesbian Social Services, 18*(2), 73–99. https://doi.org/10.1300/J041v18n02_05

Ennis, D. (2016, February 4). 10 words transgender people want you to know (but not say). *The Advocate*. http://www.advocate.com/transgender/2016/1/19/10-words-transgender-people-want-you-know-not-say

Fausto-Sterling, A. (2012). *Sex/gender: Biology in a social world*. Routledge.

Fiorentino, M. C., Garrett, M. L., McBride, N. R., Palkki, J., Roseth, N., & Taylor, D. M. (2018, March 22). *A content analysis of gender in state honor choir policies*. Presented at the 2018 Biennial Music Research and Teacher Education National Conference.

Fisher, E. S., & Komosa-Hawkins, K. (Eds.). (2013). *Creating safe and supportive learning environments: A guide for working with lesbian, gay, bisexual, transgender, and questioning youth and families*. Routledge.

Frohard-Dourlent, H. (2018). "The student drives the car, right?": Trans students and narratives of decision-making in schools. *Sex Education, 18*, 328–344. https://doi.org/10.1080/14681811.2017.1393745

Ganz, M. (2011). Public narrative, collective action, and power. In S. Odugbemi & T. Lee (Eds.), *Accountability through public opinion: From inertia to public action* (pp. 273–289). The World Bank. https://doi.org/10.1596/9780821385050_CH18

Garrett, M. L. (2012). The LGBTQ component of 21st-century music teacher training: Strategies for inclusion from the research literature. *Update: Applications of Research in Music Education, 31*(1), 55–62. https://doi.org/10.1177/8755123312458294

Garrett, M. L., & Spano, F. P. (2017). An examination of LGBTQ-inclusive strategies used by practicing music educators. *Research Studies in Music Education, 39*, 39–56. https://doi.org/10.1177/1321103X17700702

Gay, G. (2013). Teaching to and through cultural diversity. *Curriculum Inquiry, 43*, 48–70. https://doi.org/10.1111/curi.12002

Gay & Lesbian Alliance Against Defamation (GLAAD). (n.d.). GLAAD Media Reference Guide—Transgender. https://www.glaad.org/reference/transgender

Gender Minorities Aotearoa. (n.d.). *Trans 101: Glossary of trans words and how to use them.* https://genderminorities.com/database/glossary-transgender/

Gender Spectrum. (2019a). About us: Our story. https://genderspectrum.org/about/our-story

Gender Spectrum. (2019b). Gender inclusive schools toolkit. https://www.genderspectrum.org/work/gisn-members-only-resources

Gender Spectrum. (2019c). Easy steps to a gender inclusive classroom. https://genderspectrum.org/articles/easy-steps-to-a-gender-inclusive-classroom

GLSEN & National Center for Transgender Equality. (2018). *Model school district policy on transgender and gender nonconforming students: Model language, commentary, and resources.* https://www.glsen.org/activity/model-district-policy-transgender-and-gender-nonconforming-students

Gordon, D. G. (2001). Classroom management problems and solutions. *Music Educators Journal, 88*, 17–23. https://doi.org/10.2307/3399737

Grant, J. M., Mottet, L. A., & Tanis, J. (with Harrison, J., Herman, J. L., & Keisling, M). (2011). *Injustice at every turn: A report of the national transgender discrimination survey.* Washington, DC: The National Gay and Lesbian Task Force and the National Center for Transgender Equality. https://transequality.org/issues/us-trans-survey

Green, J., Hoskin, A., R., Mayo, C., Miller, sj. (2020). *Navigating trans*+ and complex gender identities.* Bloomsburg.

Green, L. (1997). *Music, gender, education.* Cambridge University Press.

Grimm v. Gloucester Co. Sch. Bd., 822 F.3d 709 (4th Cir., Aug. 26, 2020). https://www.aclu.org/legal-document/grimm-v-gloucester-county-school-board-opinion?fbclid=IwAR3rFhHEoiePQRVaOR2evMAmBUDeNz-hT4TYzf6UU58zgzeuzzkVrHNoM8s

Grinberg, E., & Stewart, D. (2017, March 7). 3 myths in the transgender bathroom debate. *CNN.* https://www.cnn.com/2017/03/07/health/transgender-bathroom-law-facts-myths/index.html

Grossman, A. H., & D'augelli, A. R. (2006). Transgender youth. *Journal of Homosexuality, 51*(1), 111–128. https://doi.org/10.1300/J082v51n01_06

Grossman, A. H., D'augelli, A. R., & Frank, J. A. (2011). Aspects of psychological resilience among transgender youth. *Journal of LGBT Youth, 8*, 103–115. https://doi.org/10.1080/19361653.2011.541347

Hall, C. (2005). Gender and boys' singing in early childhood. *British Journal of Music Education, 22*, 5–20. https://doi.org/10.1017/S0265051704005960

Hallam, S., Rogers, L., & Creech, A. (2008). Gender differences in musical instrument choice. *International Journal of Music Education, 26*, 7–19. https://doi.org/10.1177/0255761407085646

Hampton, L. (2014). Supporting genderqueer youth in rural communities: A case study. In E. J. Meyer & A. Pullen Sansfaçon (Eds.), *Supporting transgender and gender creative youth* (pp. 174–189). Peter Lang.

Harrison, J., Grant, J., & Herman, J. L. (2012). A gender not listed here: Genderqueers, gender rebels, and otherwise in the national transgender discrimination survey. *LGBTQ Public Policy Journal at the Harvard Kennedy School, 2*(1). http://escholarship.org/uc/item/2zj46213

Harrison, S. D. (2007). A perennial problem in gendered participation in music: What's happening to the boys? *British Journal of Music Education, 24*, 267–280. https://doi.org/10.1017/S0265051707007577

Hawkins, P. J. (2007). What boys and girls learn through song: A content analysis of gender traits and sex bias in two choral classroom textbooks. *Research & Issues in Music Education, 5*(1), Article 5. https://commons.lib.jmu.edu/rime/vol5/iss1/5

Hearns, L. J., & Kremer, B. (2018). *The singing teacher's guide to transgender voices*. Plural.

Heath, S. B. (1983). *Ways with words: Language, life and work in communities and classrooms*. Cambridge University Press.

Hendricks, K. S., Smith, T. D., & Stanuch, J. (2014). Creating safe spaces for music learning. *Music Educators Journal, 101*(1), 35–40. https://doi.org/10.1177/0027432114540337

Henig, R. M. (2017, January). Rethinking gender. *National Geographic, 231*(1). https://www.nationalgeographic.com/magazine/2017/01/children-explain-how-gender-affects-their-lives/

Herthel, J., & Jennings, J. (2014). *I am Jazz*. Dial Books.

Heywood, A. L., & Beynon, C. (2007). Finding a voice: Why boys (don't) sing. *The Phenomenon of Singing, 6*, 108–123.

Hill, S. C. (2021). What's in a name? *Choral Journal, 61*(10), 61–69.

hooks, b. (2000). *Feminist theory: From margin to center* (2nd ed.). Routledge.

Human Rights Campaign. (n.d.). *Violence against the transgender community in 2020*. https://www.hrc.org/resources/violence-against-the-trans-and-gender-non-conforming-community-in-2020/

Human Rights Campaign. (2018). *Cities & counties w/non-discrimination ordinances that include gender identity*. https://www.hrc.org/resources/cities-and-counties-with-non-discrimination-ordinances-that-include-gender

Hunter, M. A. (2008). Cultivating the art of safe space. *Cultivando El Arte Del Espacio Seguro, 13*(1), 5–21. https://doi.org/10.1080/13569780701825195

Hylton, J. B. (1981). Dimensionality in high school student participants' perceptions of the meaning of choral singing experience. *Journal of Research in Music Education, 29*, 287–303. https://doi.org/10.2307/3345005

Ingrey, J. (2018). Problematizing the cisgendering of school washroom space: Interrogating the politics of recognition of transgender and gender non-conforming youth. *Gender and Education, 30*, 774–789. https://doi.org/10.1080/09540253.2018.1483492

interACT: Advocates for Intersex Youth. (n.d.). *What is intersex? Frequently asked questions*. https://interactadvocates.org/faq/

Irene, L., & Harris, D. (n.d.) *SOVT Exercises*. Voice Science Works. https://www.voicescienceworks.org/

Iverson, S. V. (2007). Camouflaging power and privilege: A critical race analysis of university diversity policies. *Educational Administration Quarterly, 43*, 586–611. https://doi.org/10.1177/0013161X07307794

Ivey, G. (2016). *Gender policing: Undergraduate experience and psychosocial outcomes* (undergraduate honors thesis). University of North Carolina, Chapel Hill. https://doi.org/10.17615/k23m-kt46

Jackson, J. M. (2007). *Unmasking identities: An exploration of the lives of gay and lesbian teachers*. Lexington Books.

James, S. E., Herman, J. L., Rankin, S., Keisling, M., Mottet, L., & Anafi, M. (2016). *The report of the 2015 U.S. transgender survey*. Washington, DC: National Center for Transgender Equality. https://transequality.org/issues/us-trans-survey

Järviluoma, H., Moisala, P., & Vilkko, A. (2003). *Gender and qualitative methods*. Sage.

Jellison, J. A. (2015). *Including everyone: Creating music classrooms where all children learn*. New York: Oxford University Press.

Johnson, C. M., & Stewart, E. E. (2004). Effect of sex identification on instrument assignment by band directors. *Journal of Research in Music Education, 52*, 130–140. https://doi.org/10.2307/3345435

Johnson, C. M., & Stewart, E. E. (2005). Effect of sex and race identification on instrument assignment by music educators. *Journal of Research in Music Education, 53*, 348–357. https://doi.org/10.1177/002242940505300406

Johnson, J. R. (2013). Cisgender privilege, intersectionality, and the criminalization of CeCe McDonald: Why intercultural communication needs transgender studies. *Journal of International and Intercultural Communication, 6*, 135–144. https://doi.org/10.1080/17513057.2013.776094

Kaleem, J. (2019, November 12). Latinos and transgender people see big increases in hate crimes, FBI reports. *Los Angeles Times*. https://www.latimes.com/world-nation/story/2019-11-12/hate-crimes-fbi-2018

Kean, E. (2020). Locating transgender within the language of queer in teacher education. *Multicultural Perspectives, 22*, 57–67. https://doi.org/10.1080/15210960.2020.1741371

Kelly, M. (2020, March 14). A teacher's words can help or harm. *ThoughtCo*. https://www.thoughtco.com/impact-of-words-and-actions-8321

Keo-Meier, C., & Ehrensaft, D. (Eds.). (2018). *The gender affirmative model: An interdisciplinary approach to supporting transgender and gender expansive children*. American Psychological Association.

Kim, R. (2017). *NEPC Review: Gender identity policies in schools: What Congress, the courts, and the Trump administration should do*. National Policy Education Center. https://nepc.colorado.edu/thinktank/review-gender

Kitchen, J., & Bellini, C. (2012). Addressing lesbian, gay, bisexual, transgender, and queer (LGBTQ) issues in teacher education: Teacher candidates' perceptions. *Alberta Journal of Educational Research, 58*, 444–460.

Kosciw, J. G., Clark, C. M., Truong, N. L., & Zongrone, A. D. (2020). *The 2019 National School Climate Survey: The experiences of lesbian, gay, bisexual, transgender, and queer youth in our nation's schools*. Gay, Lesbian, Straight Education Network. https://www.glsen.org/research/2019-national-school-climate-survey

Kosciw, J. G., Grestak, E. A., Palmer, N. A., & Boesen, M. J. (2014). *The 2013 National School Survey: The experiences of lesbian, gay, bisexual, and transgender youth in our nation's schools*. Gay, Lesbian, Straight Education Network.

Kosciw, J. G., Grestak, E. A., Zongrone, A. D., Clark, C. M., & Truong, N. L. (2018). *The 2017 National School Climate Survey: The experiences of lesbian, gay, bisexual, transgender, and queer youth in our nation's schools*. Gay, Lesbian, Straight Education Network.

Koza, J. E. (1991). Music and the feminine sphere: Images of women as musicians in "Godey's Lady's Book," 1830–1877. *Musical Quarterly, 75*, 103–129.

Koza, J. E. (1992). Picture this: Sex equity in textbook illustrations. *Music Educators Journal, 78*(7), 28–33. https://doi.org/10.2307/3398355

Koza, J. E. (1993a). Big boys don't cry (or sing): Gender, misogyny, and homophobia in college choral methods texts. *Quarterly Journal of Music Teaching and Learning, 4–5*, 48–64.

Koza, J. E. (1993b). The "missing males" and other gender issues in music education: Evidence from the *Music Supervisors Journal*, 1914–1924. *Journal of Research in Music Education, 41*, 212–232. https://doi.org/10.2307/3345326

Koza, J. E. (1994). Females in 1988 middle school music textbooks: An analysis of illustrations. *Journal of Research in Music Education, 42*, 145–171. doi:10.2307/3345498

Kozan, A. L., & Hammond, S. C. (2019). The singing voice. In R. K. Adler, S. Hirsch, & J. Pickering (Eds.), *Voice and communication therapy for the transgender/gender diverse client: A comprehensive clinical guide* (3rd ed., pp. 291–335). Plural.

Kruse, A. J. (2016). "Therapy was writing rhymes": Hip-hop as resilient space for a queer rapper of color. *Bulletin of the Council for Research in Music Education, 207–208*, 101–122. https://doi.org/10.5406/bulcouresmusedu.207-208.0101

Kruse, A. J., Giebelhausen, R., Shouldice, H. N., & Ramsey, A. L. (2015). Male and female photographic representation in 50 years of *Music Educators Journal*. *Journal of Research in Music Education, 62*, 485–500. https://doi.org/10.1177/0022429414555910

Ladson-Billings, G. (1995). Toward a theory of culturally relevant pedagogy. *American Educational Research Journal, 32*, 465–491.

Ladson-Billings, G. (2011). "Yes, but how do we do it?" Practicing culturally relevant pedagogy. In J. Landsman & C. W. Lewis (Eds.), *White teachers/diverse classrooms: Creating inclusive schools, building on students' diversity, and providing true educational equity* (2nd ed., pp. 33–46). Stylus.

Lambda Legal. (2002, August 28). Groundbreaking legal settlement is first to recognize constitutional right of gay and lesbian students to be out at school and protected from harassment. *Lambda Legal*. https://www.lambdalegal.org/news/ca_20020828_groundbreaking-legal-settlement-first-to-recognize

Lambda Legal. (2018). *Changing birth certificate sex designations: State-by-state guidelines. Lambda Legal*. https://www.lambdalegal.org/know-your-rights/article/trans-changing-birth-certificate-sex-designations

Larkin, B. (2018, March 21). *30 craziest corporate policies employees must follow*. Best Life. https://bestlifeonline.com/craziest-corporate-policies-employees-must-adhere-to/

Legg, R. (2013). Reviewing the situation: A narrative exploration of singing and gender in secondary schools. *Music Education Research, 15*, 168–179. https://doi.org/10.1080/14613808.2012.737774

Leonardi, B., & Staley, S. (2018). What's involved in 'the work'? Understanding administrators' roles in bringing trans-affirming policies into practice. *Gender and Education, 30*, 754–773. https://doi.org/10.1080/09540253.2018.1455967

Lessley, E. (2017). *Teaching transgender singers* (doctoral dissertation). Available from ProQuest Dissertations. (UMI No. 10598998).

Levine, J. (2020, June 23). My nonbinary journey. *Tablet Magazine*. https://www.tabletmag.com/sections/community/articles/my-nonbinary-journey

Lhamon, C. E., & Gupta, V. (2016, May 13). Dear colleague letter on transgender students. U.S. Department of Education and U.S. Department of Justice. https://www2.ed.gov/about/offices/list/ocr/letters/colleague-201605-title-ix-transgender.pdf

Liptak, A. (2020, June 15). Civil rights law protects gay and transgender workers, supreme court rules. *New York Times*. https://www.nytimes.com/2020/06/15/us/gay-transgender-workers-supreme-court.html

Lind, V. R., & McKoy, C. (2016). *Culturally responsive teaching in music education: From understanding to application*. Routledge.

Lundquist, P., & Henson, A. (2020). *OOVO*. https://oovostraw.com/

Madsen, C. K., & Madsen, C. H., Jr. (2016). *Teaching/discipline: A positive approach for educational development* (5th ed.). Contemporary.

Maguen, S., & Shipherd, J. C. (2010). Suicide risk among transgender individuals. *Psychology & Sexuality, 1*(1), 34–43. https://doi.org/10.1080/19419891003634430

Mangin, M. M. (2018). Supporting transgender and gender-expansive children in school. *Phi Delta Kappan, 100*, 16–21. https://doi.org/10.1177/0031721718803564

Mangin, M. M. (2020). Transgender students in elementary schools: How supportive principals lead. *Educational Administration Quarterly, 56*, 255–288. https://doi.org/10.1177/0013161X19843579

Manternach, B., Chipman, M., Rainero, R., & Stave, C. (2017). Teaching transgender singers. Part 1: The voice teachers' perspectives. *Journal of Singing, 74*(1), 83–88.

Manternach, J. N., Maxfield, L, & Schloneger, M. (2019). Semi-occluded vocal tract exercises in the choral rehearsal: What's the deal with the straw? *Choral Journal, 60*(1), 47–55.

Marshall, K. (2009). Brass chicks and drummer girls: Performing gender within the university marching band. *Intersections: Women's and Gender Studies in Review across Disciplines, 7*, 26–39.

Martino, W., & Cumming-Potvin, W. (2018). Transgender and gender expansive education research, policy and practice: Reflecting on epistemological and ontological possibilities of bodily becoming. *Gender and Education, 30*, 687–694. https://doi.org/10.1080/09540253.2018.1487518

Maslow, A. H. (1943). Maslow's hierarchy of needs. *A theory of human motivation. Psychological Review, 50*, 370–396. https://doi.org/10.1037/h0054346

Matzner, A. (2001). *O au no keia: Voices from Hawai'i's Mahu and transgender communities.* Xlibris.

Mayo, C. (2014). *LGBTQ youth and education: Policies and practices.* Teachers College Press.

McBride, N. R., & Palkki, J. (2020). Big boys don't cry (or sing) . . . still?: A modern exploration of gender, misogyny, and homophobia in college choral methods texts. *Music Education Research, 22*, 408–420. https://doi.org/10.1080/14613808.2020.1784862

McBride, R. S. (2021). A literature review of the secondary school experiences of trans youth. *Journal of LGBT Youth,18*(2), 103–134. https://doi.org/10.1080/19361653.2020.1727815

McCarthy, L. (2003). What about the "T"? Is multicultural education ready to address transgender issues? *Multicultural Perspectives, 5*, 46–48. https://doi.org/10.1207/S15327892MCP0504_11

McDonald, J. (2015). Gender-neutral title "Mx" added to Oxford English dictionary. *Huffington Post.* http://www.huffingtonpost.com/entry/gender-neutral-title-mx-added-to-oxford-english-dictionary_55e093e5e4b0aec9f35307f3

McGuire, J. K., Anderson, C. R., Toomey, R. B., & Russell, S. T. (2010). School climate for transgender youth: A mixed method investigation of student experiences and school responses. *Journal of Youth and Adolescence, 39*, 1175–1188. https://doi.org/10.1007/s10964-010-9540-7

McQueen, K. (2006). Breaking the gender dichotomy: The case for transgender education in school curriculum. *The Teachers College Record.* http://www.tcrecord.org ID Number: 12663

McQuillan, M. T., & Leininger, J. (2020). Supporting gender-inclusive schools: Educators' beliefs about gender diversity training and implementation plans. *Professional Development in Education, 47*(1),156–175. https://doi.org/10.1080/19415257.2020.1744685

Meizel, K. (2020). *Multivocality: Singing on the borders of identity.* New York: Oxford University Press.

Merriam-Webster. (n.d.). Singular "they." https://www.merriam-webster.com/

Meyer, E. J. (2010). *Gender and sexual diversity in schools* (Vol. 10). Springer Science & Business Media.

Meyer, E. J. (2014). Supporting gender diversity in schools: Developmental and legal perspectives. In E. J. Meyer & A. P. Sansfaçon (Eds.), *Supporting Transgender and gender creative youth: Schools, families, and communities in action* (pp. 69–84). Peter Lang.

Meyer, E. J., & Keenan, H. (2018). Can policies help schools affirm gender diversity? A policy archaeology of transgender-inclusive policies in California schools. *Gender and Education, 30*, 736–753. https://doi.org/10.1080/09540253.2018.1483490

Meyer, E. J., & Leonardi, B. (2018). Teachers' professional learning to affirm transgender, non-binary, and gender-creative youth: Experiences and recommendations from the field. *Sex Education, 18*, 449–463. https://doi.org/10.1080/14681811.2017.1411254

Millican, J. S. (2017). Band instrument selection and assignment: A review of the literature. *Update: Applications of Research in Music Education, 35*(2), 46–53. https://doi.org/10.1177/8755123315610174

Morrison, S. J. (2001). The school ensemble: A culture of our own. *Music Educators Journal, 88*(2), 24–28. https://doi.org/10.2307/3399738

Mundy, D. E. (2013). The spiral of advocacy: How state-based LGBT advocacy organizations use ground-up public communication strategies in their campaigns for the "Equality Agenda." *Public Relations Review, 39*, 387–390. https://doi.org/10.1016/j.pubrev.2013.07.021

Muñiz, J. (2019). *Culturally responsive teaching: A 50-state survey of teaching standards*. New America. https://www.newamerica.org/education-policy/reports/culturally-responsive-teaching/understanding-culturally-responsive-teaching/

Nagoshi, J. L., & Brzuzy, S. I. (2010). Transgender theory: Embodying research and practice. *Affilia, 25*, 431–443. https://doi.org/10.1177/0886109910384068

Nagoshi, J. L., Nagoshi, C. T., & Brzuzy, S. (2014). *Gender and sexual identity*. Springer New York. https://doi.org/10.1007/978-1-4614-8966-5

Namaste, V. (2000). *Invisible lives: The erasure of transsexual and transgendered people*. University of Chicago Press.

Namaste, V. (2009). Undoing theory: The "transgender question" and the epistemic violence of Anglo-American feminist theory. *Hypatia, 24*, 11–32.

National Center for Transgender Equality (NCTE). (2016). *Fact sheet on U.S. Department of Education policy letter on transgender students*. https://transequality.org/issues/resources/fact-sheet-on-us-department-of-education-policy-letter-on-transgender-students

National Center for Transgender Equality (NCTE). (2020). https://transequality.org/

National Great Blacks in Wax Museum. (n.d.). *Then and now*. http://www.greatblacksinwax.org/expansion_plans.htm

Ngo, B. (2003). Citing discourses: Making sense of homophobia and heteronormativity at dynamic high school. *Equity and Excellence in Education, 36*, 115–124. https://doi.org/10.1080/10665680303513

Nichols, J. (2013). Rie's story, Ryan's journey: Music in the life of a transgender student. *Journal of Research in Music Education, 61*, 262–279. https://doi.org/10.1177/0022429413498259

Nichols, J. (2016, September 26). Create safe people, not safe spaces. *Maryland Political Review*. http://marylandpoliticalreview.org/create-safe-people-not-safe-spaces/

Odegard, D., & Blakeslee, M. (2017, February 24). NAfME opposes rescinding of transgender guidelines for schools—National Association for Music Education (NAfME). *National Association for Music Education (NAfME)*. http://www.nafme.org/nafme-opposes-rescinding-of-transgender-guidelines-for-schools/

Olson, K. R., Key, A. C., & Eaton, N. R. (2015). Gender cognition in transgender children. *Psychological Science, 26*, 467–474. https://doi.org/10.1177/0956797614568156

Orr, A., & Baum, J. (2015). *Schools in transition: A guide for supporting transgender students in K-12 schools*. https://www.nea.org/assets/docs/Schools_in_Transition_2015.pdf

Orr, A., & Komosa-Hawkins, K. (2013). Law, policy and ethics: What school professionals need to know. In E. S. Fisher & K. Komosa-Hawkins (Eds.), *Creating safe and supportive learning environments: A guide for working with Lesbian, Gay, Bisexual, Transgender, and Questioning Youth and Families* (pp. 91–122). Routledge. https://doi.org/10.1080/19361653.2015.1077767

O'Toole, P. (1998). A missing chapter from choral methods books: How choirs neglect girls. *Choral Journal, 39*(5), 9–32.

Oxford English Dictionary. (n.d.). Heteronormative, adj. In *OED Online. Oxford University Press.* Retrieved from http://www.oed.com/view/Entry/275594

Oxford English Dictionary. (n.d.). Heterosexism, n. In *OED Online. Oxford University Press.* Retrieved from http://www.oed.com/view/Entry/59322546

Oxford English Dictionary. (n.d.). Latinx, n. and adj. In *OED Online. Oxford University Press.* Retrieved from http://www.oed.com/view/Entry/79123233

Palkki, J. (2015a). Gender trouble: Males, adolescents, and masculinity in the choral context. *Choral Journal, 56*(4), 24–35.

Palkki, J. (2015b). "Negotiating the closet door": The lived experiences of two gay music teachers. *Visions of Research in Music Education, 26*. http://www.rider.edu/~vrme

Palkki, J. (2016). *"My voice speaks for itself": The experiences of three transgender students in secondary school choral programs.* Available from ProQuest Dissertations and Theses database (UMI No. 10141543).

Palkki, J. (2017). Inclusivity in action: Transgender students in the choral classroom. *Choral Journal, 57*(11), 20–34.

Palkki, J. (2020a). "My voice speaks for itself": The experiences of three transgender students in American secondary school choral programs: *International Journal of Music Education, 38*, 126–146. https://doi.org/10.1177/0255761419890946

Palkki, J. (2020b). Rethinking gender in the choral context. In B. Winnie (Ed.), *The choral conductor's companion: 100 rehearsal techniques, imaginative ideas, quotes, and facts* (pp. 156–157). Meredith Music Publications/GIA.

Palkki, J., & Caldwell, P. (2018). "We are often invisible": A survey on safe space for LGBTQ students in secondary school choral programs. *Research Studies in Music Education, 40*, 28–49. https://doi.org/10.1177/1321103X17734973

Palkki, J., & Sauerland, W. (2019). Considering gender complexity in music teacher education. *Journal of Music Teacher Education, 28*, 72–84. https://doi.org/10.1177/1057083718814582

Palmiter, D., Alvord, M., Dorlen, R., Comas-Diaz, L., Luthar, S. S., Maddi, S. R., O'Neill, H. K, Saakvitne, K. W., & Tedeschi, R. G. (2012). Building your resilience. *American Psychological Association*. https://www.apa.org/topics/resilience

Parents and Friends of Lesbians and Gays (PFLAG). (2020). PFLAG Glossary. https://www.pflag.org/glossary

Parson, L. (2019). Considering positionality: The ethics of conducting research with marginalized groups. In K. K. Strunk & L. A. Locke (Eds.), *Research methods for social justice and equity in education* (pp. 15–32). Springer.

Pascoe, C. J. (2011). *Dude, you're a fag: Masculinity and sexuality in high school.* University of California Press.

Paz, I. G., & Astor, M. (2020, June 27). Black trans women seek more space in the movement they helped start. *New York Times*. https://www.nytimes.com/2020/06/27/us/politics/black-trans-lives-matter.html

Peitzmeier, S., Gardner, I., Weinand, J., Corbet, A., & Acevedo, K. (2016). Health impact of chest binding among transgender adults: A community-engaged, cross-sectional study. *Culture, Health & Sexuality, 19*, 64–75. https://doi.org/10.1080/13691058.2016.1191675

Pennington, S. (2019). Transgender passing guides and the vocal performance of gender and sexuality. In F. E. Maus & S. Whiteley (Eds.), *The Oxford handbook of music and queerness*. Oxford University Press. Online publication. 10.1093/oxfordhb/9780199793525.013.65

Peters, A. (2003). Isolation or inclusion: Creating safe spaces for lesbian and gay youth. *Families in Society: The Journal of Contemporary Social Services, 84*, 331–337. https://doi.org/10.1606/1044-3894.122

Peters, J. W., Becker, J., & Davis, J. H. (2017, February 22). Trump rescinds rules on bathrooms for transgender students. *New York Times*. https://www.nytimes.com/2017/02/22/us/politics/devos-sessions-transgender-students-rights.html

Pittsburgh Public Schools. (n.d.) Gender-inclusive school communities: A policy and procedure guide to ensure the success of transgender students within Pittsburgh Public Schools. https://www.pghschools.org/cms/lib/PA01000449/Centricity/Domain/1295/PPS%20Gender%20Inclusive%20Handbook.pdf

Planned Parenthood. (n.d.). Gender identity & roles | Feminine traits & stereotypes. https://www.plannedparenthood.org/learn/sexual-orientation-gender/gender-gender-identity/what-are-gender-roles-and-stereotypes

Planned Parenthood. (n.d.). What is biological sex? | Female, male and intersex. https://www.plannedparenthood.org/learn/sexual-orientation-gender/gender-gender-identity

Pollitt, A. M., Ioverno, S., Russell, S. T., Li, G., & Grossman, A. H. (2021). Predictors and mental health benefits of chosen name use among transgender youth. *Youth & Society, 53*(2), 320–341. https://doi.org/10.1177/0044118X19855898

Poynter, K. J., & Tubbs, N. J. (2008). Safe zones: Creating LGBT safe space ally programs. *Journal of LGBT Youth, 5*, 121–132. https://doi.org/10.1300/J524v05n01_10

Puchner, L., & Klein, N. A. (2011). The right time and place? Middle school language arts teachers talk about not talking about sexual orientation. *Equity and Excellence in Education, 44*, 233–248. https://doi.org/10.1080/10665684.2011.563182

Ramsey, A. (2008). Choral music in the junior high/middle school: A junior high state of mind: Considerations for composing and arranging for the middle level choir. *Choral Journal, 49*(2), 73–74.

Ramsey, A. L. (2013). *Swagger, gentlemanliness, and brotherhood: Explorations of lived experiences in a high school men's chorus*. Available from ProQuest Dissertations and Theses database (UMI No. 3568204).

Rands, K. E. (2009). Considering transgender people in education: A gender-complex approach. *Journal of Teacher Education, 60*, 419–431. https://doi.org/10.1177/0022487109341475

Rawlings, J. R. (2016). Middle school students' perceptions of bullying. *Bulletin of the Council for Research in Music Education, 209*, 7–26. https://doi.org/10.5406/bulcouresmusedu.209.0007

Rawlings, J. R., & Espelage, D. L. (2020). Middle school music ensemble participation, homophobic name-calling, and mental health. *Youth & Society, 52*, 1238–1258. https://doi.org/10.1177/0044118X19866071

Rawlings, J. R., & Young, J. (2020). Relational aggression and youth empowerment within a high school instrumental music program. *Psychology of Music*. Advance online publication. https://doi.org/10.1177/0305735620923140

Roberts, G., Allan, C., & Wells, K. (2007). Understanding gender identity in K–12 schools. *Journal of Gay & Lesbian Issues in Education, 4*, 119–129. https://doi.org/10.1300/J367v04n04_08

Rogers, A., Castree, N., & Kitchin, R. (2013). Heteronormativity. In *A dictionary of human geography*. Oxford University Press. https://www.oxfordreference.com/view/10.1093/acref/9780199599868.001.0001/acref-9780199599868-e-811

Rogers, K. (2016, February 25). Transgender students and "bathroom laws" in South Dakota and beyond. *New York Times*. https://www.nytimes.com/2016/02/26/us/transgender-students-and-bathroom-laws-in-south-dakota-and-beyond.html

Rom, R. B. (1998). "Safe spaces": Reflections on an educational metaphor. *Journal of Curriculum Studies, 30*, 397–408. https://doi.org/10.1080/002202798183549

Sadowski, M. (2016). *Safe is not enough: Better schools for LGBTQ students*. Harvard Education Press.

Saldaña, J. (2013). *The coding manual for qualitative researchers* (2nd ed.). SAGE Publications.

Salvador, K. (2019). Equity in music education: Sustaining the courage to change. *Music Educators Journal, 105*(4), 59–63. https://doi.org/10.1177/0027432119846841

Salvador, K., Paetz, A., & Lewin-Zeigler, A. (2020). Being the change: Music teachers' self-reported changes in mindset and practice. *Update: Applications of Research in Music Education, 39*(1), 17–26. https://doi.org/10.1177/8755123320925754

San Diego Unified School District. (n.d.). Nondiscrimination policy. Retrieved from https://www.sandiegounified.org/nondiscrimination-policy

Sauerland, W. R. (2018). *Legitimate voices: A multi-case study of trans and non-binary singers in the applied voice studio*. Available from ProQuest Dissertations and Theses database (UMI No. 10825714).

Sausa, L. A. (2005). Translating research into practice: Trans youth recommendations for improving school systems. *Journal of Gay & Lesbian Issues in Education, 3*, 15–28. https://doi-org.csulb.idm.oclc.org/10.1300/J367v03n01_04

Savin-Williams, R. C. (2018, July 29). A guide to genderqueer, non-binary, and genderfluid identity. *Psychology Today*. https://www.psychologytoday.com/blog/sex-sexuality-and-romance/201807/guide-genderqueer-non-binary-and-genderfluid-identity

Schilt, K., & Westbrook, L. (2009). Doing gender, doing heteronormativity: "gender normals," transgender people, and the social maintenance of heterosexuality. *Gender & Society, 23*, 440–464. https://doi.org/10.1177/0891243209340034

Schilt, K., & Westbrook, L. (2015). Bathroom battlegrounds and penis panics. *Contexts, 14*(3), 26–31. https://doi.org/10.1177/1536504215596943

Schmidt, P. (2015). The ethics of policy: Why a social justice version of music education requires a commitment to policy thought. In C. Benedict, P. Schmidt, G. Spruce, & P. Woodford (Eds.), *The Oxford handbook of social justice in music education* (pp. 47–61). Oxford University Press.

Schmidt, P. (2017). Why policy matters: Developing a policy vocabulary within music education. In P. Schmidt & R. Colwell (Eds.), *Policy and the political life of music education* (pp. 11–36). Oxford University Press.

Schmidt, P. (2019). *Policy as practice: A guide for music educators*. Oxford University Press.

Schmidt, S. (2019, June 11). Jonathan Van Ness of 'Queer Eye' comes out as non-binary. *Washington Post*. https://www.washingtonpost.com/dc-md-va/2019/06/11/jonathan-van-ness-queer-eye-comes-out-nonbinary/

Schoenberg, S. (2015, May 6). Attorney General Maura Healey calls transgender protections "the next battleground for civil rights." *Masslive.com*. https://www.masslive.com/politics/2015/05/attorney_general_maura_healey_5.html

Schumann, C. (1848). *Abendfeier in venedig*.

Sculos, B. W. (2017). "Who's afraid of 'Toxic Masculinity'?" *Class, Race and Corporate Power, 5*(3). http://digitalcommons.fiu.edu/classracecorporatepower/vol5/iss3/6

Seelman, K. L. (2014). Transgender individuals' access to college housing and bathrooms: Findings from the national transgender discrimination survey. *Journal of Gay & Lesbian Social Services, 26*, 186–206. https://doi.org/10.1080/10538720.2014.891091

Serano, J. (2013). *Excluded: Making feminist and queer movements more inclusive*. Basic Books.

Shaffer, S., & Shevitz, L. (2001). She bakes and he builds: Gender bias in the curriculum. In H. Rousso & M. L. Wehmeyer (Eds.), *Double jeopardy: Addressing gender equity in special education* (pp. 115–132). State University of New York Press.

Shaw, J. T. (2017). Toward socially inclusive music organizations: Promoting socioeconomic diversity in choral ensembles. *Choral Journal, 58*(4), 22–37.

Silveira, J. M. (2019). Perspectives of a transgender music education student. *Journal of Research in Music Education, 66*, 428–448. https://doi.org/10.1177/0022429418800467

Silveira, J. M., & Goff, S. C. (2016). Music teachers' attitudes toward transgender students and supportive school practices. *Journal of Research in Music Education, 64*, 138–158. https://doi.org/10.1177/0022429416647048

Sims, L. (2017). Teaching transgender students. *Journal of Singing, 73*, 279–282.

Singh, A. A. (2013). Transgender youth of color and resilience: Negotiating oppression and finding support. *Sex Roles, 68*, 690–702. https://doi/10.1007/s11199-012-0149-z

Singh, A. A., Hays, D. G., & Watson, L. S. (2011). Strength in the face of adversity: Resilience strategies of transgender individuals. *Journal of Counseling & Development, 89*, 20–27. https://doi.org/10.1080/19361653.2011.541347

Singh, A. A., & Jackson, K. (2012). Queer and transgender youth: Education and liberation in our schools. In A. A. Singh & K. Jackson (Eds.), *Counterpoints* (Vol. 367, pp. 175–186). Peter Lang AG. https://doi.org/10.1007/978-3-030-13483-9

Slesaransky-Poe, G., Ruzzi, L., Dimedio, C., & Stanley, J. (2013). Is this the right elementary school for my gender nonconforming child? *Journal of LGBT Youth, 10*, 29–44. https://doi.org/10.1080/19361653.2012.718521

Södersten, M., Nygren, U., Hertegård, S., & Dhejne, C. (2019). A multidisciplinary approach to transgender health. In R. K. Adler, S. Hirsch, & J. Pickering (Eds.), *Voice and communication therapy for the transgender/gender diverse client: A comprehensive clinical guide* (3rd ed., pp. 1–29). Plural.

Southerland, W. (2018). The rainbow connection: How music classrooms create safe spaces for sexual-minority young people. *Music Educators Journal, 104*(3), 40–45. https://doi.org/10.1177/0027432117743304

Sullivan, A. L., & Urraro, L. L. (2019a). Being young and trans in school. In A. L. Sullivan & L. L. Urraro (Eds.), *Voices of transgender children in early childhood education: Reflections on resistance and resiliency* (pp. 17–40). Springer. https://doi.org/10.1007/978-3-030-13483-9_2

Sullivan, A. L., & Urraro, L. L. (2019b). Where do we go from here? Dos and don'ts when working with trans children. In A. L. Sullivan & L. L. Urraro (Eds.), *Voices of transgender children in early childhood education: Reflections on resistance and resiliency* (pp. 199–226). Springer. https://doi.org/10.1007/978-3-030-13483-9_8

Steinhauser, C. J. (2017, February 23). Protection of transgender students. http://www.lbusd.k12.ca.us/Departments/Newsroom/article.cfm?articleID=2333

Steinmetz, K. (2014a, May). The transgender tipping point. *Time, 183*(22). https://time.com/135480/transgender-tipping-point/

Steinmetz, K. (2014b, December). Why it's best to avoid the word "transgendered." *Time*. http://time.com/3630965/transgender-transgendered/

Steinmetz, K. (2015, July 28). Everything you need to know about the "bathroom bill" debate. *Time*. http://time.com/3974186/transgender-bathroom-debate/

Stryker, S. (2008). *Transgender history*. Seal Press.

Sweet, B. (2016). *Growing musicians: Teaching music in middle school and beyond*. Oxford University Press.

Sweet, B. (2020). *Thinking outside the voice box: Adolescent voice change in music education*. Oxford University Press.

Sweet, B., & Parker, E. C. (2019). Female vocal identity development: A phenomenology. *Journal of Research in Music Education, 67*, 62–82. https://doi.org/10.1177/0022429418809981

Szalacha, L. A. (2004). Educating teachers on LGBTQ issues. *Journal of Gay & Lesbian Issues in Education, 1*, 67–79. https://doi.org/10.1300/J367v01n04_07

Taylor, D. M. (2011). Bullying: What can music teachers do? *Music Educators Journal, 98*(1), 41–44. https://doi.org/10.1177/0027432111411717

Taylor, D. M. (2018). Research-to-resource: Dignity for all: LGBTQ students and empathic teaching. *Update: Applications of Research in Music Education, 36*(3), 55–58. https://doi.org/10.1177/8755123318761914

Taylor, J. K. (2007). Transgender identities and public policy in the United States: The relevance for public administration. *Administration & Society, 39*, 833–856. https://doi.org/10.1177/0095399707305548

Terada, S., Matsumoto, Y., Sato, T., Okabe, N., Kishimoto, Y., & Uchitomi, Y. (2011). Suicidal ideation among patients with gender identity disorder. *Psychiatry Research, 190*, 159–162. https://doi.org/10.1016/j.psychres.2011.04.024

Thorne, B. (1993). *Gender play: Girls and boys in school*. Rutgers University Press.

Titze, I. R. (1994). *Principles of voice production*. Prentice Hall.

Titze, I. R. (2006). Voice training and therapy with a semi-occluded vocal tract: rationale and scientific underpinnings. *Journal of Speech, Language, and Hearing Research, 49*, 448–459. https://doi.org/10.1044/1092-4388(2006/035)

Trans Student Educational Resources (TSER). (n.d.). Definitions—Trans Student Educational Resources. http://www.transstudent.org/about/definitions/

Travers, A. (2018). *The trans generation: How trans kids (and their parents) are creating a gender revolution*. New York University Press.

Valentine, D. (2007). *Imagining transgender: An ethnography of a category*. Duke University Press.

Warner, L. R. (2008). A best practices guide to intersectional approaches in psychological research. *Sex Roles, 59*, 454–463. https://doi.org/10.1007/s11199-008-9504-5

Washington Office of Superintendent of Public Instruction. (n.d.). *Reviewing instructional materials for bias*. https://www.k12.wa.us/policy-funding/equity-and-civil-rights/resources-school-districts-civil-rights-washington-schools/reviewing-instructional-materials-bias

Wayne, L. D. (2005). Neutral pronouns: A modest proposal whose time has come. *Canadian Woman Studies, 24*, 85–91.

Wells, K., Roberts, G., & Allan, C. (2012). *Supporting transgender and transsexual students in K–12 schools: A guide for educators*. Canadian Teachers' Federation. https://era.library.ualberta.ca/items/213dfe4a-d5bc-4deb-bb2f-b932f74b9aea

Wernick, L. J., Kulick, A., & Inglehart, M. H. (2014). Influences of peers, teachers, and climate on students' willingness to intervene when witnessing anti-transgender harassment. *Journal of Adolescence, 37*, 927–935. https://doi.org/10.1016/j.adolescence.2014.06.008

West, C., & Zimmerman, D. H. (1987). Doing gender. *Gender & Society, 1*, 125–151. https://doi.org/10.1177/0891243287001002002

Wilchins, R. A. (1997). *Read my lips: Sexual subversion and the end of gender*. Firebrand Books.

Womack, C. (2017, April 20). Finding their true voices in the Trans Chorus. *Los Angeles Times*. https://www.latimes.com/entertainment/arts/la-ca-cm-trans-chorus-los-angeles-20170423-story.html

Wolff, E. A., & Hums, M. (2017, September 5). "Nothing about us without us"—Mantra for a movement. *Huffington Post*. https://www.huffpost.com/entry/nothing-about-us-without-us-mantra-for-a-movement_b_59aea450e4b0c50640cd61cf

Woolley, S. W. (2017). Contesting silence, claiming space: Gender and sexuality in the neo-liberal public high school. *Gender and Education, 29*, 84–99. https://doi.org/10.1080/09540253.2016.1197384

Woolley, S. W. (2019). "When you don't believe something is real, you can't actually advocate for or support it": Trans* inclusion in K-12 schools. *Intersections: Critical Issues in Education, 3*, 25–43.

Woolley, S. W., & Airton, L. (2020). *Teaching about gender diversity: Teacher-tested lesson plans for K–12 classrooms*. Canadian Scholar's Press.

Wright, D. T. E., & Smith, D. N. (2013). Bullying of LGBT youth and school climate for LGBT educators. *GEMS (Gender, Education, Music, and Society), 6*(1). https://doi.org/10.5561/5010

Wych, G. M. F. (2012). Gender and instrument associations, stereotypes, and stratification: A literature review. *Update: Applications of Research in Music Education, 30*(2), 22–31. https://doi.org/10.1177/8755123312437049

Wyss, S. E. (2004). "This was my hell": The violence experienced by gender non-conforming youth in US high schools. *International Journal of Qualitative Studies in Education, 17*, 709–730. https://doi.org/10.1080/0951839042000253676

Ziegler, K. R., & Rasul, N. (2014). Race, ethnicity, and culture. In L. Erickson-Schroth (Ed.), *Trans bodies, trans selves* (pp. 24–39). Oxford University Press.

Zimman, L. (2014). Gender and the voice. In L. Erickson-Schroth (Ed.), *Trans bodies, trans selves* (p. 127). Oxford University Press.

Index

For the benefit of digital users, indexed terms that span two pages (e.g., 52–53) may, on occasion, appear on only one of those pages.

Figures and boxes are indicated by *f* and *b* following the page number